Contours of the Illiberal State

North American Studies

Edited by the The John F. Kennedy Institute for North American Studies of Freie Universität Berlin, the Center for North American Studies (ZENAF) of Goethe-Universität Frankfurt am Main and the Department of English and American Studies of Humboldt-Universität zu Berlin.

Volume 39

Boris Vormann is professor of politics and head of the politics concentration at Bard College Berlin. *Christian Lammert* is Professor of North American Politics and Policy, chair of the politics department and director of the John F. Kennedy Institute at Freie Universität Berlin.

Boris Vormann, Christian Lammert (eds.)

Contours of the Illiberal State

Governing Circulation in the Smart Economy

Campus Verlag
Frankfurt/New York

To our students

ISBN 978-3-593-51017-0 Print
ISBN 978-3-593-44060-6 E-Book (PDF)

Cover design: Campus Verlag, Frankfurt-on-Main
Cover illustration: Seven Persons, Cypress County, Alberta. © Patrick DeDauw.
Printed on acid free paper.
Printed in the United States of America

For further information:
www.campus.de
www.press.uchicago.edu

Contents

Preface

The chapters in this volume have been written by young researchers at the beginning of their professional careers. All of them have completed their studies on US politics and North American societies and cultures at Freie Universität's John-F.-Kennedy Institute. Some of them now work in publishing houses and research institutions, others have continued to complete their PhDs in Germany and elsewhere. What unifies their essays is a fresh look at the promises of the smart economy from those who have grown up with it. Their work also offers a distinctly European look at continuities and transformations in statehood that seeks to transcend the American-centric analysis of the United States, not just by adding a transatlantic viewpoint, but by breaking open the mold of localist and nationalist thinking.

As a group, we would like to thank the John-F.-Kennedy Institute and the Graduate School of North American Studies for their support. These institutions provided a physical home for many of the discussions and debates to take place that led to this volume—and a more metaphorical home when it came to choosing a publishing outlet and preparing the ground for this publication. In particular, we would like to thank Winfried Fluck for his extraordinary support in making this volume possible. Without his help, this collection of essays might not have seen the light of day. We would also like to thank the editors of the North American Studies series at Campus; and we are grateful to Hanna Bargheer, Dave Braneck, and Franziska Riel for their copy-editing work and their support in questions regarding format and content.

Boris Vormann and Christian Lammert
Berlin, January 2019

Prologue

Assembling the Smart Economy: A Typology of State Intervention Patterns

Boris Vormann and Christian Lammert

The era of liberal ascendance seems to have come to an abrupt end—and the notion of an imminent post-national age with it. The state is back. In fact, it never left. But the smart economy and its techno-scientific promises of big data, tracing technology and the internet, as we argue, obfuscate our view from the continuing importance of government politics. We contend that this invisibility of political agency has helped prepare the ground for the rise of illiberal states. This book seeks to salvage a richer understanding of state activity at a moment of renationalization and democratic crisis. It dissects the ways in which the context of the US state, presumed to be the most-liberal and least-interventionist possible, has in fact always been more than just a market fixer.

This book fleshes out patterns of state intervention in globalization processes. It does so in historical perspective and with a planetary scope. While the smart economy for many seems on the horizon, we contend that the sanguine view of a post-statist order that it insinuates are premature. The essays collected here pull into view the active roles of governments that have been and still are necessary to make global flows of goods, people and capital across vast distances possible. While the post-Cold War era was dominated, both in academia and political practice, by the assumption of ever-integrating networks of trade and interaction that rendered the state unnecessary, this perspective was often more a normative and ideological wish than an empirical truth. As we contend, any vision of a Green New Deal or of a smart and truly sustainable economy needs to be based on an understanding of labor in global production and of the importance of the political.

In a comparative perspective that includes Canada and Mexico, we trace the active role of the US state in facilitating global circulation along the logistical supply chains, communication channels and inter-urban travel itineraries of the smart economy and its antecedents. Ultimately, in pointing out the continuities and types of state intervention as a market enabler, shaper and developer across different temporal and national orders, this book helps to sketch out the contours of a political present in which the state is again increasingly seen as the key political actor. However, while earlier state formations incorporated certain social responsibilities of the state vis-à-vis its constituencies (such as the protection of political and social rights), the illiberal state is risking to revert back to its proto-liberal functions as a mere guarantor of economic rights and a facilitator of circulation.

Liberalism in Crisis

Until very recently, the expansion of markets seemed both inexorable and desirable. Binding societies together through networks of trade, markets have been regarded in liberal thought as emancipatory and pacifying for a long time. Why would rational actors do anything but maximize their value and interact peacefully? Smith, Ricardo and many others after them gave an unequivocal answer to this question: they would not. And yet, recent counter-movements to liberal globalization are forming in Western liberal democracies. What Syriza, Brexiteers, Podemos and Trumpists share, despite their radically different political positions, is a critique of these axiomatic assumptions. Not everybody is benefitting from globalization and global trade in similar ways. In fact, certain groups are clearly losing.

This fundamental crisis of liberal democracies coincides with the rise of a new economic paradigm. New ways of amassing and analyzing data, geosensitive tracking technology and new means of communication and transportation are beginning to radically reshape the spatial and social division of labor. We use the term "smart economy" to denote those arrangements that emphasize the role of technological innovation and market solutions in the future of work. This umbrella term captures debates and narratives that fuse tropes of technological utopianism and economic determinism to create visions of what might appear as an impending, best of all possible worlds.

Building on ideas of a postindustrial knowledge society, a flurry of new terms and concepts have been coined over recent years to capture different aspects of this emergent economic structure: the sharing economy

(Sundararajan 2016; Albinsson and Perera 2018), the zero-marginal-cost society (Rifkin 2015), the green economy (Kenis and Lievens 2015), the digital platform economy (Huws 2014; Ng 2014; Dyer-Witheford 2015; Scholz 2016; Srnicek 2017), the gig economy (Mulcahy 2016; Tolley 2018), cognitive capitalism (Rindermann 2018), the second machine age (Brynjolfsson and McAfee 2014), the no collar economy (George and Buitrago 2017)—the list could easily be extended. What these terms share is a sense of novelty and a strong faith in the progressive tendencies of technological development. As the argument goes, by sharing goods and services, and by using them more efficiently through smarter allocation and re-use, we stand to develop more environmentally-friendly societies and to avert the worst effects of climate change. In a striking historical rebirth of the postindustrial society, technology- and market-driven developments are portrayed as inevitable, and ultimately beneficial to all.

We do in part agree with those more optimistic discourses of the smart economy that tracing and tracking technology, in combination with other technological advances in communication and transportation have matured into an emergent technological paradigm that has already begun to revolutionize the spatial organization of work. E-commerce and the rise of the gig economy have emphasized the importance of speed to market. Coupled with a renationalization of economic discourses as witnessed after Brexit and the election of Trump, this might foreshadow a return of manufacturing to the North Atlantic.

But while we share the assumption that technological innovation ushered in fundamental changes in the past—from the steam engine to the telegraph, the container to the internet—and might do so again, we are much more skeptical when it comes to notions of inexorable progress. We also disagree with the idea that processes of technological development and economic restructuring are external, overcoming us from the outside. In fact, they are highly political and the state remains a key actor on multiple scales—but oftentimes the enabling work it conducts is hard to trace.

The articles united in this book look back at earlier historical formations and compare different cases to sketch how the smart economy is beginning to alter the social and spatial organization of work. But unlike many other treatments of this matter, this book puts a particular emphasis on the persistent role of the state in establishing and maintaining technological networks and new divisions of labor. Foregrounding the spatial politics of emergent economies of the future in such a manner, we seek to raise questions of political legitimacy and social justice.

It might seem paradoxical to focus such an analysis of an impending economic paradigm and new state patterns on the United States. The US has typically been regarded as an exceptional case. This is the country where, at first glance, state intervention would seem most unlikely. The mythology of American exceptionalism is based on precisely that assumption of a reticent state apparatus. The land of the free was built as a contrast to the feudal absolutist states of Europe, its revolution led to government by the people—not central state power—as the key principle of societal organization (Hartz 1955; Lipset 1990). Freedom was often envisaged in these national mythologies as a correlate of markets and individual entrepreneurialism—a vision that social scientists see as a feature of US-American difference and uniqueness to this day (e.g., Hall and Soskice 2001).

Echoing a critique of American exceptionalism in state-market affairs (e.g. Eisner 2011; Panitch and Gindin 2013; Orren and Skowronek 2017), we do not buy into this narrative of the liberal market economy, but rather use the United States as a case in point to outline the materiality and political nature of global restructuring in the smart economy in the seemingly most liberal of all states. As such, the book contributes to a more recent strand in American Studies that has grown more skeptical vis-à-vis the exceptionalist paradigm (Pease 2009; Fluck 2011 and 2016). While many of the transnational literatures (e.g., Tyrrell 1991; Thelen 1998; Fishkin 2005) that have emerged since the end of the Cold War equate post-exceptionalism with postnationalism, however, we insist that we have by no means arrived at a moment where either state or nation are overcome (see also Vormann 2014 and 2018; Lammert et al. 2018). Instead, we seek to move beyond exceptionalism by highlighting the ideal-typical features of state activity that are common to all types of national contexts and that are fundamental to ensuring circulation.

The Roots of the Smart Economy

How do political actors and institutions facilitate technological change, build infrastructures and securitize circulation to make globalization work?

By shifting the attention from debates on financialization and the footloose nature of capital, so dominant in globalization literature, to the spatial and physical dimensions of economic processes, our analysis offers new vistas on the persistent role of states and on the actual viability of green economy utopias. While state-market relations, the spatial organization of production and consumption, the role of political institutions and actors, are all historically specific, we can see continuities that the smart economy shares with earlier political economies, from the 19th century rise of national economies to the Fordist and flexible economies of the 20th century. As a historical perspective reveals, the state was at no point antagonistic to the market, but always took on facilitating roles. If its visibility and patterns of intervention shifted over time, state and market have always been intricately interconnected and codependent.

How exactly the state intervenes in markets matters enormously. As we shall see, the specific constellations of state-market relations have serious implications for democracy. Broader changes in production regimes both presuppose and result from changes in the configuration of state entities. These changes are functions of many factors: shifts in the hegemonic ideological assumptions about statehood and market efficiency, transitions in the spatial set-up of production networks, exogenous crises and shocks, to name but a few. Ultimately, democratic legitimacy was at no point an essential requirement for these arrangements to produce flourishing markets. But in the past, some of them did create certain conditions that made democracy more likely than others. Those were historical periods, when liberalism was extended from its economic meaning (free markets and small states) to its political dimension (including political and social rights). A brief historical synopsis helps undergird this crucial point.

In the 19th century, the emergence of national economies coincided with the consolidation of the modern bourgeois state. The establishment of canals, postal systems, railroads and telegraphs created national systems of circulation and exchange that were heavily financed and subsidized by the state. In turn, the central state solidified and professionalized to govern and coordinate industrialization processes and to reinvent markets as large-scale abstractions (Braudel 1983; Polanyi [1944] 2001; Slater and Tonkiss 2001). The expansion of market networks to a continental scale in North America *presupposed* the actual installation of federal governing capacities and the professionalization of the administrative state (from civil administration, to the army, and business regulation; see Skowronek 1982). At that point state activity revolved mainly around the enforcement of property rights and law and order.

Security and the establishment of a framework for wealth creation also created the backdrop for what T.H. Marshall later conceived of as civil citizenship, that is, participation in society as an economic actor on the market place (Marshall [1950] 2009). In the North Atlantic world, this general framework thereby also allowed for the manifestation of new power struggles between rising interests, notably the emergent middle classes, labor and industrial capitalists. In essence, these contestations later gave rise to claims for political participation, inclusive policies and governmental responsiveness: the Marshallian idea of political citizenship (Marshall [1950] 2009). But it would be a mistake to conclude that the progression from civil to political (and ultimately social) rights were following any clear and preordained teleological progression. These rights had to be claimed and fought for.

The Great Depression was the key turning point toward a Fordist economy. New Deal legislation in the United States contained the rationale of Keynesian-Fordist macroeconomic management through (anti-cyclical) investments and redistributive mechanisms. Ensuring aggregate demand and full employment became principle targets of government intervention (Blyth and Matthijs 2017). As such, the Fordist compromise between labor, capital and the state allowed for a national nexus of mass consumption and mass production through redistribution while creating channels of responsiveness through which the state could be held accountable. This spatial arrangement of the economy also allowed labor to leverage collective bargaining powers. In this phase, state intervention was the most visible.

The emancipation of an industrial proletariat that organized in growing unions was but one dimension of a gradual integration of heretofore marginalized populations, which later included women and African-Americans, although only to a certain degree. The social and political integration of those groups gave rise to the principle—never fully realized in practice—that people needed specific economic resources in order to participate in the developing and expanding democratic system. T.H. Marshall captured the idea that some goods needed to be protected from the market—or "decommodified"—in what he called *social citizenship* rights. As redistribution, decommodification and regulation facilitated upward mobility, the state became the principle agent in mitigating social risks. The scope of this *liberal state* exceeded the tasks of ensuring economic freedom and securing trade, but reflected the principles of political liberalism (such as universal voting rights, religious and free speech) and assured the institutional mechanisms (through redistributive and regulatory measures) to socially maintain it.

The modern welfare state was openly interventionist—and therefore also vulnerable to critique from both sides of the political spectrum: From the left, which accused it of an inescapable state capitalism that subjugated all spontaneity and desire to technocratic and instrumental rationality, and from the right, which highlighted the paternalism of the state, the utility-maximization of public actors, and the fatal tendency toward totalitarianism. After the crises of the 1970s, Hayekian critiques of the central state and Friedmanite visions of a supply-side economy gained currency and entered an uncanny alliance with progressive calls for individual liberalization. New technologies in communication and transportation fully undermined the Fordist compromise and made global production networks economically possible. Ostensibly, the state retreated.

In reaction to the (partly self-imposed) global pressures, state entities from local to federal governments were reenvisioned as "competitive" (Cerny 1999), "entrepreneurial" (Harvey 1989; Mazzucato 2015) actors whose chief goals became low inflation rates and the attraction of global flows of capital and high-skilled populations. Competitiveness in the flexible economy implied downsizing and restructuring the welfare state as well as the reinvention of education and labor markets to flexibilize workers and maximize "human capital" (Becker 1964). On a macro-economic level, this shift implied the deindustrialization of major regions in the US and the rise of what some described as the knowledge-based and service-oriented "postindustrial society" (Bell 1976). On a micro-level, it led to the shift of social risks towards individual self-responsibility (Hacker 2006). As austerity became the new mantra on both sides of the Atlantic (Peck 2010; Blyth 2013), states restructured and responsiveness decreased—a development aggravated by skyrocketing inequalities and the ensuing uneven voice in the political system. The slashing of public expenditures in social services and the radically-reduced procurement of public goods also severely limited upward mobility, amplifying the lack of trust in establishment politics and the legitimacy crisis currently under way (Blyth and Matthijs 2017; Hopkin 2017).

As an increasing number of scholars point out, the state never really disappeared in the flexible economy, but simply changed in function and became less visible. "American Amnesia" (Hacker and Pierson 2016) contributed to a myth of statelessness in which the "hidden" (Howard 1997), "submerged" state (Mettler 2011) compounded the problem of lacking responsiveness, while at the same time being highly "entrepreneurial" (Mazzucato 2015) and "innovative" (Block and Keller 2011). This more recent debate stands in sharp contrast to popular notions of a powerless state beleaguered by globalizing pressures. Indeed, the *illiberal state* is highly functional—but its actions lack accountability and are reduced to the bare minimum of enabling economic exchange in a proto-liberal sense. As we argue in this book, in large part the crisis of legitimacy of political actors is a result of an invisible, technocratic illiberal state whose social and political purpose has been stripped off and whose main tasks focus on the facilitation of flow. But since the state cannot 'go away' the utopian notions of the smart economy need to be weighed against the destructive potentials of a fully depoliticized technocracy.

Is it a coincidence that the crisis of legitimacy which recently gave way to anti-establishment movements from Trump to Brexit and Syriza coincides with the emergence of the smart economy? On the surface, technological advances seem to have reached new heights, obliterating the role of the state in markets. It is perhaps not a surprise, then, that the state seems even less legitimate under conditions that seemingly render it obsolete. And so one might begin to wonder whether the smart economy could even solve the crisis of democracy in facilitating new modes of social organization beyond spatial and political constraints. We decidedly reject this claim.

A Typology of State Action

It is no news to state theorists and economic sociologists that free markets are ultimately a utopian idea. Property rights need to be ensured, currencies stabilized, and contracts enforced. Without law and order—a minimum of security for trade to happen—and without these preconditions in place, markets cannot exist. Social contract theorists and early liberal political economists of the 17th and 18th century, from Thomas Hobbes to John

Locke to Adam Smith, agreed on these basic needs. In what is one of the most well-known passages of *The Leviathan*, Hobbes maintains that without the order provided by the state, there is "no place for Industry; because the fruit thereof is uncertain; and consequently no Culture of the Earth; no Navigation, nor use of the commodities that may be imported by Sea […]" (Hobbes [1651] 2008). As Hobbes famously assumed, this state of affairs characteristically had "no account of Time; no Arts; no Letters; no Society; and which is worst of all, continual fear, and danger of violent death […]."

Hobbes shares this insight with Adam Smith who, some 120 years later and at the cusp of the industrial revolution, took the argument even further. Although often cited and credited for his concept of the invisible hand and the coordinating function of markets in expanding divisions of labor, Smith was acutely aware of the need for state protection. With reference to what today's economists would describe as cases of market failure, Smith pointed out that markets could only thrive under conditions where states provided a stable framework. Even more than that: Book V of his *Wealth of Nations* goes into great lengths to elucidate how the government needed to build infrastructures and provide national defense and other public goods (Smith [1776] 2003).

While neoliberals of the past four decades have strongly emphasized the shortcomings of the state and predicted its impending decline (e.g., Ohmae 1995; Katzenstein 2005), the 2008 financial crisis has bolstered a heterodox strand of political economy literature at the fringes of mainstream economics that points out the persistent importance of state interventions in globalization processes. Building on prior work by authors such as Theda Skocpol et al. (1985) or Fran Tonkiss and Don Slater (2001), Jamie Peck (2010), Suzanne Mettler (2011), Mark Blyth (2013), Stephan Leibfried et al. (2015), Mariana Mazzucato (2015 and 2018) and many others have pointed out in one way or another how markets always co-depend on state institutions. It would not be very difficult to extend this list, especially with titles after the global financial crisis which, at least on the level of scholarly debates, seem to have worked to profoundly question market fundamentalist thinking.

We build on this existing scholarship to outline patterns of state activity as it facilitates the building of global production networks. However, we differ from this existing literature in what we see as a crucial point. Instead of deriving our typology from institutional capabilities or an analysis of state investments in a particular policy field, we zoom in on the interactions of state actors at various levels of government and the dynamic arrangements they enter to produce new spatial economies. In other words, we focus our analysis of state intervention on a coherent whole. Rather than looking in an additive manner at individual policies of the state in different subfields and on different levels—such as its educational or transportation policies under the influence of global competition—we reverse the analytical perspective. We use circulation as a methodological tool to understand how states facilitate expanding markets by ensuring flows of people, capital and commodities. As such we can draw into one analytical universe what might otherwise be regarded as incoherent and detached individual policies. And we can do so by tapping into a burgeoning social science literature on the social functions and implications of infrastructure (Boutros and Straw 2010; Cowen 2014; Angelo and Hentschel 2015; Burchardt and Höhne 2015; Vormann 2015; Easterling 2016; Peck 2017; Chua et al. 2018; Danyluk 2018; Klinenberg 2018; Vormann and DeDauw 2018).

Ultimately, we contend that the smart economy can be governed without any necessary reference in rhetoric or practice to liberal democracy. In fact, democracy might be a hindrance to the efficient resource allocation and productivity increases—as the case of China, above all, seems to suggest. Paradoxically, given the current crisis of liberal democracy, which is an immanent crisis born of a surplus, not a lack of technocracy, political liberalism seems to be undermined by economic liberalism (Brown 2015; Lammert and Vormann 2017). The illiberal state governs the smart economy in a manner absolved from questions of democratic legitimacy and reduced in its functions to the bareknuckle role of the enabler, shaper and developer of markets and circulation. These are the three core functions that states fulfill in historically specific ways in order to make circulation possible (see table below).

The foundational work of the state includes its facilitation of a basic market framework. As a *market enabler*, the state uses its monopoly on the legitimate use of violence and its capacity to tax so as to codify property rights, enforce contracts and legal rights, ensure domestic security and order, and build the basic communication and transportation infrastructures (from railroad networks to highways) that enable circulation. In addition to constructing and institutionally stabilizing trade corridors, the state also harmonizes trade through standardization and procures the transactional environments and legal architectures that allow for frictionless circulation. Finally, the state rallies the factors of production: by mobilizing and immobilizing people and resources, by clearing, parceling and consolidating land, and by ensuring demand either through redistribution (in the Fordist context) or through subsidized cheap credit (as in the flexible economy).

As a *market shaper*, the state responds to demands by different actors—to the rising labor movements of the 19th century or 21st century financial capital—and actively shapes market behavior through regulation, redistribution, investment incentives and innovations on various levels of government. The state regulates market entry, (re)structures labor relations, compensates and mitigates between different interests, ensures or repeals worker safety and protection, ensures minimum education and health care. More globally speaking and more succinctly put: it facilitates reproduction in ways that are more or less intent on providing civic, political or social citizenship rights. Its shaping role also implies the active decision not to internalize costs and regulate certain markets, for instance, pollution on the high seas, or exploitation through labor standard arbitrage (Wallerstein 2004, 46-48). Indeed, active investments and rather invisible cost shifts along supply chains are increasingly part and parcel of state interventions in an ideological context determined by principles of austerity and market efficiency (Vormann 2015; Patel and Moore 2017).

By *market developer*, we are referring to the tasks the state fulfills to ensure the expansion of existing markets. The state invests in new technologies through direct loan programs, tax rebates, public investments in basic research and development, and sales mandates. This also implies the maintenance and securitization of trade networks beyond its territory. The state acts as a political force in expanding economic exchange, invests in technological advancement and military capability and secures chokepoints. The state manages territorial expansion and global interaction through the creation of new trade structures (trade agreements, territorial annexation, etc.) and fosters expansion through the development and deployment of globally networked technologies (internet, containerized trade, etc.). Finally, beyond its borders, the state establishes and maintains the conditions for extraction on the periphery, for instance through collaboration with (or coercion of) weak states that liberalize their resource markets or industrial sectors through tax exemptions and low tax rates.

The orthodox notion of self-healing markets and self-regulating equilibriums tends to distract us from this very political basis of the market.

Yet, as Karl Polanyi so cogently pointed out over six decades ago, the concept of the free market has always been an unattainable aspiration: "While the laissez-faire economy was the product of deliberate state action, subsequent restrictions on laissez-faire started in a spontaneous way. Laissez-faire was planned; planning was not." ([1944] 2001, 147) This holds true today. By no means has the state become a passive agent that simply reacts to external pressures created by overwhelming market powers and that pursues fixes after the fact of so-called exogenous crises.

Dimensions	*Tasks*
Market enabler Establishing basic framework and conditions of possibility	– Land clearing, enclosures, dispossession – Property rights; law and order; sound currency and contract enforcement – Harmonization of technical standards; creation of conducive transactional environments – Ensuring demand (e.g., redistribution or cheap credit) – Selectively mobilizing and immobilizing circulation of (certain types of) people and commodities – Reduction of communication and transportation costs through infrastructure provision (ports, airports, highways; pipelines and railroads, etc.)
Market shaper Guiding of growth and steering capacity	– Minimal protection (child labor, work safety, etc.) – Evolving welfare apparatus to mitigate social risk and ensure reproduction, incl. education of the labor force, health care system, old age security; but also in the inverse sense, e.g. through labor market restructuring – Economic valuation (unproductive vs. productive land) – Regulation/Deregulation (incl. licensing, re-zoning, monopolization, externalities, etc.)
Market developer Facilitating expansion, maintenance and securitization of trade networks	– Research and development; 'picking winners' – Provision of market incentives, e.g. through taxes, subsidies, grants such as land grants to ensure territorial expansion – Creating markets and trade networks beyond the political entity through direct (military, financial, etc.) intervention or external pressure (diplomacy, negotiations, etc.) – Ensuring circulation through security of logistical bottlenecks – Active externalization of costs (pollution, citizenship arbitrage)

Table 1: Typology of State Intervention: Dimensions and Tasks

As we shift our view from piecemeal state actions in individual policy fields to the necessities of circulation, it becomes clear that statehood implies active and creative aspects of intervention. Salvaging politics and state intervention in this way means to denaturalize what otherwise seems inevitable, logical or common sense (as frequently argued about globalization, technological progress, increased mobility, or, on the local level, gentrification). Some public goods are simply not procured by markets in a sufficient and (pareto-)efficient manner. States need to facilitate markets where they do not work. But while passive reaction always appears as necessary and inevitable, foregrounding state action gives relevance to questions of social justice and shifts debates from the realm of the technocratic to the democratic.

Infrastructural Statecraft: Logistics, Power and Circulation

At the risk of belaboring the point: In taking these roles as an enabler, shaper and developer of markets, the state does not stand in contradiction with globalized production networks, but is a central actor in making them possible. The first section of this volume develops this claim empirically and investigates historical functions of statecraft to flesh out some of its pivotal tasks. In a comparative manner, the chapters point out state interventions during the 19th century era of westward expansion and state consolidation all the way to the liberalizations and deregulations of international trade in the second half of the 20th century. A central question in this context is how these transitions have facilitated and shaped labor regimes, creating more or less conducive conditions for economic, political, and social emancipation.

In his essay, Patrick DeDauw looks to the United States' northern neighbor to examine the logics of late 19th century Western expansion and to systematize our understanding of state involvement in that continental annexation. DeDauw uses logistics infrastructure as an analytical lens to flesh out the rationalities of development and state intervention that were necessary for Canadian colonial settlements. Viewed from this angle, settler colonialism no longer appears to us as an opaque and ultimately inexplicable drive for expansion, but as a set of processes following their own spatial logics producing very specific repercussions for existing social relations on the ground. DeDauw's analysis confirms that similar state patterns constitute a structural response to and anticipation of the necessities of expanding markets. As such, the state was the main player in facilitating certain types of mobility over others. Historical forms of racism, DeDauw insists, are by no means only about race itself (though they certainly are that as well), but can also be seen as a correlate of putting land to its "highest and best use" in historically and geographically specific ways.

Christian Güse shifts our attention from the 19th to the 20th century. He takes a *longue durée* perspective to outline how the state has actively facilitated circulation and today's labor relations in global production networks. Taking a closer look at the role the US nation-state played in establishing global supply networks, he argues that the state strategy of the 1970s must be understood as a deliberate project to mold the rise and shape of global supply networks. The investment in specific transportation technologies as well as policies of deregulation and privatization were employed to reshape labor relations in the transportation sector so as to make global supply chains profitable for shipping corporations. Güse's main claim is that emerging supply chains and the subsequent erosion of working conditions in the transportation industry have not simply been the outcome of natural technological developments and a supposed unraveling of political institutions. Instead, the role of the state as an enabler and developer of global production has been essential and active in the rise of global production networks.

After the fall of the Berlin Wall, liberal capitalism seemed invincible and many commentators and decision-makers thought it would be a question of time until global markets would ensure global peace and democracy. As a pivotal part of this grand vision, new free trade agreements have been in the center of much scholarly debate and public contention since the 1970s. An often neglected aspect of the expansion of trade, however, has been the physical facilitation of free trade. Tommaso Burdet zooms in on how specifically the US state needed to rework its border spaces to facilitate trade with Mexico. Beyond enabling trade through harmonized technical and safety standards, ensuring seamless circulation implied the management of congestion at the ports of entry and along trade corridors through the (partial) liberalization of cabotage restrictions and major infrastructural investments, notably in the World Trade Bridge in Laredo and the Bridge of the Americas in El Paso. Burdet points out how these and other constructions also depended on investments in adjacent infrastructures and facilities to draw suppliers and factories into a network of seamless exchange.

After the terrorist attacks of September 11, 2001, the US federal government became particularly active in separating certain types of desirable flows from unwanted ones. Security initiatives such as the so-called C-TPAT and FAST programs served as parts of a multi-layered approach by government means to try and ensure circulation while seeking to avoid friction in the supply chain, fast-tracking some flows while filtering out others. In deploying these "strategic selectivities," Burdet argues, the state has actively shaped the infrastructural environment of the border space as a semi-permeable membrane—a focal site, where the state needs to manage its interactions with other actors.

The Smart City: Grounding the Economy of the Future

One of the central tropes of the smart economy is that of the smart city. Building on our understanding of infrastructural statecraft developed in the prior section, the subsequent chapters contextualize smart cities in these broader networks of exchange. Our focus shifts from the capacities and forms of intervention by the central state to the local government and its embedded position within global circulation. The chapters question the notion of market-based growth and the green economy solutions envisaged in smart city discourses. Foregrounding state activity, this research builds on and contributes to critical work on urban and city-regional governance as well as on "planetary urbanization" (Harvey 1989, Brenner 2004; Angelo and Wachsmuth 2014; Brenner and Schmid 2015; Brenner 2017; Danyluk 2018; Wachsmuth 2017).

Tobias Kalt contrasts the utopian notion of the smart city and its visions of pollution-free mobility to the ways in which states create and fuel forms of circulation. The uneven development that they sustain on a global scale, according to Kalt, is what renders sustainable cities possible in the first place. The chapter traces circuits of commodity exchange and examines socio-material flows along the supply chain from the zones of consumption of electric cars to the zones where the vehicles are manufactured and to the zones of extraction and processing of mineral resources. Specifically, Kalt highlights the political work necessary to establish and maintain these flows. He points out who is capable of chanelling socio-ecological costs to the periphery so as to capture economic benefits in the center. In excavating these global flows that commonly remain hidden from view, Kalt mounts a critique of the smart economy that calls the hopes placed in the smart city into question.

Another aspect of the smart economy that many deem a reason for optimism relates to the urban potential of the sharing economy. Jonas Pentzien's chapter shows us how politics remains important in this realm, even if it might seemingly be crowded out by an all-powerful private digital platform. In current research, the disruptive impact of for-profit sharing economy platforms on a state's regulatory capacity is often taken as a given. Empirical studies supporting this claim, however, are scant. By taking a closer look at consequences, intended or not, of Berlin's, New York City's and Barcelona's supposedly failing ban on short term rental platforms, Pentzien's essay provides evidence to the contrary. He shows that it is not so much the technological specificity of sharing platforms that negatively impacts state capacities, but opposing interests between local, regional and state governments. Based on this empirical insight, the chapter develops a scale-based analysis of the sharing economy that explains shifting state-market relations not through the purported specificity of technological innovation, but with growth-related contradictions within the state apparatus. Far from being "disrupted" Pentzien claims that seemingly-failing bans do not reflect an increasing governmental incapability of regulating technological innovation, but instead display opposing logics of growth, expressing themselves within and across different political scales.

Adding an ethnographic dimension to our discussions of the smart city, Jeremy Williams asks how urban nodal points of the smart economy are actually reshaped and reinvented as spaces of circulation. His chapter discusses the functions of public space through a case study of the High Line in New York City. An elevated park on the site of an old goods railway line running from the Meatpacking District to Midtown Manhattan, the High Line is paradigmatic of the new types of public space which are becoming increasingly prevalent across the United States, according to Williams. The chapter investigates their four key characteristics: the invisible yet contradictory role of government; the spatial manifestations of the socio-cultural process of marketization (in particular what he calls the financialization of worth); the increased level of social control which govern such public spaces; and the increased atmosphere of performance and spectacle. Williams notes that spaces with these characteristics are not only unsatisfactory from a democratic and experiential point of view, but also undermine the possibility of political or social change. As such, they contribute to the problem of depoliticizing all things political in an increasingly technologistic smart economy utopia.

Labor, Technological Utopias and Emancipatory Potentials

The third section of this book focuses on labor in the smart economy and its potentials for emancipation on a more theoretical level. As Keynesian-Fordist mass production was replaced by flexibilized short-term work in the service industries in the second half of the 20th century, many scholars have emphasized the increasingly immaterial aspects of work. As Astrid Zimmermann's essay points out, this notion is misleading at best. Her chapter addresses the role of digital technologies within the current organization of work. While important strands of contemporary research on digital labor stress the politically emancipatory potentials of digital technologies, her chapter takes an opposing stance. Zimmermann contends that a look at the underlying material conditions of production on a global scale demonstrates that the projected potentials of digitization cannot be realized through technological progress alone. Rather than having turned labor immaterial, digitization is interconnected to the continual internationalization of capital and the migration of labor-intensive industries into low-wage zones in the periphery of economic development.

It has become fashionable in recent years to point out parallels between the United States of today and at the turn of the 20th century. Dave Braneck agrees that in both periods inequalities were rampant, technological change led to disruption and restructuring, but contends that the comparison is misleading. At first brush, today's gilded age might resemble the early 20th century in these superficial ways, but in fact, from the perspective of labor, today's context is much more problematic. While the Progressive Era and the early 20th century was a period of state-building and early labor organization, producing collective bargaining powers and emancipatory potentials for the working class—or, as Braneck puts it, while labor was "ascendant"—today's realities look significantly bleaker, given the unbundling of these institutions, deunionization and economic restructuring in global production networks. Despite any superficial similarities between the periods, then, the details of the contextual shifts of each period had drastically different impacts on work and on potentials for labor organizing, to the point that the comparison obscures more than it illuminates.

Whereas Dave Braneck compares the political leverage of labor today with its capabilities of the *past*, Lasse Thiele directs our attention toward dominant visions of the *future* of work. He critiques notions of the smart, green economy as a hegemonic response to present crises. Thiele argues that questions of employment and technology are particularly illustrative of the shortcomings of such green economy models. Institutional proposals for green growth, he contends, generally follow a technocratic, sector-by-sector approach to environmental sustainability. Despite their emphasis on technological solutions, however, they pay scant attention to the conflicting requirements of capital, labor and ecology with regard to technology. Thiele compares green economy models to discourses on accelerationism and degrowth to ask whether and to what extent a "green" high-tech post-work economy is at all realizable and arrives at the conclusion that even in optimistic scenarios, irresolvable tensions persist.

The Illiberal State: Social Citizenship and the Future of Work

Pointing out the ongoing importance of the state as a political actor is not simply a reflex of an emergent progressive literature to which this book seeks to contribute. More is at stake in these debates on the future and politics of work. Traditionally, social citizenship rights and political rights have been intricately linked to the organization of work. Social policy and welfare are part and parcel of the national economy as it consolidated in the 19th and 20th century (Lammert and Grell 2013). Although the direct causal link between modernization and welfare state development has been challenged many times over, large parts of the literature on welfare states and labor market reforms do see a connection, even if indirect, between the facilitation of production networks and the systematic protection of workers.

Reindustrialization in the Global North today seems to be an ever-more viable possibility. Indeed, more and more policymakers and scholars are pointing out that globalization in the shape we have grown accustomed to since the 1980s may have reached its peak. But if global production networks undermined the Fordist compromise in the past, the fact that they might be reversed or drastically altered through a return to more local and regional forms of production does not automatically imply a return to the political and social promises of the post-World War II era. As we have pointed out, the liberal state was not an inevitable consequence of economic and technological forces. This holds true today.

As Julia Püschel outlines in her concluding remarks to this volume, we might indeed be witnessing a "recursion towards the local" in production networks that prioritize closeness to markets, and stable supply in a period of global volatility and vulnerable supply chains. Automation might provide a way to inshore production without increasing labor costs. In a context where renationalization and neo-mercantilist protectionism threaten stability in international markets, such a strategy seems to become increasingly appealing to manufacturers and corporations.

However, these current debates on reindustrialization and manufacturing—in spite of their emancipatory gesture—entirely ignore questions of political and social citizenship. Instead, North Atlantic societies across the board have witnessed the large-scale expansion of low wage service sectors and a deep polarization on the labor market, rapidly accelerated through the automation of routine work. To be sure, there is no natural law why the new world of work should not be organized in unions. But the last decades show that the protection of labor rights in services and administration will be difficult to reestablish in the smart economy, given the concentration of power in transnational corporations that has rapidly consolidated through mergers and acquisitions after the 2008 global financial crisis.

A similar scenario would of course apply if work were entirely automated. Against fantasies of the robotic city and utopias of full automation, however, the end of work seems by no means near. If past predictions are any indicator, well-known economists have been wrong before when making similar prognoses. Famously, John Maynard Keynes assumed that for his grandchildren work would only constitute a minor detail of their existence. He assumed that their biggest challenge would be how to live meaningfully with all the free time technological advances would afford them. Just as in earlier historical shifts, rather than the complete overcoming of work, it is more likely that new jobs will be created to administer and service the smart economy.

Old questions will have to be posed anew: how to ensure demand? At a moment where nobody earns a living wage from their labor? Fordist Keynesianism stabilized aggregate demand through redistribution and the state also ensured the expansion of cheap credit after Fordism collapsed. How can it be maintained in the future? Can the universal basic income (UBI) solve this problem in the smart economy? The UBI is supported on both sides of the political spectrum—and it chimes with the governance logic of the rising illiberal state. In its conservative incarnation, it implies the complete marketization of all social relations and policy fields, as it enables individuals to become market participants and buy all goods and services (including welfare) on the market place. This also means that responsibilities could be entirely devolved to the level of the individual. The role of the state as a manager and mitigator of capital-labor relations would thereby become completely obsolete.

This, in turn, might have drastic repercussions on the functioning of democracy as the illiberal state would be freed from all social responsibility. In such a context, responsiveness would lose its meaning as a base for legitimacy entirely, while elections would become a completely hollowed out ritual. If the smart economy would take that turn, output (prosperity, life expectancy, happiness, etc.) would become the only source of legitimacy whereas input through democratic institutions and accountability mechanism (such as elections) would be rendered meaningless. As such, the state would degenerate into a committee of public safety—a *comité de salut publique*. And so the difference between liberal democracies and autocratic states of the present might slowly fade from view.

If democracy is to be a governing principle to organize societies—as we think it should be—than the illiberal state cannot be a legitimate way to enter the smart economy. If the universal basic income will one day be regarded by a political majority as a valid policy instrument remains to be seen. But a progressive variant of this tool will require a more emancipatory vision and constant vigilance to avoid a fully disconnected and economized public. The same holds true for visions of a Green New Deal. As such, liberalism itself will need to be reinvented in a way that gives equal balance to the political values of the liberal tradition as it does to its economic strand. Regardless of the future contours of the smart economy, the notion of what progress means will need to be reinvented and extended. This reimagining will have to develop a new understanding of politics as an active shaping force that can be held accountable by a democratic public.

Works Cited

Albinsson, Pia A. and B. Yasanthi Perera (eds.)(2018). *The Rise of the Sharing Economy. Exploring the Challenges and Opportunities of Collaborative Consumption.* Santa Barbara, CA: ABC-CLIO.

Angelo, Hillary and Christine Hentschel (2015). Interactions with Infrastructure as Windows into Social Worlds. A Method for Critical Urban Studies. *CITY*, 19. 2–3, 306–12.

Angelo, Hillary and David Wachsmuth (2014). Urbanizing Urban Political Ecology: A Critique of Methodological Cityism. *IJURR*, 39.1, 16–27.

Becker, Gary S. (1964). *Human Capital. A Theoretical and Empirical Analysis with Special Reference to Education.* Chicago, IL: University of Chicago Press.

Bell, Daniel (1976). *The Coming of Postindustrial Society: A Venture in Social Forecasting.* New York, NY: Basic Books.

Block, Fred and Matthew R. Keller (2011). *State of Innovation. The US Government's Role in Technology Development.* New York, NY: Routledge.

Blyth, Mark and Matthias Matthijs (2017). Black Swans, Lame Ducks, and the mystery of IPE's missing macroeconomy. *Review of International Political Economy*, 24.2, 203–31.

Blyth, Mark (2013). *Austerity: The History of a Dangerous Idea.* Oxford: Oxford University Press.

Boutros, Alexandra and Will Straw (2010). *Circulation and the City: Essays on Urban Culture.* Montreal: McGill-Queen's University Press.

Braudel, Fernand (1983). *The Wheels of Commerce.* London: Book Clubs Associates.

Brenner, Neil (2017). *Critique of Urbanization: Selected Essays.* Gütersloh: Bauverlag; Basel: Birkhäuser.

Brenner, Neil and Christian Schmid (2015). Towards a new epistemology of the urban? *CITY*, 19.2-3, 151–82.

Brenner, Neil (2004). *New State Spaces. Urban Governance and the Rescaling of Statehood.* Oxford: Oxford University Press.

Brown, Wendy (2015). *Undoing the Demos. Neoliberalism's Stealth Revolution.* Brooklyn, NY: Zone BOOKS.

Brynjolfsson, Erik and Andrew McAfee (2014). *The Second Machine Age: Work, Progress, and Prosperity in a Time of Brilliant Technologies.* New York, NY: W. W. Norton & Company.

Burchardt, Marian and Stefan Höhne (2015). The Infrastructures of Diversity: Materiality and Culture in Urban Space – An Introduction. *New Diversities*, 17.2, 1–13.

Cerny, Philip G. (1997). Paradoxes of the Competition State: The Dynamic of Political Globalisation, Government and Opposition. *Government and Opposition*, 32.2, 251–71.

Chua, Charmaine, Martin Danyluk, Deborah Cowen, Laleh Khalili (2018). Introduction: Turbulent Circulation: Building a Critical Engagement with Logistics, *Environment and Planning D: Society and Space*, 36.4, 617–629.

Cowen, Deborah (2014). *The Deadly Life of Logistics: Mapping Violence in Global Trade.* Minneapolis, MN: Univ. of Minnesota Press.

Danyluk, Martin (2018). Capital's Logistical Fix: Accumulation, Globalization, and the Survival of Capitalism. *Environment and Planning D: Society and Space,* 36.4, 630–647.

Dyer-Witheford, Nick (2015). *Cyber-Proletariat. Global Labour in the Digital Vortex.* London: Pluto Press.

Easterling, Keller (2016). *Extrastatecraft: The Power of Infrastructure Space.* London: Verso.

Eisner, Marc Allen (2011). *The American Political Economy. Institutional Evolution of Market and State.* New York, NY: Routledge.

Fishkin, Shelley Fisher (2005). Crossroads of Cultures: The Transnational Turn in American Studies—Presidential Address to the American Studies Association, November 12, 2004. *American Quarterly*, 57.1, 17–57.

Fluck, Winfried (2016). American Exceptionalism: Ein Schlüssel zum Amerikanischen Selbstverständnis. In Christian Lammert, Markus Siewert and Boris Vormann (eds.). *Handbuch Politik USA,* 15–28. Wiesbaden: Springer VS.

Fluck, Winfried (2011). A New Beginning? Transnationalisms. *New Literary History,* 42, 365–384.

George, Samuel and Felipe Buitrago (2017). The No Collar Economy. Washington, DC: Bertelsmann.

Hacker, Jacob. S. (2006). *The Great Risk Shift. The Assault on American Jobs, Families, Health Care and Retirement.* New York, NY: Oxford University Press.

Hacker, Jacob. S. and Paul Pierson (2016). *American Amnesia. How the War on Government Led Us to Forget America Prosper.* New York, NY: Simon and Schuster.

Hall, Richard A. and David Soskice (eds.) (2001). *Varieties of Capitalism. The Institutional Foundations of Comparative Advantage.* Oxford: Oxford University Press.

Hartz, Louis (1955). *The Liberal Tradition in America: An Interpretation of American Political Thought since the Revolution.* New York, NY: Harcourt, Brace & Company.

Harvey, David (1989). From Managerialism to Entrepreneurialism: The Transformation in Urban Governance in Late Capitalism. *Geografiska Annaler. Series B, Human Geography*, 71.1, 3–17.

Hobbes, Thomas (2008) [1651]. *Leviathan.* New York, NY: Oxford University Press.

Hopkin, Jonathan (2017). When Polanyi Met Farage: Market Fundamentalism, Economic Nationalism, and Britain's Exit from the European Union. *The British Journal of Politics and International Relations*, 19.3, 465–478.

Howard, Christopher (1997). *The Hidden Welfare State. Tax Expenditures and Social Policy in the United States.* Princeton, NJ: Princeton University Press.

Huws, Ursula (2014). *Labor in the Global Digital Economy.* New York, NY: Monthly Review Press.

Katzenstein, Peter J. (2005). *A World of Regions. Asia and Europe in the American Imperium.* Ithaca, NY: Cornell University Press.

Kenis, Anneleen and Matthias Lievens (2015). *The Limits of the Green Economy. From Reinventing Capitalism to Repoliticizing the Present.* New York, NY: Routledge.

Klinenberg, Eric (2018). *Palaces for the People: How Social Infrastructure Can Help Fight Inequality, Polarization, and the Decline of Civic Life.* New York, NY: Crown.

Lammert, Christian, Christoph M. Haas and Simon Koschut (2018). *Politik in den USA: Themen – Akteure – Konflikte.* Stuttgart: Kohlhammer.

Lammert, Christian and Boris Vormann (2017). *Die Krise der Demokratie und wie wir sie überwinden.* Berlin: Aufbau.

Lammert, Christian and Britta Grell (2013). *Sozialpolitik in den USA: Eine Einführung.* Wiesbaden: Springer VS.

Leibfried, Stephan, Evelyne Huber, Matthew Lange, Jonah D. Levy, and John D. Stephens (eds.). (2015). *The Oxford Handbook of Transformations of the State.* Oxford: Oxford University Press.

Lipset, Seymour Martin (1990). *Continental Divide: The Values and Institutions of the United States and Canada.* New York, NY: Routledge.

Marshall, T. H. (2009). [1950]. Citizenship and Social Class. In Jeff Manza and Michael Sauder (eds.). *Inequality and Society*, 148–54. New York, NY: W.W. Norton and Co.

Mazzucato, Mariana (2018). *The Value of Everything: Making and Taking in the Global Economy.* London: Allen Lane.

Mazzucato, Mariana (2015). *The Entrepreneurial State. Debunking Public vs. Private Sector Myths.* Philadelphia, PA: Public Affairs.

Mettler, Suzanne (2011). *The Submerged State. How Invisible Government Policies Undermine American Democracy.* Chicago, IL: The University of Chicago Press.

Mulcahy, Diane (2016). *The Gig Economy. The Complete Guide to Getting Better Work, Taking More Time Off, and Financing the Life You Want.* New York, NY: Harper Collins.

Ng, Irene C. L. (2014). *Creating New Markets in the Digital Economy. Value and Worth.* Cambridge, MA: Cambridge University Press.

Ohmae, Kenichi (1995). *The End of the Nation-State: The Rise of Regional Economies.* New York, NY: The Free Press.

Orren, Karen and Stephen Skowronek (2017). *The Policy State. An American Predicament.* Cambridge, MA: Harvard University Press.

Panitch, Leo and Sam Gindin (2013). *The Making of Global Capitalism. The Political Economy of Empire.* London: Verso.

Patel, Raj and Jason Moore (2017). *A History of the World in Seven Cheap Things: A Guide to Capitalism, Nature, and the Future of the Planet.* Oakland, CA: University of California Press.

Peck, Jamie (2017). *Offshore: Exploring the Worlds of Global Outsourcing.* Oxford: Oxford University Press.

Peck, Jamie (2010). *Constructions of Neoliberal Reason.* Oxford & New York, NY: Oxford University Press.

Pease, Donald E. (2009). *The New American Exceptionalism.* Minneapolis, MN: University of Minnesota Press.

Polanyi, Karl (2001) [1944]. *The Great Transformation. The Political and Economic Origins of Our Time.* Boston, MA: Beacon Press.

Rifkin, Jeremy (2015). *The Zero Marginal Cost Society: The Internet of Things, the Collaborative Commons, and the Eclipse of Capitalism.* New York, NY: St. Martin's Griffin.

Rindermann, Heiner (2018). *Cognitive Capitalism. Human Capital and the Well-being of Nations.* Cambridge, MA: Cambridge University Press.

Scholz, Trebor (2016). *Uberworked and Underpaid. How Workers are Disrupting the Digital Economy.* Cambridge, UK: Polity Press.

Skocpol, Theda, Peter B. Evans, and Dietrich Rueschemeyer (eds.)(1985). *Bringing the State Back In.* Cambridge, MA: Cambridge University Press.

Skowronek, Stephen (1982). *Building a New American State. The Expansion of National Administrative Capacities, 1877–1920.* Cambridge, MA: Cambridge University Press.

Slater, Don and Fran Tonkiss (2001). *Market Society. Markets and Modern Social Theory.* Malden, MA: Polity Press.

Smith, Adam (2003) [1776]. *The Wealth of Nations.* New York, NY: Random House.

Srnicek, Nick (2017). *Platform Capitalism.* Malden, MA: Polity.

Sundararajan, Arun (2016). *The Sharing Economy. The End of Employment and the Rise of Crowd-based Capitalism.* Cambridge, MA: The MIT Press.

Thelen, David (1998). Making History and Making the United States. *Journal of American Studies*, 32.3, 373–97.

Tolley, Kim (ed.)(2018). *Professors in the Gig Economy. Unionizing Adjunct Faculty in America.* Baltimore, MD: Johns Hopkins University Press.

Tyrrell, Ian (1991). American Exceptionalism in an Age of International History. *American Historical Review,* October, 1031–1055.

Vormann, Boris (2018). Greater than the Sum of its Parts. The Unrealized Potentials of Interdisciplinary Area Studies. In Frank Kelleter and Alexander Starre (eds.). *Projecting American Studies: Essays on Theory, Method, and Practice,* 183–196. Heidelberg: Winter.

Vormann, Boris and Patrick DeDauw (2018). Off Shore: The Sustainable City and its Logistical Costs. In Jason Monios and Gordon Wilmsmeier (eds.). *Maritime Mobilities*, 75–90. New York, NY: Routledge.

Vormann, Boris (2015). Toward an Infrastructural Critique of Urban Change. Obsolescence and Changing Perceptions of New York City's Waterfront. *CITY,* 19, 2-3, 332–340.

Vormann, Boris (2014). Who Needs American Studies? Globalization, Nationalism, and the Future of Area Studies. *American Studies*/Amerikastudien, 59.3, 387–406.

Wachsmuth, David (2017). Infrastructure Alliances: Supply-Chain Expansion and Multi-City Growth Coalitions. *Economic Geography*, 93.1, 643–653.

Wallerstein, Immanuel (2004). *World-Systems Analysis. An Introduction.* Durham, NY, and London: Duke University Press.

I. Infrastructural Statecraft: Logistics, Power and Circulation

Logistics of Settlement: Rethinking the Political Economic Geography of Canadian Colonial Expansion

Patrick DeDauw

Struggles over land use lie at the heart of debates around settler colonialism. In these histories, we follow scene after scene of state-orchestrated and extra-legal dispossession, of Indigenous people pushed off and denied life-sustaining access to ever-larger pieces of land. These enclosed lands then provide the basis for economic development to the benefit of an invading population and the (usually European) sponsoring state. Consequently, the colonial state undertakes various means of eliminating Indigenous communities' possible interference with that economic activity, from forced assimilation to internment, from abandonment to mass murder. Oddly enough, given the centrality of economic transformations of land use to the processes under examination by scholars of settler colonialism, this history is rarely examined from the perspective of detailed economic geography. I believe we can vastly improve historical and contemporary assessments of societies formed through dispossession and settlement by carefully studying which pieces of land are targeted, at what times, and for what particular purposes. This is particularly true given the multiple, interdependent, and unevenly important uses that exist for a specific piece of enclosed land. A more nuanced account of settler-colonial territorial expansion is necessary if we are to better understand the economic conditions in which the creation, reinforcement, and enactment of specific racist conceptions of Indigenous people's "irrational" use of the land can become part of a profitable industrial expansion strategy. Most importantly, such accounts can clarify the terrain and scale on which such struggles are waged, particularly given the many speculative sunk costs that depend on the success of dispossession at specific sites. For those serious about mounting effective challenges to racist projects of dispossession, such a detailed understanding of the economic stakes is strategically indispensable.

To illustrate this approach, I will focus on several episodes throughout the history of the Canadian state, with a particular eye to land dispossession for the construction and securitization of transport infrastructure. These state-led infrastructural projects, I argue, serve as linchpins for larger economic development strategies. Physical infrastructures allow colonial states to import and provision a labor force to a specific productive location, export its products, and "pacify" the region by military and civilian means. In serving each of these functions, infrastructures are critical to the capitalist valuation of land. By linking and thus changing the relationships between places, by shaping and enacting markets in goods and in labor, the political decisions to build infrastructures dialectically form the land markets to which they respond. From their own swathes of hyper-securitized land corridors—and their massive externalization into the ocean—they create new possibilities for the "highest and best" uses a planetary market in land will deem worthwhile for any particular fenced-in slice of the Earth's surface. Thus the construction of infrastructure is quite literally path defining: their high costs and slow turnover create powerful forms of path dependency, as other investment horizons in various related land uses come to depend on the paths that infrastructure provides. Examining these political decisions enforced and enacted through the state not only gives nuts-and-bolts detail to the histories of colonial violence understood through the model of "accumulation by dispossession" (Harvey 2003; Coulthard 2014), but also sheds light on their interrelation with the shifting land-use needs of "infrastructural regimes" undergoing creative-destructive transformation (Vormann 2019). Understanding these dynamics of interdependent economic geographies can provide a key point of leverage for grasping variations in the intensity with which state actors and owners of capital pursue racialized land dispossessions, and what the restructuring of access to those lands means in practice, both for a broader capitalist economy and for those it seeks to exclude.

These political-economic calculations make up the texture of the much-discussed centrality of land enclosure to settler colonialism. Patrick Wolfe, paradigm-forging historian in settler-colonial studies, has famously described a "logic" of Indigenous "elimination," whereby "[t]he primary object of settler-colonization is the land itself rather than the surplus value to be derived from mixing native labour with it" (1998, 163). Thus the expanding European capitalist economy, protected by the settler state and its property regime, seeks land as new sites of investment, a fundamental underlying structural relationship between settler and native that crystallizes in anti-Indigenous racism (Wolfe 2016). This much-commented formulation has helped found settler-colonial studies and has been widely commented upon in the overlapping fields of Indigenous and Native American studies (Kauanui 2016; Rowse 2014). In her *Indigenous People's History of the United States*, Roxanne Dunbar-Ortiz (2014) also identifies the enclosure of Indigenous land as crucial to the globalization of European capital. Glen Coulthard's influential approach draws explicitly on David Harvey's concept of "accumulation by dispossession" (an update of Marx's critical take on "primitive accumulation") to argue that state-managed conflict over the Mackenzie Valley Pipeline and the Dene people's self-determination was fundamentally a struggle "for the land" (Coulthard 2014, 51). Even those writing in a less Marxist vein, like the psychoanalytically inclined Lorenzo Veracini, regularly assert that land grabs lie at the root of the settler-Indigenous relationship (2010). This insistence on the primacy of land enclosure to settler colonialism should thus immediately open a research agenda in economic geography to explore which land is targeted for commodification, when, and to what ends. These fundamental questions are too often blackboxed in such histories (see Veracini 2010; 2015).

Before Wolfe's interventions, scholars in the Marxist tradition of critical historical geography often undertook detailed analyses of the "agrarian question" in settler colonies, which, "simply stated, asks how the land is to be productively organized. On what basis and in what combinations will labour and capital be applied to land, and for what ends?" (Beilharz and Cox 2007, 117). While recognizing the centrality of extensive and expanding staple-crop and livestock frontiers produced for export is indeed important (Denoon 1983), it is nonetheless crucial to understand how similar political struggles have been waged over the allocation of enclosed land to other uses, if at less uniformly expansive scales. The entire field of mainstream economic geography known as industrial location theory asks the question of where productive activities can most efficiently and thus profitably be located. Since Alfred Weber's 1909 *Standardtheorie* ("an algorithm that purported to specify the ideal location for a manufacturing plant taking into account freight rates, the agglomeration of industrial facilities, and labor costs"; Neilson 2012, 323), there have been many attempts in economic geography to trace the transformations of firms' calculations regarding the "highest and best uses" of each potential parcel of land, and the consequences of such speculative calculations on the production of economic space (see Cowen 2014). Critical interventions by Neil Smith (2010) and David Harvey (2006) have since emphasized the structural unevenenness of space and location under the disequilibrium growth of capitalist territorial development. Most rigorously, Richard Walker and Michael Storper (1989) have argued that revolutions in production techniques both require and enable the spatial extension to "growth peripheries" and reshuffling central to capitalist geographical-territorial industrialization, from the US Rust Belt to the Asian Tiger economies.

It is absolutely and importantly true that much work, critical and mainstream, on the geographical expansion of industry has taken the territorial land mass now forming the United States as a blank slate, a virgin terrain for the experiment of industry's unfettered unfolding in space, from the Eastern Seaboard, to the South, to the Pacific Coast. They take little account of the many acts of territorial dispossession basic to its consolidation as a laboratory for industrial and agricultural production innovation. The resonance of such thinking with *terra nullius* discourse (Veracini 2010), however, should not be grounds for its categorical dismissal by those interested in understanding the colonial violence that clears the literal ground for—and maintains the security of—such forms of invasive productive activity. Instead, it should be taken as an extremely fertile starting point for empirical analysis. We can, in fact, renovate such scholarship for our own uses (Gilmore 1993), both to explain the directions of territorial industrialization (i.e. why specific land is targeted by specific industries at specific times) and to further explore the conditions surrounding state-directed and -sanctioned violence and other means of assimilation and land pacification. If we are to understand how speculations as to the highest-and-best-use for land emerge within a dynamic spatial political economy, a theory of territorial dispossession for economic development must have some kind of account for why the expansion of particular industrial frontiers can speculatively command sufficient money power and coercive force to make such visions a reality—and how the costs of the violence required to securitize them for those particular uses are unevenly distributed.

Any such calculation includes, at the very least, the qualities of land for agricultural production (a measure contingent upon the context of existing techniques and technologies and market prices); the presence and ease of access of primary resources, renewable or not (likewise determined in a context of technology and market prices); the suitability of the scale of land available to existing techniques of production; the regional availability of suitable labor power or the availability of suitable land to house and retain those imported to do so within commuting distance; and of course, the ability to connect such land to primary input providers, to labor pools, and finally to markets. The relative positioning of such land to transport and communication infrastructure (as both space and time can be effectively shrunk, see Harvey 1989) is itself classically experienced by firms or potential firms as a factor of cost in input prices, shipping, and wages (Storper and Walker 1989; Cowen 2014). This tremendous matrix of shifting conditions is the context in which decisions about siting and production take place, and to which an expanding market in land would speculatively respond (Harvey 2006).

While such research may seem dull or even naively empiricist, these are absolutely crucial strategic questions for those moved to oppose the violence of a settler state. Settlement did not expand in all directions at once: settlers who chose to move to what is now the Yukon when there was no gold rush would be hard pressed to find even the most fanatically ethnonationalist of states willing to subsidize their life choices and pay to transport the necessaries of life to them. As Harvey writes, "Everyone who moves to establish difference in the contemporary world has to do so through social practices that engage with the mediating power of money. […] [A]ny 'interpretive' or 'political' community which seeks to forge a distinctive identity in place has to accommodate it. […] [P]ossession of sufficient money power is a necessary condition for exploring difference through place construction" (Harvey 1996, 319). For an expanding settler capitalist economy, the financial and practical ability to provide for the survival and security *in situ* of those benefiting from the state's nominal protection depends on some sort of expected return.

Further, enclosure of land as real estate depends on owners being able to effectively enforce monopoly excludability—to ensure that the land is only used or occupied according to the owner's (leasable) wishes. The costs required for defending such territorial claims have historically not only been shouldered directly by the capitalist, farmer, or landlord individually, but are often collectivized in the form of a para-military or police force—that is, a state's repressive capacity. At the same time, having the economic and political resources to capture that arm of the state, or to articulate one's industrial or agricultural expansion with the interest of the "national economy" is a contingent, historical struggle. This is why it is necessary to have some specific understanding of the nature of location choices for productive and reproductive activities—the anticipated and achieved "highest and best uses"—that give substance to Thorstein Veblen's claim, as rendered by Harvey, that

> "the whole settlement pattern of the United States should be understood as one vast venture in real estate speculation. […] To say, therefore that place construction is given in the logic of capitalism's production of space is not to argue that the geographical pattern is determined in advance. The success or failure of speculative investments is largely worked out a posteriori through spatial competition between places." (Harvey 1996, 296)

This framework introduces a host of other empirical questions such as: what do land prices in a settler colony look like immediately before "frontier" expansion, state-led and informal, and what effect does the addition of newly enclosed land have on land prices? What makes this or that piece of land an asset? How does each wave of enclosure and land consolidation create value within a market? How are the costs of dispossession distributed? Relatedly, how much of what kinds of labor power do such land uses require? What sources of laborers (appropriately skilled, compliant, or altogether coerced) are available nearby or within a financially feasible distance for import?[1] In short, the economic, political, and military activities that make up a process of settlement take place within a whole matrix of fluctuating costs. While each of the above questions is indeed crucial

1 The structural irrelevance of Indigenous labor to the settler industrial economy has quite often been schematically overstated, given the striking variation between cases of freeholding Māori in New Zealand, enslaved Indigenous miners in Chile, various forms of racialized land- and labor-management in the Dutch and English colonies of southern Africa (Denoon 1983), not to mention India and Kenya. In the specifically Canadian case, Indigenous labor has been central to various moments in the history of Canadian industrialization well beyond the fur trade (see Adams 1989; Tough 1997; Hall 2016; Bourgeault 1983), and continues to be the target of human-resources recruitment and retention campaigns (see, e.g., Fiscal Realities Economists 2016). Lutz (2003) gives a particularly illustrative example in his examination of the early salmon canning factories up the British Columbian coast: as steamships and refrigeration allowed for greater distances between catch and processing, the dispersed network of upwards of 75 majority-Indigenous–staffed canning factories up and down the coast centralized into a handful of megacanneries in Vancouver and Prince Rupert, from which Indigenous workers less dependent on the wage were largely excluded. Transport infrastructures and possible production geographies create opportunities and limits for markets in labor as much as for markets in land, and these variations also beg a greater degree of historical and geographical nuance, particularly for those concerned about actually existing histories of racial capitalist exploitation—though this is beyond our scope here (see DeDauw 2016).

and deserves a great deal more elaboration, our focus on a certain form of land use, a keystone for so many others, requires in particular that we come to see texture within the geography of conquest more specifically.

Sovereign and Geoeconomic Territory, or the Uneven Facts of Conquest

The role of state capacities in the organization and securitization of territories is indispensable to understand for any serious analysis of conquest. Indeed, conceptualizing the relationship of economic space to the sovereign cartographic unit of the nation-state is particularly crucial when considering the uneven extraterritorial land grabs involved in the expansion and consolidation of state territories, colonial and otherwise. By examining the messiness in practice of the monopolization of legitimate force in sites of colonial expansion, we can grasp the variegated relationship between corridors of conquest and the wealth of nations.

It may be tempting to imagine settlement as the outcome of a bottomless hunger for land on the part of settlers, who then manage to fund and execute an omnidirectional expansion across Indigenous territories until militarily halted; in reality, however, specific speculations about potential productive and profit-turning uses for specific pieces of land underlie the state's attempts to violently reorganize space. The resulting economic and demographic unevenness within such territories is not epiphenomenal but constitutive of the settler-state as a container of multiple productive and reproductive activities. Indeed, the crude use of geopolitical models of territorial expansion in even critical histories of the territorial expansion of imperial capital and settler societies underdescribes the meaningful dynamics of the process. By glossing over the question of the utility of a specific plot of land (inherent, relational, and capitalized), we are left with a reductive model where simply staking a cartographic claim to vast swathes of uneven and unsettled land automatically produces wealth.

Influential late 19th century German geographer Friedrich Ratzel imagined "geopolitics" as essentially a Darwinist struggle between nation-states over space. Ratzel sees states as organic outgrowths of pre-existing nations, themselves "naturally avaricious," each struggling with the others to maximize "its rightful *Lebensraum*" to ensure its defence and flourish, with natural land barriers forming speed-bumps, and rival peoples acting as the only temporary fetters on the spread of a powerful, inherently imperial population across the globe (Cowen and Smith 2009, 26). German National Socialists' uptake of the concept in justifying their own invasion-and-agricultural-settlement plan to extirpate Slavic peoples in the Nazi East (Kakel 2013) certainly has resonances with American history.[2] However, Ratzel's vague, ahistorical naturalization of the nation–state connection (Tilly 1990) is likewise a problem in the critical literature on the settler state, naturalizing an unproblematic connection between a unified settler "nation" and "their" state. The credulity of some critics (see, e.g., Veracini 2010) regarding the natural and omnidirectional land-hungriness of a settler state—even if such imperialism is being deplored—provides an overview of settler colonial history at an unhelpfully coarse level of resolution.

Geographers Deborah Cowen and Neil Smith argue that there has been an observable transition in the historical relationship between space, sovereign violence, and trade. They contend that the "territorially demarcated system of nation-states" that has formed the basis of the "geopolitical social—the assemblage of territory, economy and social forms that was both a foundation and effect of modern geopolitics—is currently recast by an emerging geography of economy and security that might best be captured as geoeconomics" (Cowen and Smith 2009, 23). While not proposing a strict periodization, they draw our attention to a reorganization of economic and political geography beyond nation-state containers, and an increasing military securitization of the physical ties that bind far-flung economic activities together through the world market. Cowen and Smith examine the formal decolonization of classic franchise colonies to show how uneven international economic relationships survived decolonization through market means (see Césaire 2001), as the expensive formal politi-

2 Similarly, while evidence of mutual admiration by Frederick Jackson Turner—famed author of the "frontier thesis" of American culture—and Ratzel has a certain salacious character to it, especially for those who wish the genocides and other violent injustices undertaken in the settlement of the US West to be commemorated with the gravity of the Nazi Holocaust (Kakel 2013; see Madley 2013), the relationship of discourse to practice here cannot be taken too mechanistically. For those seeking to understand the relationship of this ideology to the project of agricultural settlement and the mass murder of racially targeted populations, it is important to note that Turner's thesis was delivered in 1893, three years after the Massacre at Wounded Knee commemorated as the end of formal armed conflict between the USA and its Indigenous peoples (Brown 1970).

cal-territorial administration of colonies by European powers reconsolidated into extraterritorial, imperial force aimed at securitizing the chokepoints and channels of global trade, like ports, railways, and key canals, often under the aegis of US capital and military oversight (Cowen and Smith 2009, 38–42). The concentration of force on specific pivots thus enables the predictable and uninterrupted operation of the trade corridors that link the exploitation of lands and laborers with capitalist heartlands, old and new.

Donald Denoon argues persuasively in *Settler Capitalism* (1983) that different settler colonies' divergent land policies and Indigenous policies (which can be, though is not always, a euphemism for physical extermination organized, incentivized, or sanctioned by the state) were forged in the crucible of struggles over the implementation of very different visions for the productive organization of land. Many classical settler colonies began as isolated naval port garrisons with negligible territorial and productive ambitions, given few easily coercible local labor forces and prohibitively high transport costs relative to European markets. Instead, they were rather used largely as byways and military outposts, only initially and tentatively expanding into the hinterland to grow food to supply passing ships (Denoon 1983, 25–27). The first sustained ventures of European commercial capital into the region now claimed by the Canadian state, the expansion of offshore cod fisheries from the overfished Celtic Sea to yearly voyages to waters off of what is now Newfoundland, utilized different production methods—offshore banks fishing and inshore platform fishing—that likewise dictated different land uses: only the inshore installations employed occasional Indigenous labor, and likewise only the inshore installations built weaponry into their production plan (Harris 2008, 31–37). These different production techniques, blurring here as they do with transport technologies, value terrestrial property in the colony differently and eventually create pressure for different land policies. This sets the stage for different formal and informal relations with Indigenous people. In the territory that would later be claimed by central Canada, the network of forts and waterways that made up the economic and effective state geography of the Hudson's Bay Company fur trade (Daschuk 2013, 14; Harris 2008, 107) likewise had its own very limited needs for land. The kinds of all-encompassing settlement required, as Denoon wrote, for an expanding agricultural frontier or post–gold-rush settlement are not the same as that required for other activities. The violence needed to secure a key strait is not the same as that needed to secure an extensive commercial sheep walk, let alone a coal mine, a fish cannery, a family subsistence farm, or a common beaver-hunting ground.

In other words, the organized violence of settler-state sovereignty does not merely spread like a noxious gas in all directions, evenly saturating every piece of land it can until it reaches the unsurpassable borders of an evenly matched sovereign entity. Specific policy decisions by historical blocs to undermine and dissolve Indigenous national consciousness and claims to sovereignty as potential sources of resistance to colonial expansion (Simpson 2014; Coulthard 2014) are contingent, and often horrific, responses to challenges to specific economic activities, not expressions of a pathological drive to extinguish a competing nation (see Harris 2002). By de-Darwinising settler-state expansion, we can begin to see the territorial intricacies of how force has been used to create, destroy, and reroute circuits of economic mobility and ways of living across the same territories.

The question of sovereignty does not entirely disappear in such an analysis, but it ceases to be the taken-for-granted first and last question we ask in our study about capitalist economic expansion in its settler-colonial variation.[3] Adopting this approach allows us to disaggregate the phenomena poorly represented by the clash-of-the-titans (or David-and-Goliath) metaphysical turf war of Ratzelian analysis into the much more consequentially intricate and uneven geographies of geoeconomic violence. The important moral and political argument that the land in its entirety was stolen (as renovated by different ideas about the shared use of the land, see Dunbar-Ortiz 2014; Coulthard 2014) can at times make it seem as though devouring sovereign communities was the end goal of nation-state expansion in Europe or abroad. But an adaptation of Barbara Fields's famous argument regarding US chattel slavery can be useful here, as settler colonialism was not "about" the creation of the settler-colonial relation of triumphal sovereignty.[4] This is not in any way to minimize the gravity of these injus-

3 See Pasternak 2017 for a careful consideration of struggles over sovereignty and invasive circuits of capital accumulation among the Algonquin people of Barriere Lake.

4 "Probably a majority of American historians think of slavery in the United States as primarily a system of race relations—as though the chief business of slavery were the production of white supremacy rather than the production of cotton, sugar, rice and tobacco. One historian has gone so far as to call slavery 'the ultimate segregator.' He does not ask why Europeans seeking the 'ultimate' method of segregating Africans would go to the trouble and expense of transporting them across the ocean for that purpose, when

tices. Instead, it demonstrates the necessity of clarifying the nature of the process in order to explain historical variations in expanse and intensity, and consequently be better poised to challenge them.

Infrastructures, Market Expansion, and the Logistics of Settlement

Particular geoeconomic spaces emerge as focal points within the more amorphous outline of the borders of the settler colony. When discussing the geography of settler capitalism, an attention to these effective corridors can clarify vague understandings of the expansion of market society. Once private property regimes and market dependency have been forcefully installed (Luxemburg 2003), these logistical infrastructures link the fates of distant regional economies to each other and render them vulnerable to riches and ruin through the turbulence of fluctuations and competition on the global market. Moreover, the social transformations of land access these infrastructures enable have profound effects undermining Indigenous ways of life (Coulthard 2014). The benefit of this approach, however, is in highlighting of "forgotten spaces" (Sekula and Burch 2011), the material infrastructures and logistical corridors *between* these uneven spaces, and the labor of making those market connections work.

Indeed, in all of the literature about the expansion of markets and market-dependency, and the many waves of globalization discussed therein (e.g. Foster-Carter 1978; Wallerstein 2011; Brenner 1978; Warren 2016), it can be easy to forget their material existence. Capitalist mindsets and comportments, like possessive individualism (Thielen-Wilson 2012; Sharma and Wright 2008), are certainly a part of the process, but an isolated Robinson Crusoe would hardly be worth the trouble of schooling in possessive individualism if there was no means to funnel the outcome of his increase in productivity off the island. Markets are brought into being by labor, living (transport and retail workers) and past (construction workers, shipbuilders, surveyors), that brings diverse areas of production into competition through the possibility of their goods, people, and services reaching

they could have achieved the same end so much more simply by leaving the Africans in Africa" (Fields 1990, 99).

one another relatively quickly. This labor enables the socio-spatial relations through which the phenomena of "time-space compression" (Harvey 1989) can revolutionize living conditions. These capacities, and not the intercontinental evangelism of a wicked idea, make it possible for a consumer on one continent to decide between commodities produced on two others, enabling the rule of the law of value (Marx 1959; see Elson 2015) and the ensuing pressure toward ever-increasing productivity rationalization (given the appropriate social-property relations, see Brenner 1978). Further, they allow new "higher and better" land uses through the connection of particular pieces of land ("remote" but fertile, for instance) to distant markets, and thus propel both surges and collapses in land prices.

David Harvey's path-breaking intervention in *Limits to Capital* (2006) theorized how the construction of the built environment of infrastructure (slow-turnover, fixed-in-the-ground capital) facilitates the speed-up of turnover and hypermobility for other forms of capital, as goods get to market more quickly and profits can be more rapidly reinvested in expanded reproduction. The use of the state to socialize liabilities in such high-risk, high-cost, and slow-turnover investments—supplementing market failures, issuing and backing monopolies, and so on—is central, as is its speculative, political intervention into markets in privatized land:

> "Land price movements [...] now enter into the picture because those who organize investments in immobile transport infrastructures can often appropriate the benefits of rising land values in the areas served (this is as true for the state as it is for associated capitalists).This means that it is beneficial (from the standpoint of capital in general) to let loose land speculation and the appropriation of rents and land taxes as a means to pull, push and guide transport investments. [Thus] the creation of transport infrastructures depends upon speculative and political mechanisms rather than upon more usual market mechanisms." (Harvey 2006, 379)

The role of infrastructure construction in land markets—where history shows clearly that not every speculation bore fruit—highlights the profound interdependence of different kinds of land use: urban production needs rural extraction, expansive commercial wheat farms need millions of acres of railway concessions (see Luxemburg 2003, 391, on Canada), and vice versa, in hundreds of combinations. These logistical infrastructures enable markets and allow both the so-called rational allocation of resources and land, and the rational (i.e. profitable) arrangement of activities in space. This is far from a technological determinism: a highway "does" none of these things outside of the socio-economic spatial relations in which it is embedded.

Scholars have recently been examining the military-commercial management rationales that govern such infrastructures under the name of "logistics" (Cowen 2014). Reinhardt Jünemann synthesizes the science of logistics a strategic effort to ensure the delivery of "the right quantity, of the right thing, in the right place, at the right time, in the right quality, at the right price" (to which many add, to the right customer) (qtd. in Mathar and Scheuring 2012). This interrelated matrix of concerns is of course not necessarily particular to capitalism (food must reach its eaters before it spoils, see Daschuk 2013) but takes on particular forms under the intensity and speed-up of capitalist competition (Cowen 2014; Neilson 2012). At the same time, the commonplace meaning of logistics is simply the way that something gets done. In both senses, settlement is a tremendous logistical undertaking. People are imported (free, unfree, and indentured), and resources exported. Land is cleared (of devalued people, animals, and vegetation), enclosed, and irrigated for subsistence and cash crops, while capital goods and weaponry are imported to facilitate those processes. Ports, railroads, and other means of transport are constructed to allow for the import and export of all of the above. Grand undertakings in import provisioning aim to ensure the survival of people doing the specific forms of labor coercively incentivized by the market, while state and non-state activity isolates, contains, and plows and builds across competing modes of life, targeting them for various forms of removal as obstacles to a new spatial economy.

The much-discussed intertwining of military and commercial developments in the history of logistics, like the shipping container honed in the Korean and Viet Nam wars (Cowen 2014), is particularly notable in the variety of arrangements required to geographically extend the means of survival for an occupying migrant labor force, while displacing, circumscribing, redirecting, and absorbing circuits of Indigenous mobility and production. As Cowen writes, "This military history reminds us that logistics is not only about circulating stuff but about sustaining life. It is easy today to associate logistics with the myriad inanimate objects that it manages, but the very sustenance of populations is a key stake in the game" (2014, 3). It is thus crucial to understand the role of transportation and communications technologies (as infrastructures) not only in bringing production processes and territories under the rule of the market (through the possibility of the movement of goods), but also in enabling the migrations (military and civilian) that allow for the fictitious commodification of land as productive real estate through speculation and land-access reorganization. Settler logistics produce and reproduce the lives of those whose survival and prosperity comes to be linked with the task of making those particular land uses into a reality (see Evans 2016).

Pipelines and Railroads: A History of Blockades on Growth

Given the centrality of resource extraction to the history of many settler colonies (Denoon 1983), the logistical means of getting workers and products to and from such sites are key components of their economies. These land uses for uninterrupted flow are both chokeholds for the profitable expansion of such industries and key sites of conflict with Indigenous peoples (Cowen 2014). Recent blockades by some Indigenous people and others affected by the risk of potential spills in oil and gas infrastructure have sprung up in the "Cowboys and Indians" coalitional protests against the Keystone XL Pipeline (Nicks 2014); the Unist'ot'en blockade camp has now long stood in the way of Northern Gateway pipeline construction (Pablo 2014); the 3.8 billion US dollar Dakota Access Pipeline, which has served as a flashpoint for pan-Indigenous movement building from across the Americas (American Horse 2016); and Kinder Morgan's Trans Mountain pipeline's cost horizons have been altogether upended through Indigenous-led waves of construction disruption (Monga 2018). Indeed, Prime Minister Justin Trudeau's offer to nationalize the imperilled Trans Mountain expansion project to finish its construction sets the stage for even more direct conflict between opposed Indigenous groups and the Canadian state than was occurring when it was a nominally private venture (Flanders 2018). These movements constitute place-based interventions into the development of pivotal infrastructures within broader production geographies of resource extraction. Each highlights not only the tremendous risks to key water sources and land uses caused by the overlay of the infrastructure, but also the host of global environmental and social problems linked to fossil fuel extraction and combustion (Malm 2016).

Some observers have noted the historical resonance between struggles over pipeline paths and the armed conflict between Indigenous people and the Canadian state in its late 19th century railroad expansion (Henaway 2013; Kipfer 2018, 9). Even today, pipelines and railroads not only criss-cross each other, but are in direct competition as means of transporting oil, each with particular advantages and liabilities (Atkins 2015). But we must be cautious in drawing such connections and look more closely at contemporary conditions surrounding the struggles over dispossession for logistical land use.

The project of territorial expansion that began in earnest with Canadian confederation in 1867 hinged upon the completion of the Canadian Pacific Railway as a means to redirect and consolidate economic circuits East–West, away from the rapidly expanding United States to the south (Harris 2008, 450–54). The emerging vision for solving the crisis of the collapse of the fur trade—land, people, and resources between the Great Lakes and the Rocky Mountains rendered "unproductive" to the world market by a collapse in fur demand—was of turning the region into a breadbasket worked by favoured immigrants (many from Eastern Europe) with the necessary agricultural skills (Evans 2016). Merchants, industrialists, realtors, and politicians consolidated into a powerful political bloc in Toronto and Ottawa, fomenting enthusiasm for this vision and winning the government over to undertake "Western expansion" by pitching, in a series of publications, a reimagining of the territory: no longer a cold and distant wasteland, the interior was in fact a lush and profitably cultivable terrain (Toews 2015). The state here acts as an active harmonizing force, hitching several levels of class interest (homesteading peasants, merchants, and manufacturers) into a broader project of economic development. This vision, of course, absolutely needed infrastructure to enable its execution: a cost-effective and reliable means to get people and capital goods in and wheat out in a market-appropriate amount of time, and this took the form of the federal commissioning of the Canadian Pacific Railway (Adams 1989). Thus the expansion of Canada as an enforceable national territory, its geopolitical space, depended fundamentally on this geoeconomic corridor.

The land-clearing dispossession required for this state-managed agricultural frontier was not in itself the most intense of the state's assault on Indigenous peoples. In fact, the brutal confinement of the Cree, Assiniboine, Blackfoot, and Métis peoples off of their lands—which lay directly in the southerly path selected for the railroad—to reserves well north of the corridor was accomplished using both the iron fist of military force and the velvet glove of purposefully precarious aid in food (given the collapse of the bison population; Daschuk 2013). This pivotal episode in the reshaping of the continental interior's human geography shows how the transformation of broad swathes of land for commercial agriculture depended fundamentally on the state property in reserves. The government used these reserves most intensively and urgently to incarcerate populations threatening the smooth operation of the public-private land corridor of the railroad. Moreover, these coercive and incentivizing tactical approaches themselves depended on the ability to import weaponry and food to the right place at the right time, with the latter largely brought in by a private merchant, I.G. Baker&Co., as bonded cargo through the Erie Canal to Montana and then northward by ox train, to fill the feeding gap until the rail connection was completed (Daschuk 2013, 127–33). Similarly, the unfinished CPR was rescued from the brink of bankruptcy and funded to completion precisely by the political goodwill it drummed up by being able to import the soldiers, provisions, and arms necessary to suppress the Indigenous, Métis, and settler uprisings against this spatial reorganization in 1885 (Adams 1989, 91). The functional imbrication of war logistics, colonial supply lines, and commercial logistics is readily apparent in this foundational moment, enabling profitable agricultural enclosure and the creation of a manufactured-goods market for Eastern Canadian manufacturers. The creation of a geoeconomic landscape of Indigenous confinement and secure commodity flow enabled the transformation of the prairies into the Canadian export breadbasket. This vision for development therefore depended on the creation of political will (particularly as a promise of return on investment) in order to fund the infrastructure necessary for effective market expansion.

Canadian historical geographer Cole Harris famously commented about the transition of Canada from a mercantile fur trapping field to an agricultural export economy in the second half of the 19th century, "the fur trade had not required a land policy" (2002, 54). His observation reminds us that different infrastructure-enabled production geographies place very different pressures on new rural settlement and land use. When considering the connection between uprisings against railroads and those against pipelines, we cannot ignore that each takes place in not only a very different legal and political context, but likewise in a different technological and spatio-economic one. To take one example, geographer Keith Storey (2016) has described the 1970s transition from "new town" to "no town" labor-importation models in Canadian and Australian mining, timber, and oil and gas extraction. As relative transport costs and shipping times fell, and the pressure on firms to remain as lean and flexible as possible in a volatile commodity market increased, these dynamics pushed extractive capitalists to strategize to lay down as little as possible of the slow-turnover capital in the immovable fixed infrastructure required by permanent settlement—for long-term, extensive land uses for the infrastructures of social reproduction. The "no town" solutions, not unlike the offshore sand banks fishing mentioned above, employed different commuting models and non-permanent settlement types like mining camps, which then depend on a very different spatial distribution and linkages between spaces of labor reproduction (where workers and their families live, recreate, and reproduce) and those of production (see Katz 2001).

But just as the fur trade did in fact require certain directly administered pieces of land in the form of trading forts and safe river passageways, so will a twenty-first century no-town resource camp, however restricted in surface. Storey describes a process of unbundling of the channels and agglomerations necessitated by the transport technologies and costs in the past (resource towns and public highways) toward hyper-specialization (school-less camps, airstrips, ice and logging roads, and pipelines). This "splintering" process will likewise mean a distinctly different kind of intensive "land policy" than a frontier of permanent extensive agricultural settlement (cf. Graham and Marvin 2002). The separation of spillover benefits of infrastructural investment to local communities—especially Indigenous ones—has tangible consequences: the little open-access infrastructure that is built, as in the James Bay / Attawapiskat diamond mining region, "do not connect communities to one another. They connect resource and regional centres to the provinces underneath them" (Hall 2011, 390). Understanding the kinds of geoeconomic bypass spaces produced by such arrangements, and how they bind together local economies not even connected by land, let alone roads, is crucial. Depressed ex-fishing communities in Newfoundland send workers to bitumen extraction camps in Northern Alberta (Storey 2016, 591) as the scale of the area from which high-return industries can afford to quickly import their workers—including specially mandated Indigenous labor forces (Caine and Krogman 2010)—increases, with various distributions of those costs between the firm, the state, the worker, their family, the land, the water, and the atmosphere. This means that mass settlement, as classically understood, may not be the default form industrial territorialization takes, for intensive or extensive land uses.

Understanding exactly how profitability margins work within intra-industrial competition is likewise important. Upswings in the value of crude oil broke the seal on the viability of poor-quality Athabaska tar-sands bitumen development, while the phenomenally capital-intensive production methods required (1.4 million Canadian dollars per job) and the cost-technical requirement for non-stop production mean that even downswings in price have made it a worthwhile gamble to continue key components of production at a loss (Vettese 2016). That is, the damage to idled machinery in the cold climate would, up to a point, outweigh the costs of continued unprofitable production on a skeleton staff (Vettese 2016).[5] These sunk costs in tar-sands infrastructure have consequences in terms of proximate land use for housing following the oil bust (Will workers ever come back? How many and for how long? Will they bring their families?), and more distant infrastructural land use, as they continue to motivate investors to apply pressure for oil pipeline construction even as global oil prices have dropped. Indeed, TD Bank (2012) issued a report (during the heady days of higher oil prices) on the crucial importance of oil and gas pipelines to Canada's overall economic development, warning that the strangulation of extraction by blocked pipeline expansion would force Canada to forego as much as "$1.3 trillion of GDP (in 2010 Canadian dollars) and $276 billion in taxes from 2011 to 2035." Having a nuanced understanding of the fundamentally relational nature of economic pressures at many scales (e.g., how bitumen competes with shale oil, see ibid.), and of the many investment horizons depending on infrastructural projects' completion, expands our understanding of the conditions that turn the spatial expansion of the tar sands and its far-flung infrastructure into viable sites of investment.

This general model holds not only for mercantilist and "post-Fordist" periods—with their differing emphases—but even for episodes at the

5 As Andrew Carnegie himself argued, "[I]n enormous establishments with five or ten millions of dollars of capital invested and with thousands of workers, it costs the manufacturer much less to run at a loss per ton or per yard than to check his production.... Twenty sources of expense are fixed charges, many of which stoppage would only increase. Therefore, the article is produced for months and, in some cases that I have known, for years, not only without profit or without interest on capital, but to the impairment of the capital invested" (qtd. in Botwinick 1993, 144).

height of national Fordism, where dispossession for transport infrastructures likewise had its own effects in crystallizing certain forms of oppositional Indigenous consciousness. Anthropologist Audra Simpson argues, writing on her own Mohawk community facing Montréal on the south banks of the St. Lawrence River, the "modern political consciousness in Kahnawà:ke has its impetus in the construction of the St. Lawrence Seaway canal in 1957, […] the first [settler-state] interaction perceived to jeopardize Mohawk identity and culture as it tore through the site of Mohawk economic and cultural activity: the riverfront" (2014, 51). Thus the decision by the Canadian state, in tandem with that of the USA, to ease transport between Lake Erie and the Port of Montréal through changes in the land (see Cronon 2003) meant that high-investment routes of transport that were decidedly *international* were being carved out of government-ceded reserve territory, through a renewal of legalized dispossession (Simpson 2014). Indigenous people were once again treated as "in the way" of this emergent geoeconomic corridor, with the suppression of their opposition becoming a cost of production for the many industries depending on this expansion—costs of repression absorbed here by the US and Canadian states.

Today, a 7 billion Canadian dollar expansion project for the St. Lawrence Seaway's fleets and infrastructures (to accommodate larger ships) is planned. This project aims to take advantage of a boom in grain prices caused by increased demand in China and India (Almeida 2016); a weak Canadian dollar making the country's exports particularly competitive (Dawson 2015); the correlative rise of the Port of Hamilton since 2010 as an agricultural-commodity feeder hub; a global trade slump cheapening ships themselves; and a decision by the Canadian government to remove a 25 percent duty on imported ships (Atkins 2015). As the Vice President of Canada Steamship Lines Group said, the "removal of the duty made all the stars align and made it possible to build new ships and bring new tonnage to our fleet" (qtd. in Atkins 2015). The work of understanding how owners of capital and state actors chart the alignment of these economic and political stars is, I argue, exactly what those examining dispossession should do. Through it, we can pinpoint objective pressures pushing states and owners of capital toward plans for specific territorial reworkings that will calculate the political and economic costs of, for example, further "preempting" even more land by the rapids that give Kahnàwa:ke its name. From the perspective of capitalist logistics, then, the formal and informal political power of populations being plowed through to refuse the externalization of costs in transport, becomes a factor in "total cost," where the timely completion and reliable operation of logistical chokepoints are central to their successful competition as logistical hubs (Cowen 2014; Monios and Wilmsmeier 2015).

Shiri Pasternak notes that, in the landscape created by the initial implementation of the Canadian reserve system, "forced settlement resulted in a unique spatial phenomenon that unwittingly placed Indian reserves on the frontier of vital national and regional boundaries: frontiers, for example, for natural resource extraction, suburban development, military training grounds, oceans and in-land waterways, state borders, and energy generation" (2014; see Hall 2015). What was a solution for one spatial regime of capital accumulation becomes a barrier to another (Smith 2010). In the particular case of newly needed infrastructure space, the particular kinds and scales of land uses required for these channels and nodes have, as we have seen, led to several of the most dramatic conflicts between Indigenous peoples and the Canadian state. From the side of some Indigenous people, such massive and risky land uses not only interrupt subsistence economies and sites of reproduction, but also enable other intensifications of environmentally damaging land uses elsewhere, that are life-threatening on multiple spatio-temporal scales (LaDuke 2016).

This helps us think carefully about the specificities of anti-Indigenous racism in these shifting contexts. Cowen and Smith argue that Ratzel's imperialism was "environmental" rather than "biological" because his view was that "[i]nferior races deserved to be crowded off the earth by Europeans not because of their race per se but because of their irrational use of the land" (Cowen and Smith 2009, 29). This recalls more generally how a capitalist market in land is designed to dispossess and redistribute by market means any land user falling short of a speculatively quantified "highest and best use," particularly in a world of accelerating enclosures (see Hall 2015). Ruth Wilson Gilmore adds, "[r]acism functions as a limiting force that pushes disproportionate costs of participating in an increasingly monetized and profit-driven world onto those who, due to the frictions of *political* distance, cannot reach the variable levers of power that might relieve them of those costs" (2002, 16, emphasis hers). It is not a matter of geographic distance from the riches that pass through the seaway to the port, as for those who live through a fresh-water shortage in the shadow of the Panama Canal (Parenti 2017; Bogdanich et al. 2016). "Race-connected practices" through time (Wilson 2000, 1) have provided political resources that enable the conversion of an asset into a liability via the geographic hyperproximity of the Kahnawà:ke Mohawk people's land base to a key node in an infrastructural expansion plan on which many capitalist investment horizons in many countries depend. From the point of view of state actors and many owners of capital, these pivotal infrastructural undertakings are absolutely crucial to broader visions for economic development, and are thus the subject of major investment and a proportionate level of legal maneuvering (up to and including armed force) to ensure they are reliably and securely executed. This uneven economic interface—a profound and unbridgeable asymmetry between what is destroyed and what is gained—measures uncomfortably on a balance sheet, even when "damages" are paid.

Conclusion

A geoeconomic analysis allows us to grasp a great deal about how changes in land use and production and transport techniques, particularly in a setting with as much uncommodified Crown and reserve land as Canada, can renew and intensify the many of the deleterious effects on Indigenous people and others long after the formal frontier has been closed. Since conditions change significantly depending on the kind of productive activity in question, a framework as multifaceted as that described above is necessary: not all land is becoming luxury real estate, thousand-acre factory farms, mines, indemnified toxic waste dumping grounds, or transcontinental canals, though most fee-simple landowners are likely to feel the pressure of property taxes to seek some "highest and best" use for it (Harvey 2006, 348). The form such land-use restructuration takes depends on many other things, not least the restructuring of other parcels of land connected to it, near or far.

As we have seen with the Concorde and the sweatshop, certain capital-intensive modes of hyperflexibility in transport are not a done deal: they depend on cheap energy, a whole world of externalities, and the absence of reliable cheaper alternatives. Like any technology, transport automation does not march irreversibly in one direction. Perennial questions of land use and transport loom as long as people need to eat, sleep, and drink in places far from abundant sources of food, shelter, and potable water. Space has not entirely been annihilated by time, and the earth is not flat. The anchoring of container ships outside of ports with the 2016 bankruptcy of Hanjin, the world's seventh-largest maritime shipping carrier, shows just how precarious the networks of speculative capital that underwrite the labor of space-time compression actually are (Wright and Song 2016; see Neilson and Rossiter 2010).

The logistical problem of the many reorganizations of space, lives, and land, for which "settler colonialism" has served as shorthand, extends unevenly within and extensively beyond the borders of the settler state itself. But grasping it in its specificity means understanding how the geographies of production, reproduction, transport, and consumption shuffle and evolve, and how lands currently abandoned or ignored by capital may come to be viable options for investment—if enough speculative political will is marshalled—through technological or economic changes (see Vormann and DeDauw 2018). A metaphorical or literal desert (or tundra) may suddenly develop new value as a prime location for a new production technique or transport corridor, and such a considered approach will be necessary to understand what the effects are of such uses being superimposed over the ways of life that criss-cross, inhabit, and interact with the area in question.

Shifting conditions in the spatial organization of the global capitalist economy have led, for example, to the development of data and mapping infrastructures designed to make the arctic more navigable (Ruiz 2016) with the always-lingering option of Arctic oil extraction (Milne et al. 2015) and the possibility (however remote) of commercial shipping crossing the North Pole given global-warming related ice melt (Vidal 2016). These possibilities, and the dynamic and co-determinate cost limits to their realization, bring brand new questions for Northern Indigenous peoples whose lives have already been quite differently shaped by the formal territorial expansion and administration (without large-scale settlement) of states like Canada, the USA, Greenland/Denmark, Iceland, Sweden, Finland, Norway, and Russia. Environmental change (like the flooding and desertification of formerly temperate regions) and technological change (like the employment of new methods for producing energy or transport) open up new problems and opportunities for reordering space economies through the upending of current cost calculations. Critics of the many injustices that capitalist settler colonization has incurred, of the devaluation of lives and the offloading of costs, of the projects of encirclement and abandonment, of dispossession and exploitation, must develop and spread a critical literacy in these kinds of questions.

Not unlike the joke that Marxists "have predicted correctly the last twelve of the last three crises" (Harvey 2010), scholars in the settler-colonial studies tradition would probably be right in many of these cases by predicting some further dispossession at some point. It is unclear, however, exactly how helpful so general an analysis is toward understanding the specific directions, rhythms, and levels of intensity such dispossession takes, especially long after the formal, territorial "closure" of the frontier. But by situating the study of racism (as "the state-sanctioned or extralegal production and exploitation of group-differentiated vulnerability to premature death," Gilmore 2007, 28) within an historical-geographic materialist context, we may, as Ruth Wilson Gilmore puts it "develop richer analyses of how it is that radical activism might most productively exploit crisis for liberatory ends" (2002, 22). As I have argued, accounting for the shifting economic geography of a settler colony from a logistical perspective can provide the kind of spatio-temporal texture that can serve as the basis of understanding when, where, and how it may become profitable for a state to target people for eviction on capital's many internal frontiers. These complications are not "surface complexity" (Wolfe 1998, 164) but rather precisely the terrain on which genuine contingent struggles have been—and are—waged about the tolerable collateral damage of capitalist industry's expansion into spaces of life and the rounds of creative and not-so-creative destruction this has entailed. Such an analysis can, hopefully, contribute to strategies for intervention into our current historical, geographic, and material environments, assisting struggles to bring about new ways of organizing productive and reproductive labor, of "making, moving, growing, and caring for things and people," (Gilmore 2012), in which the looting of lives and lands could not become an opportunity for the accumulation of wealth.

Works Cited

Adams, Howard (1989). *Prison of Grass: Canada from a Native Point of View*. Regina, SK: Fifth House Press.

Almeida, Isis (2016). Emerging Markets Behind Agriculture Boom Now Driving a Bust. *Bloomberg*, Apr. 10.

American Horse, Iyuskin (2016). 'We are protectors, not protestors': Why I'm fighting the North Dakota pipeline. *The Guardian*, Aug. 18.

Atkins, Eric (2015). Pipelines winning as crude slump hits oil by rail. *The Globe & Mail*, Jun. 8.

Beilharz, Peter and Lloyd Cox (2007). Settler Capitalism Revisited. *Thesis Eleven*, 88, 112–124.

Bogdanich, Walt, Jacqueline Williams, and Ana Graciela Méndez (2016). The New Panama Canal: A Risky Bet. *The New York Times*, Jun. 22.

Botwinick, Howard (1993). *Persistent Inequalities: Wage Disparity under Capitalist Competition*. Princeton, NJ: Princeton University Press.

Bourgeault, Ronald (1983). The Indian, the Metis and the Fur Trade: Class, Sexism and Racism in the Transition from 'Communism' to 'Capitalism.' *Studies in Political Economy*, 12, 45–80.

Brenner, Robert (1978). The Origins of Capitalist Development: A Critique of Neo-Smithian Marxism. *New Left Review* I/104, 25–92.

Brown, Dee (1970). *Bury My Heart At Wounded Knee: An Indian History of the American West*. New York, NY: Bantam Books.

Caine, Ken, and Naomi Krogman (2010). Powerful or Just Plain Power-Full? a Power Analysis of Impact and Benefit Agreements in Canada's North. *Organization & Environment*, 23.1, 76–98.

Coulthard, Glen (2014). *Red Skin, White Masks: Refusing the Colonial Politics of Recognition*. Minneapolis, MN: University of Minnesota Press.

Cowen, Deborah (2014). *The Deadly Life of Logistics: Mapping Violence in Global Trade*. Minneapolis, MN: University of Minnesota Press.

Cowen, Deborah and Neil Smith (2009). After Geopolitics? From the Geopolitical Social to Geoeconomics. *Antipode*, 41.1, 22–48.

Cronon, William (2003). *Changes in the Land: Indians, Colonists, and the Ecology of New England*. New York, NY: Hill and Wang.

Césaire, Aimé (2001). *Discourse on Colonialism*. Trans. Joan Pinkham. New York, NY: Monthly Review Press.

Daschuk, James (2013). *Clearing the Plains: Disease, Politics of Starvation, and the Loss of Aboriginal Life*. Regina, SK: University of Regina Press.

Dawson, Allan (2015). Canadian 2014–15 wheat exports exceed US for first time in years. *Manitoba Co-operator*, Mar. 31.

DeDauw, Patrick (2016). Logistics of Settlement: Uneven Markets in Land, Labour, and Infrastructure in Canadian Colonial Expansion. Master's thesis, Freie Universität-Berlin.

Denoon, Donald (1983). *Settler Capitalism: The Dynamics of Dependent Development in the Southern Hemisphere.* Oxford, UK: Oxford University Press.

Dunbar-Ortiz, Roxanne (2014). *An Indigenous Peoples' History of the United States.* Boston, MA: Beacon Press.

Elson, Diane (2015). *Value: The Representation of Labour in Capitalism.* London, UK: Verso.

Evans, Jessica (2016). The uneven and combined development of class forces: migration as combined development. *Cambridge Review of International Affairs,* 29.3, 1061–1073.

Fields, Barbara Jeanne (1990). Slavery, Race and Ideology in the United States of America. *New Left Review,* I/181, 95–118.

Fiscal Realities Economists (2016). Reconciliation: Growing Canada's Economy by $27.7 Billion. National Aboriginal Economic Development Board. Nov.

Flanders, Stephanie (2018). Justin Trudeau on Trade, Gender Equality, and the Pipeline He Just Bought. *Bloomberg Businessweek,* Jun. 7.

Foster-Carter, Adrian (1978). The Modes of Production Controversy. *New Left Review,* I/107, 47–77.

Gilmore, Ruth Wilson (1993). Public enemies and private intellectuals: Apartheid USA. *Race and Class,* 35.1, 69–78.

— (2002). Fatal Couplings of Power and Difference: Notes on Racism and Geography. *The Professional Geographer,* 54.1, 15–24.

— (2007). *Golden Gulag: Prisons, Surplus, Crisis, and Opposition in Globalizing California.* Berkeley, CA: University of California Press.

— (2012). Interview. *Democracy Now,* May 2.

Graham, Stephen and Simon Marvin (2002). *Splintering Urbanism: Networked Infrastructures, Technological Mobilities, and the Urban Condition.* London, UK, and New York, NY: Routledge.

Hall, Rebecca (2011). Diamond Mining in Canada's Northwest Territories: A Colonial Continuity. *Antipode,* 45.2, 376–93.

— (2016). Reproduction and Resistance: An Anti-colonial Contribution to Social-Reproduction Feminism. *Historical Materialism,* 24.2, 1–24.

Harris, Cole (2002). *Making Native Space: Colonialism, Resistance, and Reserves in British Columbia.* Vancouver, BC: UBC Press.

— (2004). How Did Colonialism Dispossess? Comments from an Edge of Empire. *Annals of the Association of American Geographers,* 94.1, 165–182.

— (2008). *The Reluctant Land: Society, Space, and Environment in Canada before Confederation.* Vancouver, BC: UBC Press.

Harvey, David (1989). *The Condition of Postmodernity: An Enquiry into the Origins of Cultural Change.* London, UK: Wiley.

— (1996). *Justice, Nature, & the Geography of Difference.* Maldon, MA: Blackwell.

— (2003). *The New Imperialism.* Oxford, UK: Oxford University Press.

— (2006). *The Limits to Capital.* London, UK, and New York, NY: Verso.

— (2010). Explaining the crisis. *International Socialist Review,* 73.

Henaway, Mostafa (2013). *Capitalism on the Edge: the Crisis that came and the crisis yet to come.* Montréal, QC: Howl Arts Collective.

Kakel, Carroll P., III (2013). *The American West and the Nazi East: A Comparative and Interpretive Perspective.* London, UK, and New York, NY: Palgrave Macmillan.

Katz, Cindi (2001). Vagabond Capitalism and the Necessity of Social Reproduction. *Antipode,* 33.4, 709–728.

Kauanui, J. Kēhaulani (2016). 'A structure, not an event': Settler Colonialism and Enduring Indigeneity. *Lateral,* 5.1.

Kipfer, Stefan (2018). Pushing the Limits of Urban Research: Urbanization, Pipelines and Counter-Colonial Politics. *Environment and Planning D: Society and Space.*

LaDuke, Winona (2016). What Would Sitting Bull Do? *Yes! Magazine,* Aug. 29.

Lutz, John Sutton (2009). *Makúk: A New History of Aboriginal-White Relations.* Vancouver, BC: UBC Press.

Luxemburg, Rosa (2003). *The Accumulation of Capital.* London, UK, and New York, NY: Routledge.

Malm, Andreas (2016). *Fossil Capital.* London, UK, and New York, NY: Verso.

Marx, Karl (1959). *Capital.* Vol. I. Moscow: Foreign Languages Publishing House.

Mathar, Hans Joachim and Johannes Scheuring (2012). *Unternehmenslogistik: Grundlagen für die betriebliche Praxis mit zahlreichen Beispielen, Repititionsfragen, und Antworten.* Zürich: Compendio Bildungsmedien.

Milne, Richard, Christopher Adams, and Ed Crooks (2015). Oil companies put Arctic projects into deep freeze. *Financial Times,* Feb. 2.

Monga, Vipal (2018). Kinder Morgan Threatens to Halt Pipeline Expansion. *The Wall Street Journal,* Apr. 8.

Monios, James, and Gordon Wilmsmeier (2015). Identifying material, geographical and institutional mobilities in the global maritime trade system. In T. Birtchnell et al. (eds.). *Cargomobilities: moving materials in a global age,* 125–148. Abingdon: Routledge.

Neilson, Brett (2012). Five Theses on understanding logistics as power. *Distinktion: Journal of Social Theory,* 13.3, 322–339.

— and Ned Rossiter (2010). Still Waiting, Still Moving: On Labour, Logistics, and Maritime Industries. In David Bissel and Gillian Fuller (eds.). *Stillness in a Mobile World.* London and New York: Routledge.

Nicks, Denver (2014). Cowboys And Indians Descend on Washington To Protest Pipeline. *Time,* Apr. 22.

Pablo, Carlito (2014). Wet'suwet'en people disagree about Pacific Trail Pipelines project. *The Georgia Straight,* Apr. 7.

Parenti, Christian (2017). If We Fail. *Jacobin,* Aug. 29.

Pasternak, Shiri (2014). Occupy(ed) Canada: The Political Economy of Indigenous Dispossession. In Kinno-nda-niimi Collective (eds.). *The Winter We Danced.* Winnipeg, MB: ARP Books.

— (2017). *Grounded Authority: The Algonquins of Barriere Lake Against the State.* Minneapolis, MN: Minnesota University Press.

Rowse, Tim (2014). Indigenous Heterogeneity. *Australian Historical Studies,* 45, 297–310.

Ruiz, Rafico (2016). Locative Media and the Production of Georesources: a Pan-Arctic Spatial Data Infrastructure. *Spheres: Journal for Digital Cultures,* 3, 1–16.

Sekula, Allan and Noël Burch (2011). The Forgotten Space. New Left Review, 69.

Sharma, Nandita and Cynthia Wright (2008). Decolonizing Resistance, Challenging Colonial States. *Social Justice,* 35.3, 120–138.

Simpson, Audra (2014). *Mohawk Interruptus: Political Life Across the Borders of Settler States.* Durham, NC: Duke University Press.

Smith, Neil (2010). *Uneven Development: Nature, Capital, and the Production of Space.* London, UK, and New York, NY: Verso.

Storey, Keith (2016). The evolution of commute work in the resource sectors in Canada and Australia. *The Extractive Industries and Society,* 3, 584–593.

Storper, Michael and Richard Walker (1989). *The Capitalist Imperative: Territory, Technology, and Industrial Growth.* New York, NY: Basil Blackwell.

TD Bank (2012). Pipeline Expansion is a National Priority. *TD Economics,* Dec. 17.

Thielen-Wilson, Leslie (2012). White Terror, Canada's Indian Residential Schools and the Colonial Present: From Law Towards a Pedagogy of Recognition. PhD diss., Ontario Institute for Studies in Education.

Tilly, Charles (1990). *Coercion, Capital, and European States, A.D. 990–1992.* New York, NY: Blackwell Books.

Toews, Owen (2015). Resettling the City? Settler Colonialism, Neoliberalism, and Urban Land in Winnipeg, Canada. PhD diss., City University of New York.

Tough, Frank (1997). *'As Their Natural Resources Fail': Native Peoples and the Economic History of Northern Manitoba, 1870-1930.* Vancouver, BC: UBC Press.

Veracini, Lorenzo (2010). *Settler Colonialism: A Theoretical Overview.* London, UK, and New York, NY: Palgrave Macmillan.

— (2015). *The Settler Colonial Present.* London, UK, and New York, NY: Palgrave Macmillan.

Vettese, Troy (2016). At All Costs. *Jacobin,* Jul. 13.

Vidal, John (2016). Arctic shipping passage 'still decades away.' *The Guardian,* Feb. 9.

Vormann, Boris (2019). City Limits: Sustainable Urban Governance in Planetary Infrastructural Regimes. In Helmut Aust and Anél Du Plessis (eds.). *The Globalization of Urban Governance,* 79-84. New York, NY: Routledge.

— and Patrick DeDauw (2018). Off Shore: The Sustainable City and its Logistical Costs. In Jason Monios and Gordon Wilmsmeier (eds.). *Maritime Mobilities.* London, UK, and New York, NY: Routledge.

Wallerstein, Immanuel (2011). *Historical Capitalism.* London, UK, and New York, NY: Verso.

Warren, Rosie (ed.). (2016). *The Debate on Postcolonial Theory and the Specter of Capital.* London, UK, and New York, NY: Verso.

Weizman, Eyal (2006). *Hollow Land: Israel's Architecture of Occupation.* London, UK, and New York, NY: Verso.

Wilson, Bobby J. (2000). *America's Johannesburg: Industrialization and Racial Transformation in Birmingham.* Lanham, MD: Rowman and Littlefield.

Wolfe, Patrick (1998). *Settler Colonialism and the Transformation of Anthropology.* London, UK, and New York, NY: Continuum.

— (2016). *Traces of History: Elementary Structures of Race.* London, UK, and New York, NY: Verso.

Wright, Robert and Song Jung-a (2016). Hanjin bankruptcy brings chaos but no capacity cut. *Financial Times*, Sep. 1.

Guaranteeing the Flow: How State Politics Shaped Global Logistics Systems

Christian Güse

At the turn of the century, proponents of globalization were quick in declaring the nation state dead and replaced by a flat, globalized world of competing markets (Ohmae 1995; Friedman 2005). Nearly two decades later nation states are not only still around. They are back in the spotlight, due to their importance for global markets, be it in the form of trade agreements, fixing financial markets, or the management of migration This chapter looks at how the US state has actively facilitated and shaped globalization processes by constructing infrastructures and reorganizing labor in global production networks.Since the late 1970s, a dramatic change has occurred in the way we deliver, produce and consume goods. With the emergence of global supply networks, connecting producers and retailers around the globe via train-ship-truck chains, a physical global market has developed that seems to make national borders more and more irrelevant and less and less governable by the state. It is not only finished products that are increasingly shipped worldwide. Global supply chains have enabled production itself to change from Fordist models of large scale production towards a global flexible production system in which a company outsources the production and assembly of various parts of their product to other, often foreign, companies.

As trade has been re-organized in global flows of goods, located in the logistic-space of the supply-chain, national territories seem increasingly irrelevant (Cowen 2014). As widespread explanations have it, changes in production and technology are at the heart of this restructuring. Technologies such as container shipping and modern communication technology, as well as the introduction of systemic logistical thinking to private transportation, became the core of the global coordination of goods that increased speed and reduced transportation costs to almost zero (Reich 2007; Levinson 2008). These innovations became the key module in global supply chains, and subsequently in flexible production processes. They allow everything to be transported quickly and flexibly on trains, trucks and ships without any significant friction time, creating seemingly uninterrupted flows of goods from production to point of sale. As such, container transportation alone has grown into a $210 billion industry over the past 50 years. According to the World Trade Organization (WTO), the freight industry transports approximately $13 trillion in goods every year, good for 70 percent of all world trade (Hakim 2014).

To be sure, technology played an important role in global economic restructuring. But that this is only part of the story. As Edna Bonacich and Jake G. Wilson contend, the changes in transportation result from a complete overhaul of the transportation sector's labor relations. Since transportation has always been a labor-intense industry, the majority of its costs are comprised of transportation rates and workers' wages. Ever since the late 1970s, the sector has increasingly shifted from a more stable-employment-based system to one characterized by independent contractors, heavy competition, and precarious working conditions, which has led to a massive decline in wages and contributed to rising inequalities within the sector (Bonacich and Wilson 2008). For Bonacich and Wilson, these changes in transportation have not simply reduced costs and changed how goods are produced, they have been the basis for more general economic changes and power shifts, with consumers and retailers as the big winners and manufacturers and workers as the losers (Bonacich and Wilson 2008, 241-242).

This explanation of changes in material globalization is certainly less technologically deterministic. What is almost entirely overlooked, even in these more hesitant arguments, is the role of the nation state in these changes. If mentioned at all, the state is depicted either as a hindrance to private development and the extension of markets, or as a reactionary actor, unable to regulate these changes (Friedman 1999). In these accounts, the development of supply chains is depicted as a process taking place outside of the political sphere and portrayed as almost inevitable. Subsequently, these accounts, which often focus on technological development paint an image in which the outcomes of the changes in logistics are natural and apolitical.

In this essay, I argue that the US state played an active and central role in the development of global supply chains. In a mutually-dependent relationship between political-institutional and economic market actors it determines the form of these supply chains to this day. The state did not just react to private economic and technological developments. Instead it established a specific arrangement between labor, business and state actors that led to a reorganization of the transportation sector, from an institutional regulatory organization to a system structured around market-based competition.

To make this argument, I will provide a critical historical analysis of the developments in the trucking and the maritime transport industries from the 1950s until today. I concentrate specifically on the relationship between state and market actors, especially workers, shippers (meaning the retailers and producers that order goods to be shipped) and carriers (the operators that actually transport goods, including third party logistics businesses) and in which ways changing power structures between these actors influenced state strategies and led to the subsequent restructuring of labor relations in the transportation sector by the state.

Before the 1970s: The Fordist State as Investor and Stabilizer

Prior to the changes in transportation in the late 1970s, the various sectors that would later be conceptualized as interwoven components of an overall global supply network were considered mostly independent transportation industries following their own respective development trajectories. One of the most central of these industries for the inland transportation of goods (next to railroads) was the trucking industry. While commercial trucking in the US had been around since before World War One, it did not become a stable industry until after the end of the Second World War, under an era of economic production and regulatory state strategies usually referred to as Fordism (Perry 1986).

As a principle of labor organization, Fordism marked an age of taylorized assembly-line production, in which large-scale corporations produced standardized goods in ever-increasing quantity (cf. Lipietz 1996). The enormous increase in production under this system, coupled with new redistributive policy measures, led to rising wages and the need for continuously-expanding investment and growth. To cope with that growth and to generate adequate purchasing power, the state typically utilized strict regulation, Keynesian strategies of government investment, the provision of public goods, and a strong welfare state. These methods established an institutional compromise between state, labor and business that ensured stability and consumer power.

This mode of regulation, often referred to as the Fordist compromise, or simply Fordism, became the predominant state strategy until the late 1970s. Within this rationale, transportation, specifically access to public transportation and affordable freight traffic, was seen as an indispensable part of the economy and if not a public-, then at least a merit good. Providing stability to the trucking sector was already a key concern for the US state by 1935. This is when the US state's Fordist mode of regulation began playing an important role in the development of overland haul in at least two major ways: investment in infrastructure and stability through entry and price regulation.

Trucking

The American Trucking Association described the trucking industry before 1935 as "unstable and chaotic" (Perry 1986, 21). Trucking was an extremely labor-intense industry. However, entrance into the industry was easy, since it required no education and only the capital necessary to invest in one's own truck. The number of potential truckers was consequently too high, leading to an atomized structure of mostly owner-operators (wherein the truck is privately owned and operated by a trucker) and smaller for-hire carrier companies (private companies that employ several truckers), constantly undercutting each other in rates. This extensive undercutting not only lowered truckers' profits to unsustainable rates, but also constantly sent trucking companies out of businesses, while new businesses continuously entered the sector, creating an industry that was so volatile and unreliable that shippers would only contract truckers ad hoc on a very small scale. The Motor Carrier Act (MCA) in 1935 introduced regulations on entry, rate setting and operation to abandon the sector's atomized structure and crippling competition, establishing a stable institutional framework around the Interstate Commerce Commission (ICC) and Teamsters' union.

First, the ICC regulated entry into the sector by issuing certificates granting operating authority. Under the grandfather clause, preexisting for-hire businesses could demonstrate that they had operated as a trucking business before the implementation of the MCA and would then be allowed to continue along existing routes (Perry 1986, 23). New carriers trying to enter the industry had to justify the need for their operation in ICC hearings. In these hearings, truckers had to provide proof of the public need for their service and safety standards while presenting routes that were not yet overused by other truckers (Childs 1985, 143). Second, the ICC negotiated rates for carriers through rate bureaus and set minimum and maximum limits. Changes in rates would have to be reported to the ICC, and discounts were not permitted to prevent undercutting. William Childs describes the role of the ICC in setting rates as both broker and referee. Initially the ICC brokered rates between shipper and carrier in their hearings, and they would then act as referees in enforcing the rates (Childs 1985). Finally, the ICC controlled the operational structure of carriers. They issued certificates which restricted operations to specific routes and were official records of the conditions of the operation. If carriers wanted to change their operational structure (e.g. extend their routes or set new conditions for shippers), they would have to apply to modify the certificate with the ICC.

New structures controlling entry into trucking were generally highly protective of existing operations, and ICC rulings typically sought to prevent instability in the sector through new entries. The majority of carriers operating in the mid-1970s had initially been granted their certificate through the grandfather clause (Perry 1986, 25). Applicants would have to prove that they could provide a service not manageable by existing businesses. This stopped the constant new entries in the industry, and thereby also prevented the extensive rate cutting. Furthermore, it reshaped the atomized structure of the trucking industry. Carriers began to invest in more trucks and tried to expand or merge with other companies. The number of regulated carrier companies, referred to as common carriers, declined about 20 percent between 1950 and 1975, while the value of freight increased six-fold during that period (Perry 1986, 31). Finally, entry restrictions prevented new non-unionized operators from undercutting established businesses and made the number of operators more manageable for the Teamsters (the trucking union; Belzer 2000, 34).

The rates negotiated by the ICC's rate bureaus also gave enormous bargaining power to the Teamsters' union in setting wages. With discounts being prohibited, wages were no longer based on market competition, but negotiated centrally by the union. This led to a rapid growth in the Teamster's influence, and in the 1950s wages rose steadily until they peaked in 1973, when union leaders managed to negotiate a real wage increase of 20 percent. While competition through rates was impossible under the rate bureaus, carriers would still compete over the quality of services (Belzer 2000, 25-27).

The 1935 MCA represents an early and important example of a state strategy that would become common within the Fordist compromise. Because of its vital role in providing growth for the US economy, transportation was seen as a merit good, which justified state policies that promoted stability and lowered rates to open access for a broader (though still paying) public. Further, huge investments in highways under the Eisenhower Administration provided additional jobs and allowed for a higher volume of overland freight traffic.

Workers and unions profited most from the stable rates through higher wages. Carrier companies also benefitted from the new regulations, since stable conditions enabled significant growth, even with greater unionization and fixed rates limiting profits. And thanks to the now-steady trucking landscape, shippers could establish more reliable contracts of guaranteed quality with existing truck operators. While there were only 100,000 trucks on US roads in 1914, this number jumped to one million in 1920 and exploded to 18 million by 1970.

Maritime Transport

The maritime transport sector saw the state similarly curb aggressive price undercutting with the Shipping Act of 1916 and its 1961 amendments. The act established conferences (regional carrier alliances that could collectively negotiate rates), while competition was maintained by regulating conference bargaining power through the Federal Maritime Commission (FMC) and by providing subsidies for common carriers. But even more important for the sea transportation sector was the US states' involvement in the emergence of container shipping. Container technology is an integral and central part of modern supply chains, as it enables the modulation[1] of the whole transportation chain and therefore near frictionless transportation from manufacturer to consumer (Levinson 2008; Rodrigu 2017). The

1 Refers here to the practice of equalizing different links in the supply chain, as well as the form of shipments, into easily manageable units or modules for organization and accounting.

technological development of the container, along with its subsequent widespread adoption, is part of a broader historical process tightly linked to the development of the American sea transportation sector which was duly shaped by state political processes. Government regulation in the sector laid critical groundwork for the emergence of container-focused flexible supply chains in the 1970s.

In fact, long before today's standardized 20ft long container became the major unit for handling freight all over the globe, it was the US military that first used containers (called "transporters" or later CONEX) in significant numbers during World War II (Pepper 1988, 223-225). However, these early steel containers were heavy, expensive and mostly considered a hindrance rather than a benefit in transporting goods. They were mainly used to transport the soldiers' personal belongings safely to the front.

In 1956, Malcolm Purcell McLean's Sea-Land was one of the first companies trying to implement container technology in the private shipping sector. McLean's outfit initially began as a small trucking company, and he focused on reducing transportation costs for both his ships and trucking lines. He saw the container as a potential solution to the problem of latencies at the ports and as a way to utilize the space on his freighters more efficiently (Pepper 1988, 53-52). And while, as Levinson suggests, the departure of McLean's first container ship, the *Ideal-X*, was certainly an important moment (Levinson 2007, 1), it is not as though the container revolutionized the transportation sector on that very day.

Similar to how trucks and roads have to be considered within the transportation system as a whole, the container must be understood as only a part of a set of technologies and systems of governance. In order to function as what Neil Coe, Philip Kelly and Henry Wai-Chung Yeung define as space-shrinking technologies, the container must be incorporated into a wider system of various technologies (Coe et. al. 2010, 125). For instance, capacity shortages on freighters is strongly linked to the capacity of related technologies at the port, such as cranes or the size of docks (Jackson 2005, 16). When McLean first began using containers in 1956, related technologies at the ports were not compatible with his container ships. Changing ships, cranes and docks to fit the new technology would have been an enormously costly investment. Therefore, during the first years, Sea-Land and its competitor Matson Navigation were the only fairly large firms that used container ships. The incentive for other shipping corporations to adopt container technology was simply not strong enough.

A related impediment to investment in containers, apart from the enormous costs in port technologies, was the fact that there was no standard size for containers. In the 1950s, small companies and bigger outfits like Sea-Land and Matson Navigation used entirely different sizes and joints for their containers (Levinson 2008, 127). As Neil McBride argues, the accessibility of a technology is the major factor for people to adopt or invest in it (McBridge 2003, 266). Not knowing which container size or joint system would survive, after all, made containers an even less-attractive investment. One New York-based manufacturer offered no fewer than 30 different models of containers. In order to stabilize this young sub-sector of ocean transportation, the United States Maritime Administration (Marad), and the Federal Maritime Board (the FMC's predecessor) decided in 1958 to standardize container sizes and joint systems. Under the 1916 Shipping Act, Marad and the Maritime Board subsidized shipbuilding for US vessels, as well as their operation on international routes, as long as they complied with their strict regulations. In fact, under the Jones Act, only Marad-approved vessels could handle cargo between US ports. Having the right to commandeer ships in wartime, the navy strongly encouraged Marad's standardization efforts. If a container size would become US standard, it would therefore not only be subsidized by the FMC but its use would be required for international vessels to trade in American Ports (Levinson 2008, 128).

The standardization process of container sizes began in 1958 under Marad in the US and internationally in 1961 through the International Standardization Organization (ISO). The process did not initially involve any shipping corporations, but instead consisted mainly of government actors of all eleven member states, including the US National Defense and Transport Associations. Finally, in 1965, the 10ft, 20ft and 40ft container became both the US and international standard. However, the standards were not immediately able to encourage private investments. Despite strong lobbying, the ISO committee rejected Sea-Land's proposal for a joint system and instead favored a system and a container size that would accommodate the European port system and fit better into already-established infrastructure at US ports, advancing military efforts towards supporting Europe within the Cold War. Corporations who decided to use the new ISO standard were massively subsidized, leading to a strong increase in businesses that were willing to invest in containers. However, the standards still failed to initiate massive investment. All told, only about 8 percent of cargo was handled in containers (Levinson 2008, 160).

Given all these interventions, fixes and nudges, it is hard to see the development of the shipping container as its often painted: an example of private ingenuity in a context where private interests overtake the state on the way to establishing a free global market, in turn rendering the state itself obsolete in the process. Instead, its development was deeply embedded within the US state's strategy of investing in infrastructure as public good and a basis for trade expansion. But if it was publicly supported—what parts of the public actually benefitted?

Overall, some of the biggest winners of the Fordist compromise were in fact the shippers themselves. Despite their critique of high rates and the inability to establish longer transportation chains through door-to-door rates directly with carrier companies[2], shippers profited massively from the stability and investment in transportation that made ever-increasing volumes of trade and economic growth possible. Between 1950 and 1970, the value growth rate of merchandise exports and imports was 6.48 percent (UNCDAT 2014a). Accounted for inflation, the total value of merchandise traded by the US rose from $12.05 billion in 1948 up to $108.8 billion in 1975 (UNCDAT 2014b). In 1948, the US alone made up 21.6 percent of all world trade (although there was a boom in this post-war period that might have inflated the number; UNCDAT 2014b).

Large-scale corporations, steadily growing, characterized the Fordist era. General Motors' annual revenue grew from $9.9 million in 1955 to $11.2 million in 1960 and $24.3 million in 1970, keeping it at the number one spot on the Fortune 500 list throughout this period. Second on the list, Exxon, grew from $6.7 million in 1955 to $14.9 million in 1970. But most astonishingly Ford Motors, the company for which the period is named, wasn't even in the top 100 in 1955, and then skyrocketed to third place with an annual revenue of $14.8 million in 1970 (Fortune 2014). It is exactly this increase in shipper's power that would play a central part in the changes in state strategies towards transportation in the late 1970s.

2 The term "door-to-door rates" refers to rates that allow shippers to contract a single carrier or 3PL to deliver goods from the plant to the retailer for a fixed rate. These deals often require carriers to work exclusively for one shipper in exchange for long-term mileages.

The Vietnam War: Establishing the First Global Supply Chain

In the late 1960s, container supply chains had slowly become more popular, but were still limited to corporations who owned several links in the chain, e.g. trucks and ships. The enormous investment required in ports and ship manufacturing were part of the reason why other carriers were not yet willing to establish similar chains. Today, the container travels never empty and without pause along seemingly frictionless logistic corridors to its destinations. In the late 1960s however, container transportation was still marked by empty back-hauls, various unnecessary on- and off-loads, and time-consuming inspections when moved from one vehicle to the next, leading to long friction times at the ports.

Under the Fordist mode of regulation the state had played a vital role for the growth of the individual transportation sectors by providing the regulatory framework, as well as for the new container technology by pushing for a global standard. But in 1966, in a private-public partnership between Sea-Land and the State Department, the US also helped to establish a precedent for the effectiveness of global container-supply systems. By embedding them for the first time within a new logistics approach, this partnership showed how these various points of friction could be avoided and what the potential of global supply chain could look like. It was an external event that provided an opportunity for this partnership to form in the first place: the Vietnam War.

Started in 1955, the Vietnam War increasingly became a logistics catastrophe. By 1966, sixteen different logistic strategies were tested in Vietnam (Marolda 2017, 357-358), almost all of them based on the old "push-system," which tended to deliver the wrong amount of supplies, later than needed (Pepper 1988, 220). A systemic logistics approach would have introduced a "pull-system" of production and distribution in which the consumer (retailer) requests the amount and kind of material needed, which is then produced and delivered, exactly when needed (Bonacich and Wilson 2008, 4). Instead of shipping X from point A to B as cheap as possible by minimizing the rates of each step in the chain, this systemic approach looked at production, transportation, and distribution as a whole, and tried to maximize X (the profit).

Various academic publications and analytic reports of this new distribution method had already gained traction after World War II and research into logistics was heavily pushed by Secretary of State Robert McNamara.

Especially the *Weeks report* to President Truman and the *Doyle report* under President Eisenhower highlighted the new possibilities offered by this new approach. Both reports introduced a paradigm shift away from a simple cost-minimizing approach, towards a systemic conception of logistics (Allen 1997, 107; Cowen 2014, 23-24). The main problem in implementing such a system alongside container technology (as a way to turn different kind of freight into easily calculable modular units) was the insufficient infrastructure at the ports in Saigon and Da Nang, which could not handle bigger vessels.

McNamara decided to massively restructure the docks in Da Nang and build an additional US port in Saigon, later followed by another in Cam Ranh Bay. They were intended to be specifically designed to handle freighters transporting the military's 7-foot CONEX containers, and to establish a standardized and systematic "pull-system" of supply chains. However, in late 1966, McLean convinced McNamara and the Pentagon that his corporation, being the only one to incorporate container systems on ships and trucks on a large scale, could solve the military's logistic problem. These new container ports primarily benefitted huge vessels used by the US military, and later, international trade.

After workers learned how to best utilize the container's space as part of a military-sponsored training program in 1968, Sea-Land's container transportation line to Vietnam could finally operate at full capacity. Around the same time, new communication technologies, such as computers, were also used in the Vietnam War to coordinate the supply efforts, with Sea-Land quickly adopting the new technologies to track their container movement (Pepper 1988, 246). This quickly made wasted capacity apparent, as freighters were sent back to the US empty. Sea-Land's contract with the military allowed for private profits on the side, as long as it did not lower the capacity for sending supplies to the front. Therefore, McLean began to use the empty space and imported goods on the way back from Okinawa to the U.S., boosting profits enormously. The new potential of systemic container transportation exposed by Sea-Land's operations in Vietnam did not go unnoticed.

The foreign investment in Vietnamese ports by the US state, although justified through the war effort, was a major break with the preexisting rationale and would become exemplary for the American state's new role in private transportation after the 1970s. The investment in foreign ports can already be seen as an early example of what Saskia Sassen describes as the unbundling of the *national* as equating *national territory*. This unbundling is, as she describes, an example of a global dynamic inhabiting national institutions (Sassen 2007, 4f). But more importantly, it highlights the role state institutions play in setting up the necessary infrastructure for these global, supposedly private, systems to exist in the first place.

By implementing container ships in a logistical pull-system of production, the military highlighted the enormous efficiency and benefits of this new form of supply chains to the private economy. The private-public partnership between Sea-Land and the US military can therefore be understood as creating a massive positive externality in the form of a knowledge spillover to the private sector. And indeed, shippers quickly adapted to this new transportation system and saw its benefits for expanding their own trade capacities. While container transportation was still a niche industry in 1966, the demand for container shipping boomed by 1969, and the equivalent of 3,400 TEU of commercial imports and exports passed through US ports on a weekly basis, coming to and from as far and wide as Rotterdam, Bremen, Yokohama, Saigon and Cam Ranh Bay. Sea-Land's revenue increased from $102 million in 1965 to $227 million in 1968, as the company expanded its routes to Vietnam, Western Europe and Japan (McLean Industries 1968).

However, this new alignment of containers and logistics was still a far cry from the global, flexible production system of today. Long-term contracts and discounts between carriers and shippers were still mostly prohibited to prevent unfair competitive advantages and to sustain the public good character of transportation, making the door-to-door rates that shippers wanted to implement impossible. The transportation sector had shown its potential for effective fast and precise delivery during the Vietnam War, but to shippers it had also revealed its enormous profitability. Ironically, through the constant growth that shippers had experienced under the strong regulatory systems of the past decade, they would aim at abolishing set regulation in order to access this new potential. The crisis of stagflation, which occurred throughout the 1970s, would give them an opportunity to advocate a shift in state strategy towards deregulation and privatization, thereby putting access to and control over the supply chains firmly in the hands of the private sector.

The Crisis of Stagflation and the Reorientation towards a Neoliberal State Strategy

It is not the state, as a coherent entity, that executes power, but various forces within society that struggle to exercise power through the state (Jessop 2010; Skocpol 2010; Gilens and Page 2014). The struggle of these forces (e.g. economic, social or cultural groups or interests) is in turn determined by the form of the state (e.g. representative democracy, dictatorship), and in turn its favoritism towards certain dominant groups. This is what Bob Jessop and others describe as "*form determined condensation*" (Jessop 2010, 45). At the same time, interest groups that gain access to the state can push for and implement institutional changes that reshape the state itself, further expanding or embedding their access to and power within the state. Jessop speaks here of a "*material condensation*" of the relationship of forces (ibid, 44). Over time, this condensation establishes an "*evolutionary perspective*", or path dependency, in the form of the state (ibid, 46).

As long as the power relations between groups are balanced, or at least stable, state strategy is expected to be relatively coherent and to create durable institutional structures that reflect those relationships.[3] It is in these times, Jessop argues further, that the state exercises power most effectively. In the transportation sector, the Fordist mode of regulation constituted such a period of relative stability in state strategy which reflected the power relations between shippers, carriers and workers. Not only were institutions such as the ICC, conferences, and port authorities established to negotiate between the different groups, but unions gained influence as well, representing the workers' bargaining power.

Changing balances of political forces can in turn influence the effectiveness of state power, and in extreme cases lead to complete shifts in the state's course of action (see Baumgartner et al. 2008). These changes are in part conditioned by the specific institutional structures and procedures of the state apparatus, which might, intentionally or not, benefit certain groups more. Within the transportation sector, as shown before, the stability generated by institutions under the Fordist era provided stable rates and

3 Coming from the regulation school himself, it should be noted that the stable periods that Jessop describes are very similar to the regulation school's idea of stable modes of regulation.

wages for carriers and workers, but massively benefitted shippers by ensuring a continuous increase in their output and revenue. But the additional power for shippers alone was not enough to initiate a change in state strategy. While shippers had some success in advocating an increase in port investment to lower terminal rates, their attempts to implement door-to-door rates and establish long-term contracts with carriers failed, in part, as it contradicted the Fordist rationale of providing transportation as a public rather than an exclusive good.

And yet, change happened. Another opportunity for strategic reorientation can arise out of external events (e.g. economic crisis, war). Those events, although themselves subject to inscribed strategic selectiveness, can possess path-shaping aspects and become opportunities for groups to exercise power and initiate strategic reorientation and reorganize specific structures. One such opportunity for shippers arose in the 1970s with the crisis of stagflation.

By the late 1960s, Fordism in the U.S., and embedded liberalism on an international scale, already seemed to be exhausted. Unemployment and inflation were starting to increase drastically, introducing a phase of "stagflation" that would last throughout the 1970s (Harvey 1999, 28). Big corporations and their large-scale distribution through production were the basis of Fordist production. But, as no expansion into new markets or growth was in sight, the Fordist push-system of production started to break down. This was particularly true of the transportation sector, where the 1973-1974 energy crisis put additional pressure on shippers and carriers to reduce their costs in order to generate any profit at all, leading to a race to create bigger ships within nautical manufacturing, since fewer, larger vessels were more fuel-efficient. After a number of mergers and bankruptcies, the carrier industry was dominated by a smaller number of large carrier companies, such as Sea-Land and Matson, many of which utilized container technology. As a moment of strategic reorientation, the crisis of stagflation influenced the balance of shippers, carriers, and workers in two ways: it reduced the credibility of unions and helped shippers to undermine the dominant state strategy of Fordist regulation.

Transportation unions had been under suspicion and allegations of corruption since at least the post-World War II period. Shippers argued that corrupt unions kept rates artificially high and therefore hindered the efficient transportation of goods. Fiercely anti-union shipper groups, such as the Ship Owner Association and the Industrial Association of San Francisco, campaigned heavily against transportation unions and put forward the narrative stressing the inefficiency of transportation because of union demands and artificially high wages (Bonacich and Wilson 2008, 161).

In the trucking sector, the Teamster's credibility had declined steadily since the 1970s under these longstanding allegations of corruption. Various Teamster leaders were charged with allegations of bribery, and James R. Hoffa, the Teamster leader since the 1950s, was embroiled in a highly-publicized incident when he was sent to prison in 1967 for corruption (Belzer 2000, 26-28). By 1979, non-union trucking was on the rise and the amount of freight handled by the Teamsters had decreased by about 20-25 percent between 1967 and 1977 (Perry 1986, 59). The West-Coast based International Longshore and Warehouse Union (ILWU) managed to keep longshore workers among the better-paid transportation workers, but this was often at the sacrifice of other factors, such as benefits and full employment. Under the increasing influence of containerization, the demand for longshore labor decreased by 60 percent. For example, employment at the port of New York/New Jersey dropped from 30,000 longshore workers in 1970 to 7,400 in 1986 (Talley 2002).

Shippers not only managed to utilize the crisis by imposing a narrative of union corruption and inflated wages on it, but they also used it as a strategic moment to initiate a change in state strategy, away from the Fordist compromise itself. In the 1970s, the failing of the old economic system generated strongly-polarized debates on the nature of state involvement in free markets in general. On one hand, social democratic movements advocated along Keynesian lines for more government intervention, spending and a strengthening of the Fordist compromise, while on the other, corporate interests, among them shippers, argued to liberate corporate and business power, arguing that government regulations were in fact the problem that hindered economic growth (Harvey 2007, 13). They found their alternative in the ideas of neoliberalism.[4]

Deregulation and privatization, which became the prime mechanisms of neoliberal state strategy, should not be understood as a *retreat* of state

4 In the U.S., neoliberal ideas were defined as an economic paradigm by the Chicago School under Milton Friedman and found, as David Harvey argues, financial and political support in a group of wealthy business owners (Harvey 1999, 21-22). Privatization and deregulation, meaning the alleged drawback of state intervention, became the key features in implementing neoliberal ideas in the 1980s (Jamie Peck and Adam Tickell refer to this as the "roll-back phase"; Peck and Tickell 2008, 384).

involvement, but as *tools* to restructure the transportation sector towards a market-based form of organization.[5] In the transportation sector, the Fordist compromise, with its strong institutional regulations, had been long critiqued by shippers and carriers alike. In the late 1970s and early 1980s, shipping corporations were still mostly operating on their few, established routes and had to constantly renegotiate contracts with port workers and other transportation corporations that utilized trucks and trains. The inability to negotiate long-term door-to-door contracts was a particular concern. Shippers typically negotiated with carrier firms on a short-term basis, which frequently led to their making costly last-minute detours. Long-term contracts with producers, prohibited under state regulations, could have enabled shipping corporations to plan the most efficient routes beforehand, establish lasting supply-chains and make full use of the container-logistics system.

Supported by the constantly-growing number of owner-operators, which for the longest time claimed to be structurally disadvantaged, shippers, manufacturers and trade associations started to lobby extensively for deregulation. In 1968, the Brookings Institute in Washington, D.C., received $1.8 million in funding from the Ford Foundation for an eight-year research program on regulation. In total, the Brookings Institute published 22 books, 65 journal articles and 38 doctoral dissertations, all of which advocated almost exclusively for regulatory change. Further, throughout the late 1960s and early 1970s, a number of court decisions ruled in favor of various transportation businesses that wanted to enter the industry as owner-operators (Madar 2000, 39ff).

In the trucking sector, the ICC was under heavy critique by the public and the government. Owner-operators, especially contract carriers, had

5 Neoliberalism's general emphasis on free markets and entrepreneurial freedoms does not entail an overall decline of the nation state or a reduction of state involvement in the transportation market. As Don Slater and Fran Tonkiss explain, the 'private market' is not some form of innate social structure opposed to the state as a form of human-made over imposed political institution. Instead, they argue, markets must be considered "[…] as a historical form; a type of exchange that developed in particular context and became integrated into a larger social and economic system. Markets were linked to the emergence of modern—and, more specifically, capitalist—modes of social and economic organization." (Slater and Tonkiss 2001, 36). Every market is therefore a form of social and economic organization that is dependent on the historically specific social and political structure of the state it is embedded in. As such, a supposed 'free market' without any state involvement is complete fiction.

criticized the ICC from the beginning for implementing discriminatory regulations that favored established carriers (Madar, 2000, p. 83). The ICC was further criticized for promoting a cartel-like structure that kept rates artificially high and made trucking too costly and inefficient. In 1977, the Council of Wages and Price Stability concluded that rate bureaus made independent ratemaking almost impossible. Therefore, trucking rates were generally extremely inflexible and competition was impossible, leading to an inefficient trucking sector (Perry 1986, 29).

This not only contradicted the now prominent perception that markets can best reflect the needs of society, but efficiency was additionally considered a major problem in the ongoing energy crises. In the sea transportation sector, similar arguments of inefficiency and bribery were directed towards the conferences and the FMC. Again, under supposedly emancipatory claims, shippers and carriers argued that the established conference structure discriminated against smaller owner-operators or terminal operators, and subsequently hindered competition, inflated rates and prevented the emergence of a more capable and dynamic transportation sector.

Overall, shippers and owner-operators inscribed a very effective narrative of inefficiency and discriminatory practice to the debate, and identified Fordist institutions like the ICC and FMC as causes for the crisis, within the larger public discourse. With the additional power and influence shippers had gained, ironically through their prospering under Fordist regulation, and the growing anti-union sentiments aimed at organized labor, the power balance in transportation had shifted massively; away from the workers towards carriers and shippers. Deregulation, it was widely argued, was therefore the best way to fix these problems of inefficiency and overcome the crisis.

After the 1970s: The Neoliberal State as Deregulator and Compensator

The shift from a Fordist state approach, marked by institutional regulation, towards a free market approach, initiated by deregulatory policies, largely restructured the transportation sector as a whole. Most notably, this shift influenced the organization and conditions of labor within transportation. Table 1 provides an overview of this shift in the state's approach and its impact on the sector. In the following part, I will outline more closely how it affected the trucking and maritime transportation industry.

The most important deregulatory state measure in the trucking sector was likely the Motor Carrier Act of 1980 (1980 MCA). Under Section 5, it lowered the entry barriers for owner-operators into the trucking industry by shifting the burden of proof towards already established carriers that wanted to protest against new applicants (Anderson 1989, 144). Under Section 11, authority over ratemaking was reformed both in the ICC's role as broker and referee to promote "fair competition." Rate constrains, set by the ICC, were now only partially obligatory. Not only were discounts allowed, but rates could now also be set by carriers within 10 percent of the rate of the previous year. Furthermore, the ICC's authority in checking the accuracy of rates was limited to cases where the ICC had reasonable doubt of fraud. The 1980 MCA also allowed carriers to bypass the rate bureaus and broker rates directly with the shippers (cf. Anderson 1989, 75ff).

As the burden of proving a public need for services shifted to the protestors, entry restrictions were essentially a formality. Between 1976 and 1979, the number of applicants for operating authority increased from 6,800 to 12,800 and rose after the 1980 MCA to over 29,000 applications (Anderson 1989, 76). Actual grants of authority increased from 690 in 1979 to 2,452 just twelve months after passing the Act. Heavy competition was again introduced into the sector, and since trucking was an easy sector to get into, a large reserve labor force began to form. Shippers and third party logistics companies strategically exploited this situation by subcontracting truckers instead of employing them. That way they could offer much lower rates, which truckers were forced to except if they wanted to stay competitive.

Today, truckers work an average of 12 hours per day and earn an average annual income of $28,000. Although there was a slight uptake in the last couple of years, their wages have overall declined by a third since the 1970s (Krugman 2018). In an attempt to reduce their costs, this contracting system also encouraged owner-operators to violate safety and health regulations and constantly work longer hours. David Bensman argues that this must be understood as a form of negative externalities for the public (e.g. over use of highways, traffic accidents, pollution), which are ultimately compensated through the nation state in the form health care, low-income tax exemptions and safety measures (Bensman 2009, 4f). While often hailed as the policy that made trucking more efficient (Madar 2000; President Carter 1980), the 1980 MCA lowered costs for shippers mainly by pushing them down the hierarchy to the individual truck operators and, in the form of pollution, to the broader public.

In the maritime transportation industry deregulation measures came most notably in the form of the 1984 Shipping Act. Section 5 of the act redefined the antitrust immunity for conferences. First, it required all conferences to be open to any kind of carrier, not just common carriers, to prevent discrimination of contract carriers. Second, it gave conference members the right to set independent contracts outside the conference. And finally, no third-party interventions in tariff filings were allowed, meaning that any long-term contracts or time/volume contracts with shippers and intermodal contracts[6] with other carrier were permitted (Lewis and Vellenga 2000, 28). In turn, section 5 effectively rendered conferences useless. The initial idea, as mentioned earlier, was to prevent discount wars and competition over back-haul rates. But now, not only was any steamship line able to contract indefinitely with any shipper, even outside the conference, but discounts on back hauls were possible as well and became the new norm.

Additionally, section 10 weakened regulation through the federal maritime commission (FMC). Not only was the FMC now prohibited from denying non-common carriers access to conferences, but the burden of proof for filing complaints or prohibiting tariffs now fell on the FMC as well. The FMC had to prove within 45 days that a tariff conformed to national regulations. If they were not able to do so, which was usually the case, the tariff went into effect (Lewis and Vellenga 2000, 28). And finally, the Shipping Act allowed shippers to form shipper associations to, as Congress argued, provide fair bargaining rights for shippers and carriers. Similar to deregulation in trucking, the Act introduced heavy competition into the sector and made back-haul rates the new norm for overall shipping rates, as every route was covered as a back-haul route by some carrier. And those back-haul rates often barely covered the price for fuel.

6 Intermodular contracts are long-term contracts that establish a kind of alliance between two carrier firms providing different kinds of transportation to offer door-to-door rates to shippers.

	Regulation / Deregulation & State Investments	*Development of Container Supply Chains*
1910-1940s	1916 Shipping Act: entry into Steamship line sector is regulated by the conference system 1935: Motor Carrier Act Late 1940s: US military trains Japanese port workers	
1950s	1950: Korean War as a first experience of multinational logistic effort / Recession creates need for logistics 1956: Weeks and Doyle reports 1958: Container Standardization Processes under the United States Maritime Administration	1956: McLean and Matson; early, individual attempts at container shipment ICC deregulates "piggyback" rides 1958: beginning of container standardization processes
1960s	Early 60s: increase in logistic institutions in the US 1961: The FMC is established 1961: founding LMI / Systemic approach introduced to private sector 1965: Cam Ranh Bay 1968: computers were utilized in Vietnam to coordinate supply chains Late 1960s: beginning of the crisis of embedded-liberalism Late 1960s: Urban Crisis	1965: container standards are established 1966: first transatlantic container shipping route established by McLean 1968: McLean utilizes empty containers on their way back from Vietnam Late 1960s: Singapore starts to build container ports
1970s	1970s: fiscal crises Founding of the G7 Mid 1970s: stopping government spending for urban projects under Nixon 1976. Nobel prize for Freedman 1978 Chicago 5 restructure Chile End of 1970s: deregulation of international investment	1970s: container-shipment industry in recession Late '70s: strong lobbying for transportation deregulation
1980s	Early 1980s: massive deregulation in trade, transport and port regulation under Reagan International deregulation under IMF supervision 1990: Washington Consensus	1980: Toyota begins JIT production mid 1980s: Long term contracts become common Toyota assembled cars for GM, beginning of JIT on a global scale

Table 1: Regulation and Investment in the US Transportation Sector

The non-discriminatory nature of the new act also eroded the protectionist tendencies of the 1961 Shipping Act and made entry into US conferences easier for foreign vessels (even if they violated regulations the FMC was often unable to file claims fast enough). This not only increased competition even further, but intensified the already-harsh working conditions on the vessels themselves, through the use of flags of convenience (FOC). FOC describes a practice in which steamship lines register their vessels in countries with weaker or nonexistent regulations, especially in the workplace. In 2003, 33.9 percent of all container vessels operating mainly in the US were registered in foreign countries (Bonacich and Wilson 2008).

As a result, according to the International Transport Workers Federation, FOCs became a vehicle for paying low wages and forcing longer work hours and unsafe working conditions (Bensman 2009, Vormann 2015). Also, since these vessels do not belong to any definitive nationality (the company is often not based in the country of which the ship is flying its flag), they are beyond the reach of most unions, which tend to have national, not international reach. And finally, the vessels themselves are often old, badly maintained and unsafe, further exacerbating safety, health and environmental issues. Or put differently, the sector creates costs that have to be compensated for by the state.

In general, within this new and highly competitive market, shippers were able to use their scale to present take-it-or-leave-it deals to the steamship lines. Under Fordism, shippers needed to find carriers for each part of the supply chain (inland, overseas etc.), because long-term- and intermodal-contracts where prohibited in order to ensure the public goods character of transportation. But with the changes to regulation throughout the 1970s, shippers can offer steamship lines or 3PL businesses exclusive door-to-door rates for the entire chain, shifting the responsibility for the whole supply chain to the carriers. If the carrier was previously only operating in trucking or sea transportation, they are now forced to subcontract other carriers to guarantee the delivery of the goods in order to stay competitive. On the other side, carriers who did cover the whole transportation line tended to outsource parts of the chain to lower costs. Similar to the trucking industry, the dismantling of the FMC and the increase of shippers' bargaining power, alongside increased competition among carriers, created a hierarchy of outsourced and subcontracted businesses. Shippers sit at the top of those hierarchies, able to demand rates that are barely profitable for any carrier below them.

Conclusion

Economic globalization is a political process, shaped by the interdependence between state and market actors within the transportation sector. Global supply-networks did not develop *despite* the US state's intervention into a supposedly free market. Their formation only became possible *because* of a shift in the US state's course of action towards the transportation industry. Under the Fordist mode of regulation, the state used strong institutional regulation to restrict competition, stabilize the transportation sector and ultimately provide access to transportation for a larger public. This was a course of action that reflected the power balance between shippers and organized labor at the time. And while certainly protectionist, and also fueled by a post-war boom, it was under this regime that producers and retailers managed to massively increase trade and expand their influence. Meanwhile, as exemplified by the container, the US invested heavily in technology and tried to establish its use beyond its national borders. And by implementing them in private-military partnerships, the US highlighted the possibilities of modern supply chains to the larger public.

Ironically, it was the growth that shippers experienced under Fordism that then empowered them to utilize the crisis of the 1970s, where they were well-positioned to create a narrative for the crisis and ascribe blame for broader economic struggles on union inefficiency and restrictive Fordist regulations. This shift in the balance of power eventually influenced a reorientation in state strategy towards policies of deregulation. But deregulation does not mean a retreat of the state, but must be understood as a different kind or regulatory mode, one that deliberately gives certain organizational responsibilities to market mechanisms. And this new regime came with a complete restructuring of labor relations that has been organized around competition.

Transportation is cheaper today than ever before, so much so that it has made offshoring not only feasible, but the norm. It has allowed for the emergence of highly flexible supply networks between various specialized transportation companies. This cost reduction in transportation did not simply come from technological advancements or more efficient logistics practices. The largest part of this cost reduction is due to a decrease in wages. As companies have outsourced each step of the supply chain to various subcontractors, they have managed to use their size to essentially push costs down to the individual workers. Even more, because of safety violations and the environmental impact of the industry, a large part of the costs associated with transportation are foisted onto the public and then reabsorbed by the state.

State policies of deregulation and privatization as well as investments in new infrastructure have established the direction in which the global logistics system has moved—and will have repercussions on the ways it will move in the future. The state has shaped the character of labor relations in the sector and set them on a path of declining wages and precarious working relations that are necessary for this global system to function. Given its role, not only in investing, regulating and mitigating risks in the construction of global infrastructure, but also in fixing market failures and compensating for negative externalities of the market, it is unlikely—yes, even impossible—for the state to become obsolete in economic globalization. The cost shifts that facilitate global trade networks today make it inherently unstable and unsustainable in the long run, without the state providing these essential release functions. Therefore, the question for the future of circulation is not one of an outmoded state, but one of whose interests will be represented by the state.

Works Cited

Allen, Bruce (1997). The Logistics Revolution and Transportation. In *Annals of the American Academy of Political and Social Science.* Thousand Oaks, CA: Sage Publications, Vol. 553.

Anderson, Dale G. and Felton, John Richard (1989) (eds.). *Regulation and Deregulation of the Motor Carrier Industry.* Ames: Iowa State University Press.

Baumgartner, R. Frank et al (2008). *Lobbying and Policy Change – Who Wins, Who Loses, And Why.* Chicago, IL: University of Chicago Press.

Belzer, Michael H. (2000). *Sweatshops on Wheels: Winners and Losers in trucking Deregulation.* New York, NY: Oxford University Press.

Bensman, David (2009). *Port Trucking Down the Low Road: A Sad Story of Deregulation.* New York: Demos.

Bonacich, Edna and Jake B. Wilson (2008). *Getting the Goods. Ports, Labor and the Logistics Revolution.* Ithaca and London: Cornell University Press.

Carter, Jimmy (1980). *Motor Carrier Act of 1980 Statement on Signing S. 2245 Into Law.*

Childs, William R. (1985). *Trucking and the Public Interest, the Emergence of Federal Regulation 1914-1940.* Knoxville: University of Tennessee Press.

Coe, Neil M; Philip F. Kelly, Henry Wai-Chung Yeung (2010). *Economic Geography: A Contemporary Introduction.* Hoboken. NJ: Blackwell.

Cowen, Deborah (2014). *The Deadly Life of Logistics – Mapping Violence in Global Trade.* Minneapolis, MN: University of Minnesota Press.

Friedman, Milton (1962). *Capitalism and Freedom.* Chicago, IL: The University of Chicago Press.

Friedman, Thomas (1999). *The Lexus and the Olive Tree: Understanding Globalization.* New York, NY: Harper Collins.

— (2005). *The World is Flat: A Brief History of the Twenty-first Century.* New York, NY: Farrar, Straus and Giroux.

Fortune (2014). Fortune 500 – Archive. *Fortune.com.* Time Inc, web.

Gilens, Martin and Benjamin I. Page (2014). "Testing Theories of American Politics: Elites, Interest Groups, and Average Citizens." *Perspectives on Politics.* American Political Science Association.

Hakim, Danny (2014). Aboard the Cargo Colossus. *New York Times – Business.*

Hamilton, Gary G. and Petrovic, Misha (2006). Making Global Markets: Wal-Mart and Its Suppliers. In Nelson Lichtenstein (ed.). *Wal-Mart: The Face of 21st Century Capitalism.* New York, NY: The New Press.

Harvey, David (1999). *Limits to Capital.* New York, NY: Verso Books.

Jackson, Eric C. and Maloni, Michael (2005). North American Container Port Capacity: A Literature Review. *Transportation Journal.* Philadelphia: Penn state University Press, 44.2.

Jessop, Bob (2010). Redesigning the State, Reorienting State Power, and Rethinking the State. In Kevin T. Leicht, and J. Craig Jenkins (eds.). *Handbook of Politics. State and Society in Global Perspective*, New York City: Springer.

Krugman, Paul (2017). Trucking and Blue-Collar Woes. *The New York Times,* May 23.

Levinson, Marc (2008). *The Box: How the Shipping Container Made the World Smaller and the World Economy Bigger.* Princeton, NJ: Princeton University Press.

Lewis, Ira and David B. Vellenga (2000). The Ocean Shipping Act of 1998. *Transportation Journal,* 39.4.

Lipietz, Alain (1996). Social and Ecological Impact of Globalization. *Das Argument.*

Madar, Daniel (2000). *Heavy Traffic: Deregulation, Trade, and Transformation in North American Trucking.* Vancouver: UBC Press.

Madrik, Jeff (2014). Our Misplaced Faith in Free Trade. *New York Times,* Oct. 4.

Marolda, Edward J. (2017). *The United States Navy and the Vietnam Conflict, Vol. 2: From Military Assistance to Combat, 1959-1965.* London: Forgotten Books.

McBride, Neil (2003). Actor-Network Theory and the Adoption of Mobile Communications. *Geography.* Sheffield: Geographical Association, 88, 4.

McLean Industries (1968). *Annual Report.*

Ohmae, Kenichi (1995). *The End of the Nation State: The Rise of Regional Economies. New York City, NY: Simon and Schuster.*

Peck, Jamie and Adam Tickell (2008). Neoliberalizing Space. In Neil Brenner (ed.). *Spaces of Neoliberalism. Urban Restructuring in North America and Western Europe.* Malden, MA: Blackwell.

Peppers, Jerome G. Jr. (1988). *History of United Sates Military Logistics: 1935-1985.* Huntsville, AL: Logistics Education Foundation Publishing.

Perry, Charles R. (1986). *Deregulation and the Decline of the Unionized Trucking Industry.* Philadelphia, PA: University of Pennsylvania.

Reich, Robert B. (2007). *Supercapitalism. The Transformation of Business, Democracy and Everyday Life.* New York, NY: Knopf.

Rodrigue, Jean-Paul (2017). *The Geography of Transport Systems.* New York, NY: Routledge.

Sassen, Saskia (2007). *A Sociology of Globalization.* New York, NY: W.W. Norton & Company.

Skocpol, Theda (2010). Bringing the State Back In: Strategies of Analysis in Current Research. In Peter E. Evans, Dietrich Rueschmeyer and Theda Skocpol (eds.). *Bringing the State Back In.* Cambridge: Cambridge University Press.

Slater, Don and Fran Tonkiss (2001). *Market Society. Markets and Modern Social Theory.* Cambridge: Blackwell Publishers.

Talley, Wayne K. (2002). Wage Differences of US Ports and Transportation Industries: Deregulation versus Regulation. *Economic Inquiry.* Oxford University Press, 39.3, 406–29.

UNCTAD (2014a). Merchandise trade balance, annual, 1948-2003. UNCTADstat. Web 27.

— (2014b). Values of shares of merchandise exports and imports, annual,1948-2013. *UNCTADstat,* Web Oct 27.

Vormann, Boris (2015). *Global Port Cities in North America: Urbanization Processes and Global Production Networks.* New York, NY: Routledge.

Circulation Needs, State Selectivities and Technostructures: The Case of NAFTA

Tommaso Burdet

The state retains a central role in organizing the mobility of the contemporary capitalist economy. Nonetheless, it is sometimes difficult to assess the state's position when ceaseless and frictionless economic exchanges seem to be dependent solely on free market mechanisms. Specifically, influential laissez-faire economists have argued that the state lacks the necessary instruments to cope with the hyper-complexity which characterizes contemporary economic interactions, and active regulation would only mark a devious alteration from the natural equilibrium provided by free market self-regulation. The state's regulating function over the organization of the economy needs to be framed in the context of the seemingly-unrestrained and unregulated coordination which the economy is able to set forth all over the world.

The concept of circulation allows us to analyze the state's regulating function within the contemporary organization of the economy. The notion of circulation implies a plan over the organization of its open-ended flux, "the setting in place of control systems through repeated patterns of movement and the building of stable structures to channel this movement" (Boutros and Straw 2010, 6). In other words, it implies the regulation over movement by a structuring entity. Circulation, the outcome of the organization of movement within a certain structure, is first and foremost a spatial concept: it has to do with the organization of space and the direction given to the entities which move within it. At the same time, the concept of circulation carries a fundamental ambivalence. On one hand, circulation is defined by the struggle to shape and channel the movement of certain entities, giving them standardized, circular form. On the other hand, circulation, as the aggregate result of different movements, always implies the possibility of a break in its order, meaning that circulatory movements always represent a concern for those who wish to form and govern them.

This essay examines the US state's involvement in structuring movement across its southern border in order to unpack these governing capacities. There are two prominent circulation policy concerns along the US-Mexico border, which, at times, can conflict with one another: (1) the securitization of the border and (2) the improvement of trade circulation as as a result of the North America Free Trade Agreement (NAFTA). These policies target a wide array of different actors—local communities and migrants, international logistic firms and transnational crime organizations, etc.—which share one common ground: they all produce different kinds of flows and, as such, they are targeted by the state with policies of circulation in different ways. Above all else, however, a specific and crucial scalar concern within the American southwestern border space has been particularly pressing for policymakers: the tradeoff between dominance of the "global reach" for trade and nation-based security concerns.

One of the state's main strategies to deal with these border circulation policy issues has been to apply a precise selectivity on targets of circulation by constructing a set of institutions and infrastructures which deal with each particular circulation need. The kind of response generated on the border space in terms of circulation will depend on the state's stance on it, thus aiding or abridging circulation. In this respect, this paper argues that the main instrument used to deal with trans-border circulation has been an infrastructure policy which aims to create a balance between multiple circulation needs while ensuring the reproduction and the dominance of the global scale for the needs of trans-border trade.

Circulation represents the state's regulatory concern over the government of moving entities upon space. As will become clear in the next section, in order to regulate circulation the state delimits its space of action by referring to a precise spatial capacity, a geographical scale, which constitutes the limit of the state's regulation over circulation. The regulation of circulation, in turn, is spatially realized by an ensemble of physical infrastructures, the *technostructure*, which serves the state's regulatory goals on circulation within its scale of reference. In this regard, the hegemonic status of the global as the best perspective for economic circulation assigns a renewed importance to the technostructure, which now transcends the limits of nation-based regulations and must be projected toward global grids of circulation.

Technostructures and Connectivity

As Michel Foucault stressed in his lecture series "Security, Territory, Population" (Foucault et al. 2009), the regulation of circulation, as a political concern for those who wield power, has represented a key goal in the structuration of modern forms of state power. The design of modern cities, the construction of roads and canals within nations, the definition of territorial sovereignty itself: the history of the implementation of these political measures coincides with the history of the modern state which, in turn, represents a territorially defined space of circulation. This rather immaterial notion of power, which Foucault conveniently defines as "security", consists of the direction, the pace and the occurrence itself of circulation, which, in order to happen, needs structures, rules and enforcement. Among their functions, therefore, modern states regulate circulation. The means and ends of this regulatory project will be dependent on the specific space/time frame in which the state operates.

Foucault's remarks on the birth of the nation state have another important implication: circulation is always projected upon one (or more) geographical scales of reference. The concept of scale is used here to highlight the direction and the size of the state's decision-making process when it comes to regulate circulation. Just as the notion of circulation always implies the presence of a structure which enables it to occur within space, it is always necessary to consider what are the spatial limits in the extension of the web of connectivities. Therefore, when the state considers the problem of circulation, it will decide how to regulate it by considering the spatial boundaries of its endowments, hence the geographical scale of reference. For example, a political system which is organized around the principle of territorial sovereignty will produce a system of circulation based on the national scale: the state builds a structure which is designed to serve the purposes of national circulation (Jessop 1999).

Presently, as Peter Dicken underlines in "Global Shifts" (Dicken 2007) the changes undergone by the system of economic production have triggered a reorganization of the frontier of circulation. Production circuits and economic networks are now displaced across the world and the economy has undergone a process of globalization. The circulation of economic factors, for its part, needs to be projected and extended beyond nations in order to establish and reproduce this kind of organization of the economy. The way in which this system is organized implies that the nation-state cease to be the fundamental unit in the regulation of economic exchanges.

Contemporary policies of circulation therefore challenge the state with a new task: facing the relativization of the national as the best perspective for the organization of circulation and the emergence of a new global context for the organization of economic activities. And yet, the hegemonic status of the global scale for the organization of economic exchange does not imply that pre-existing forms of spatial organization will simply be swiped away. If globalization has put into question the role of the national scale in managing circulation, at the same time Jessop (2003, 179-196) points to the fact that "the global" as a social/economic/political perspective has not yet acquired that hegemonic status which would determine a substantial shift in the way in which these activities are organized. The security of national borders or the decisions regarding immigration policies, for example, are still a matter of sub-global regulation.

The simultaneity which characterizes the state's efforts to manage multiple scalar concerns is expressed by Jessop's concept of a "relativization of scale," that is, the absence of a well-settled consensus over the best and most-preferred scalar perspective to organize the state's efforts over its activities upon space (and the subsequent proliferation of "discursively constituted and materialized and embedded spatial scales" (ibid., 181) which followed the end of the hegemony of the national scale).

Yet, looking at the figures of world trade since the 1980s[1] till the present days seems to tell us that, despite the fragmentation which characterizes the state's scalar policy, the condition of global circulation of economic factors has never looked better. These data also tell us that the state, amid the decline of the national as the dominant perspective in its political endowments, has been able to create and reproduce a functional environment for the circulation of economic factors across the world. In this chapter, I contend that the reproduction of the hegemonic status of the global scale for the circulation of economic factors has been made possible through a specific spatial arrangement, organized by the state—an ar-

1 The contribution of trade to the global GDP was 58.3 percent in 2015 (World Bank national accounts data, and OECD National Accounts data files (object name: Trade % of GDP, http://data.worldbank.org/indicator/NE.TRD.GNFS.ZS). Moreover, trade has outpaced production in every year since the 1960s (World Trade Organization, "Volume of world merchandise exports and gross domestic product, 1950-2013", https://www.wto.org/english/res_e/statis_e/its2014_e/charts_e/chart01.pdf).

rangement which I call, borrowing from Henri Lefebvre, the technostructure.

Within a system of states where capitalism is the dominant form of economic organization, infrastructures fulfill the function of materially and spatially establishing networks of connection which are needed to establish a structure of circulation. Infrastructures are certainly a peculiar case, in that they represent one of the most prominent interventions of the state on space and yet are so central in the reproduction of capitalist economies. When Lefebvre talks about the contradictions of capitalism in relation to space (Lefebvre 2003), he emphasizes the inability of the capitalist economy to produce by itself the means of connection which are so central for the reproduction of its own circulation.

Lefebvre therefore envisions the system of states' spatial endowments, which he calls the "technostructure," as a complex array of infrastructures with the function of overcoming capitalism's inability to provide for its own circulation needs through the state's spatial aid by constructing of a web of connections. The Lefebvrian technostructure comprises the totality of the state's intervention directed toward the creation of a space of circulation which may comprise different kinds of infrastructures such as motorways, canals, railroads, networks of highways, air traffic routes and the production and distribution of energy. The space which results from these arrangements is the space of capitalist circulation, where the hegemonic status of the capitalist mode of production and its global circulation needs is established and reproduced.

This structure, nonetheless, is not built to serve the goals of capitalist circulation alone. According to Lefebvre, the state's technostructure is so designed as to target with specific territorial measures all the state's goals upon circulation, sub-global ones included. On the border, for example, the state's technostructure guarantees the primacy and the reproduction of global flows while keeping out potential threats for national security. And if scales may have been relativized with the hegemonic decline of the nation, the state equips itself with a multi-function, complex technostructure in order to both sustain capitalist global circulation while aiming for its own territorial goals. In other words, the technostructure enables the state to cope with the simultaneity which characterizes its actions on space given the relativization of scales, when multiple (and sometime contradictory) goals must be attained at the same time.

The construction of the technostructure represents a direct territorial aid to the capitalist needs of circulation. This relation develops out of the capitalist market's circulation needs and it has been described by David Harvey's in the theory of the "spatial fix", which explains the expansion of the capitalist mode of production in space and the active role of the state in setting forth the spatial conditions for its occurrence. The construction of transportation infrastructures, key for their ability to abridge the detrimental space/time constraints to capitalist production, is considered by Harvey as one of the most central spatial conditions in the expansion of the capitalist mode of production. Once the market's circulation needs overcome the national space, new frontiers of accumulation need to be opened in new spaces and territories.

Amid the expansion of supra-national, free-market arrangements, such as NAFTA or the European Single Market, state's facilitation to capitalist circulation takes a spatial turn: the technostructure's capacity is expanded in order to allow economic factors to circulate across the world. As such, globalization prompts the state to rework its regulation of circulation beyond the limits of the national scale. And yet, the national still remains a meaningful perspective for matters that escape the functioning of global trade, such as security. In the next section, the case of the U.S.-Mexico border will serve as an example to flesh out the inner logics and tensions of such circulation needs in a context of free trade. The condition of the U.S.-Mexico border under NAFTA carries a special interest for the study of the regulation of circulation because it allows to observe how the state, through the construction of a border technostructure, manages to fulfill the needs of global circulation while, at the same time, pursuing the goal of maintaining the border as a security barrier.

Circulation Policies: The Case of NAFTA

Borders are perhaps the most interesting sites to observe the relativization of scales and the increased dominance of the global scale for capitalist circulation upon space. Borders may be defined as "instruments of communication aimed at reifying, but at the same time [depersonalizing] power" (Newman and Paasi 1998, 187), which is to say they signal the purposes of the entity which they demarcate: state's sovereignty. Depending on the kind of activity which engages them and the particular space/time frame in which a given border policy is situated, different kinds of responses will be triggered on the border space. Borders, as every aspect of the state apparatus which deals with circulation, must accommodate the global circulation needs of the capitalist economy, a policy goal which has brought, in some cases (Ohmae 1995), the request of their very dismantlement. And yet, states have been reluctant to abandon their regulating function over the barriers separating their national territory from their neighbors.

Rather than representing a contradiction, the border's present state points to the fact that the state is challenged with different circulation concerns simultaneously: facilitating the flow of global trade while halting the penetration of foreign threats into the national territory. In the case of the U.S.-Mexican border, the American border technostructure has served the function of applying a multi-scalar circulation strategy which selects what kinds of subjects are allowed to circulate across the border. In a free-trade regime such as NAFTA, the transborder trade community has been the first beneficiary of the expansion of the infrastructural environment on the border.

The growth in number of incoming trucks from Mexico, the most used means of transportation for cross-border trade, makes it clear how the elimination of the tariff regime has not exhausted the matter of cross-border regulation of circulation, shifting the regulation concern over circulation from tariff collection to spatial management (see Figure 1 below).

In terms of South-North movement, the signing of NAFTA has functioned as a catalyst for trade circulation, particularly for certain ports of entry (Otay Mesa[2], California and El Paso and Laredo, Texas). The increased pressure at these ports of entry required a particular approach in the state's management of circulation. The state has accordingly reacted to the growth of trade circulation by focusing on infrastructural-specific border practices at the ports of entry.

The signing of NAFTA represents, in this regard, a way to sanction the prominence of the global scale over nationally embedded circulation regimes. NAFTA has worked toward the removal of trade barriers among its three signatory nations, with a particular emphasis on lifting tariffs and the liberalization of services. The three nations established a policy of free trade in practically every economic field[3] with notable exceptions in certain

2 Otay Mesa is one of the two ports of entry of the San Diego-Tijuana border area, which also served by the San Ysidro port of entry (Davidson et al. 2010).

3 "Nafta embraces not only trade in goods (with focus on comprehensive rule of origin), but services (as broadly defined and as also sectionally dealt with in some industries),

activities still considered to be a matter of national protection.[4] This reorganization has been especially significant for Mexico, which had a historically more pronounced tariff policy in respect to foreign trade than Canada or the US.[5]

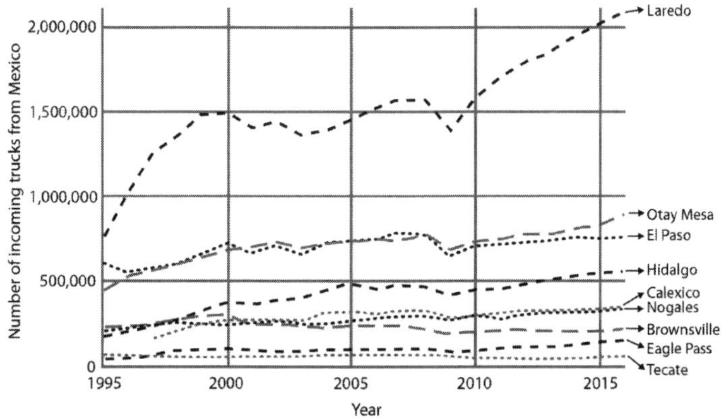

Fig. 1: North American Transborder Freight by Year (Southern Border Land Ports, Incoming from Mexico); Source: Bureau of Transportation Statistics [database], https://www.bts.gov/, accessed 15 April 2018.

The three signatories to NAFTA agreed on the phase-out of the majority of tariffs within 15 years, even though most of them ceased to be in effect 10 years after the signing (Villarreal and Fergusson 2017, 5). This constituted a major advantage for the United States, whose penetration into the Mexican economy after NAFTA has been particularly pronounced (Kennish 1995, 1). Under NAFTA's investment regulation, "all forms of ownership and interest in a business enterprise, including both majority and minority interests, intangible property and contractual investment interests" (ibid., 19) could be freely exchanged across the United States, Canada

substantive issues of direct investment that bridge international difference between the U.S. and Mexico, environmental and labor issues, a dispute resolution system that goes beyond that existing under the GATT, and the most comprehensive intellectual property regime yet encapsulated in treaty format" (Norton 1995, 6).

4 The most notable exceptions to the NAFTA agreement are related to the energy sector for Mexico, which substantially maintains a protectionist approach to the extraction of oil and gas domestic resources (Maxwell and Tomlin 2002, 37), and the protection of Canadian cultural industries, which are exempted from the NAFTA provisions (ibid., 50).

5 "In 1993, Mexico's average tariffs on all imports from the United States was 10%" (Villarreal and Fergusson 2017, 5).

and Mexico. NAFTA accomplished the consolidation of a "continental hub" (Morales 2014, 77) for the circulation of trade within North America. Between 1993 and 2013, the exports of merchandise between the US and its NAFTA partners increased 250 percent, whereas imports increased 278 percent in the same time period (Hufbauer et al. 2016, 16).

From the point of view of border circulation management, one of the most important infrastructures for NAFTA's trade transportation is the port of entry. A port of entry is defined as "a port at which foreign goods are admitted into the receiving country [or] an air terminal or land access point (customs) where foreign passengers and freight can enter a country," (Rodrigue et al. 2006, 270). The importance of a land port of entry is dependent upon the network of infrastructures which serve a certain port of entry, which are part of a land transportation corridor. A transportation corridor is the ensemble of transportation and commercial infrastructures that bring the transportation of trade to take a specific geographic distribution (Boske and Harrison 1995, 13-14). Every national section of a transnational transportation corridor, thus, would eventually serve a particular port of entry (Vadali et al. 2011, 17). The port of entry serves as a funnel for incoming/outcoming circulation inside the greater national/regional system of circulation (see Figure 2 below).

After NAFTA was signed, the function of the American port of entry as an infrastructure of circulation was overturned. If, in the pre-NAFTA years, the existence of the port of entry revolved around the collection of tariffs from foreign freights, the introduction of NAFTA introduced a new duty to the port of entry due to its territorial status as a bottleneck for commercial circulation. Speeding up the passage of goods and avoiding congestion, that is, the overuse of infrastructure (Frischmann 2014, 136-138), became main concerns of circulation policy. Congestion was targeted specifically after NAFTA was signed because it was perceived as the major obstacle in the state's effort to guarantee an expedite and frictionless transborder flow of trade.

Sources of infrastructural congestion at the U.S.-Mexican border ports of entry depend on the enforcement of particular rules of circulation and certain infrastructural deficiencies. Two main periods can be identified in the analysis of port of entry congestion: pre- and post-9/11. This periodization is proposed in order to observe how different circulation concerns are being resolved by the state when it comes to regulate border access. Despite the fact that the U.S.-Mexico border has a long history of being identified as a source of security threats by both the national communities (St John 2011), 9/11 represents a watershed in the history of border circulation policies because it was the first time that security intertwined with logistical concerns on the border space, thus producing new kinds of infrastructural arrangements.

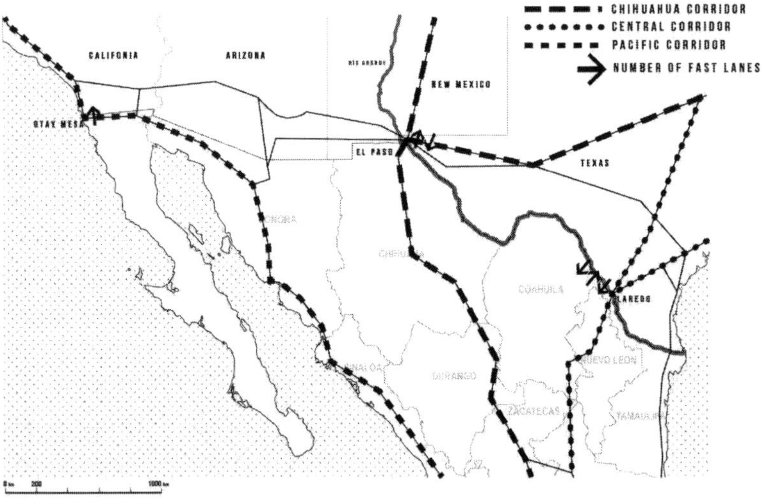

Source: Boske, Leigh B., and Harrison, Robert, U.S.-Mexico Trade and Transportation: Corridors, Logistics Practices, and Multimodal Partnerships, (Austin: Lyndon B. Johnson School of Public Affairs, 1995); Austin, Rose, and Davidson, David, "Atlas of the Land Entry Ports as the U.S.-Mexico Border", in Border Policy Brief, 5, no. 4, (2010).

Fig. 2: Major Transportation Corridors and Ports of Entry; Source: visualization by author, based on Boske and Harrison 1995/Austin and Davidson 2010

In a regime of free trade where tariffs cease to represent a friction against transborder trade circulation, there is a shift in the ways in which transborder circulation is regulated: from tariff-collection to congestion management. As will be shown in the next paragraphs, the United States has dealt with this new challenge by expanding the border technostructure. And while some national-based rules of circulation are still found among the sources of frictions for border crossers, as in the case of cabotage rules6, the importance of border infrastructures of transportation has become

6 Cabotage refers to the ability of foreign vehicles and labor to transport goods within a country (Lakshmanan and Anderson 1999, 18).

even more central in the efforts to guarantee the global flow of trade passing through its borders.

Addressing NAFTA-related Congestion

Before 9/11, the border infrastructural deficiencies were twofold: on one hand, the transportation infrastructures serving the port of entry were not considered sufficient to handle the amount of traffic going to the border, thus generating congestion (Turnbow 1991). On the other hand, some of the ports of entry themselves were not equipped to properly handle traffic without generating congestion, due to the structure of the port itself in terms of limited infrastructural capacity (U.S. Department of Commerce,2008, 5).

Admittedly, port of entry border congestion had already been an issue even before the signing of NAFTA. Already in 1991, public officials had been concerned that the "existing facilities [could] not adequately accommodate the current flow of commercial traffic" (Conahan 1991, 8), and they underlined how the construction and improvements of border infrastructures, such as highways, bridges, and ports of entry, was crucial to avoid congestion along the United States southern border (ibid., 34). But with the implementation of NAFTA, infrastructural congestion became a much more immediate problem.

Despite the fact that trade was liberalized *de jure* among NAFTA partners, the three countries kept their national laws for technical and safety regulations within the private transportation sector (Lakshmanan 1999). The matter was especially pressing on the border between the United States and Mexico, where the enforcement of American rules on cabotage and safety specifications for carriers created delays when crossing the border (Scheinberg 1996).

The harmonization of technical and safety standards, was therefore another important task of the state to allow for seamless transportation flows. As part of the efforts to coordinate NAFTA's regional technical standards for the trucking industry, the three signatories established the Land Transportation Standards Subcommittee, which was charged with creating a compatible regulatory environment for land transportation in Mexico, the United States and Canada (Department of Transportation 2000). The work of the committee focused mostly on the dissemination of information on the standards of custom inspections and the regulations on the profile of truck drivers (minimum age, sobriety, etc.), as well as the establishment of common rules for the transport of freight across borders (Potter and Kruger 2018).

Meanwhile, the rules regarding cabotage were used as a political tool for pressuring the US Congress upon the maintenance of a national rule of transportation, which resulted in further pressure on the cross-border infrastructural system.

Cabotage restrictions were used to protect national transportation industries by prohibiting foreign carriers from exploiting a country's domestic transportation markets (Barry and Ojah 2001, 8). The liberalization of transportation is part of NAFTA's provisions on the liberalization of trade (Harrison 2000). Nonetheless, this sector, due to the resistance of the International Brotherhood of Teamsters (Richman 2009), was never really liberalized: heavy restrictions for Mexican carriers still exists—they are not allowed to operate beyond a 20 km bandwidth along the border—, and efforts to liberalize the sector have been inconsistent from the inception of NAFTA to the present days (Alexander and Soukup 2010, 313).

The enforcement of rules on cabotage eventually produced new logistical arrangements on the border area, which caused further pressure on the ports of entry and their related infrastructures (Pastor 2011, 127-128). Most of the transport along the border is now dependent upon drayage, a logistical practice which refers to "the U.S.–Mexico movement of truck-tractors transferring loaded and empty trailers between distribution centers and truck transfer facilities located close to the border." (Harrison et al. 2009, 37). Drayage is one of the congesting factors on the ports of entry(Ojah et al. 2002). Freight coming from Mexico changes either two or three trucks depending by its origin. If the freight is from outside the border zone, it will go through three different carriers: it is first transported to the border area, re-loaded on a dray carrier, which transports it to the United States, where it is then loaded on a long-haul carrier, which delivers it to its final destination. If freight originates in the border area, as in the case of maquila productions, it will be transported by a dray carrier into the United States, where a long-haul trailer will pick it up. In this case, the same freight is shipped using two different tractors. Moreover, dray carriers usually originate in Mexico. Therefore, they are likely to congest the port of entry twice: in outward voyages, when they are loaded, and inward, when they are empty.

The persistence of national rules of circulation determined a shift in how cross-border circulation was operated: unable or unwilling to change regulations on cabotage, the United States shifted the question of the management of border congestion on infrastructural policy. The technostructure, therefore, has compensated for the limits posed by national-based restraints on frictionless circulation amid an institutional reconfiguration of the border as a gateway.

Therefore, the United States' role in the management of NAFTA's circulation before 9/11 could not be limited to the changes in the enforcement of the border rules. The modification of the dominant trade regime between the signatories of NAFTA prompted the United States to make some infrastructural endowments in the first years of NAFTA's implementation.

Overall, between 1994 and 1998 state and federal expenditures on roadway infrastructures projects in southwest border states (California, Arizona, New Mexico, Texas) totaled 3.2 billion US dollars (Hutton 2000, 44-51), with California and Texas as the larger recipient of federal and state aids, for a total of 2.56 billion dollars, 78 percent of the total sum. The federal government provided the largest amount of funds for border infrastructural improvements in these two states: 1.1 billion dollar out of a total of 1.2 billion dollars spent between 1994 and 1998 in California and 670 million dollar out of 1.2 billion dollars in Texas in the same time lapse. As of 1998, the ownership of the majority of the ports of entry (19 out of 25) was trusted to the federal government via the General Service Administration.

Just as the rest of the southwestern border facilities, the busiest ports of entry in the southwestern border, Laredo, Otay Mesa and El Paso, underwent a process of expansion of their capacity in the immediate post-NAFTA years. In the case of Laredo and El Paso, which are served by the Central and the Chihuahua Mexican transportation corridors, respectively (Boske et al. 1995, 24), the strengthening of the infrastructural capacity was realized through the construction of additional transportation infrastructures to decongest existing ones: the World Trade Bridge in Laredo (opened in 2000) and the Bridge of the Americas in El Paso (completed in 1998; Texas Department of Transportation 2015, 38). The port of entry of Otay Mesa, served by the Pacific Corridor, was conceived as the main hub for incoming trade from Mexico into California and was opened for commercial import in 1994 (General Service Administration 2018). Otay Mesa was constructed to divert commercial traffic from the San Ysidro port of entry, which was subsequently closed to commercial traffic from the early nineties. These three initiatives were born out of the need to ease infrastructural congestion, which worsened after the approval of NAFTA and the ensuing increase in northbound traffic from Mexico.

Although the project of the World Trade Bridge was first conceived of in 1991, the Presidential authorization for it did not come until 1994 (Texas Department of Transportation 2015, 38), the year in which NAFTA went into effect. The construction of the World Trade Bridge was funded by direct aid from the US federal government, to which the city of El Paso ceded ownership of the bridge area through a lease-to-own arrangement (Phillips and Manzanares 2001, 13). Although the bridge's construction costs were relatively moderate—approximately 2.2 million dollar—the costs of the surrounding infrastructures, such as the General Service Administration facilities and roadway improvements, reached 115 million dollar (Texas Department of Transportation, 2015, 38). The bridge was officially opened on April 15, 2000 and connects Interstate 35, one of the major North-South transportation corridors of the United States (U.S. Department of Transportation 2017), with the Central transportation corridor, which serves Monterrey and Mexico City. The Central corridor's role in the U.S.-Mexican commodity chains primarily consists of the trade of raw materials and other non-maquila exports (Vadali et al. 2011, 17), hence the high pressure on the Laredo port of entry, as seen in the chart above.

The Bridge of the Americas (1998) resulted from the renovation of a crossing facility which was first built in 1967 as part of the Chamizal Treaty (Texas Department of Transportation 2015, 63). The construction of the new bridge included two two-lane bridges for truck traffic and four four-lane bridges for other vehicular traffic (Center for Transportation Research 2012, 31). It cost the United States government 6 million dollar, financed through fee collection from commercial traffic (Texas Department of Transportation 2015, 63). After its construction, the Bridge of the Americas became the busiest port of entry in the El Paso area, handling more than half of the international commercial traffic passing through the city (Vadali et al. 2011, 13). Most of the commercial traffic crossing the Bridge of the Americas comes from the high concentration of maquiladoras in the direct proximity of the bridge. The high traffic on the bridge, therefore, depends on the location of the bridge itself, which, as part of the twin-city urban context, channel the traffic coming from the processing factories in its vicinity (ibid., 37).

The Otay Mesa land port of entry was first opened in 1984 in an effort to decongest the San Ysidro port of entry (Gray 1999). The newly-opened land port of entry initially allowed only northbound cargo operations (Soden 2006, 21). However, the development of a binational industrial cluster revolving around the expansion of maquiladoras on the Mexican side of the border near the port of entry (Sosa 2008, 175-176) eventually led to a change in operations. The profitability of the maquiladora model of production depended and depends on precise logistical practices, such as drayage, which involves many charges and discharges of freight between two or more different plants, thus resulting in the need for maintaining an open and expedited circulation channel between the maquiladoras' production facilities. Before the renovation of Otay Mesa, trucks returning from the United States had to pass through San Ysidro, thus further congesting the port of entry. With the stimulus provided by NAFTA (Boedeltje 2012) and the development of the maquila industry, further pressure was placed on the border urban area.[7] In 1994, a southbound commercial lane was finally opened at Otay Mesa, along with other kinds of renewal projects needed to sustain the increase in traffic at the port of entry (Soden 2006). Moreover, all the commercial traffic was diverted from the San Ysidro port of entry, which was reserved for non-commercial and pedestrian crossing. The cost of the project was 27 million dollars (Hutton, 2000, 44). From the 1990s on, Otay Mesa has been the busiest port of entry in California for incoming/outgoing commercial trucks (California Department of Transportation and California State Transportation Agency 2014, 176).

The specificities of these infrastructural arrangements suggest that the state does not regulate circulation blindly, but rather that the construction of a system of infrastructures is heavily influenced by the territorial and logistical practices which are already well-settled within the border territory. And yet, as in the case of cabotage restrictions and drayage, the state has positively shaped trans-border circulation by accommodating the logistical practices and other circulation needs which are carried on within specific regional/urban border contexts.

Just as the abandonment of the tariff regime was paired with an expansion of the technostructure, the prominence of security concerns on the border represented a chance to advance the state's facilitation of trade circulation. After 9/11, United States' border circulation policies were

7 During the 1990s, Tijuana almost doubled the number of maquiladoras, from 388 in January of 1990 to 742 in January 1999 (Economics Research Associates 2005, 57).

hardened in order to securitize the border space against the penetration of foreign threats. However, the new security needs did not lead to the dismantlement of the trade-friendly circulation regime which characterized the early NAFTA years. Rather, as will become clear in the coming pages, the technostructure itself incorporated the state's needs of security by creating a separated space of circulation for trade. In so doing, the state has further expanded its agenda of easing global trade circulation while at the same time pursuing the goal of national security.

Post-9/11 Restructuring

After the terrorist attacks of 9/11, the border policy of the United States prioritized the securitization of different forms of circulation (immigration, transportation, trade), which were perceived as vehicles for potential threats (Jones and Seghetti 2015, 10). A number of measures were taken to reduce risks coming from foreign sources even though some of them proved to be shortsighted—like the proposal to scan 100 percent of incoming containers, which produced mixed results.[8]

In general, 9/11 highlighted the double function of the border as both a gateway and a barrier for circulation. With the Homeland Security Act of 2002, customs officials merged with border patrol agents in the Customs and Border Protection under the Department of Homeland Security and were charged with a "dual mission" of protecting national security while allowing for a smooth circulation of goods across the border (Lee et al. 2013, 78). Facing the possibility of an increase in congestion at the ports of entry (one of the immediate effects of the 9/11 attacks; Andreas 2009, 154), countermeasures were developed through the addition of a new, multi-layered, infrastructural environment, which sought to reconcile security with circulation facilitation. In this regard, some preexisting, trusted traveler and shipper programs were strengthened on the US-Mexico border, as in the case of SENTRI, Secure Electronic Network for Travelers

8 From 2005 to 2013, an average of 90 percent of cargo transported by train has been inspected at the port of entry. The initiative was nonetheless less successful for what concerns other forms of transportation: only the 28 percent of the containers transported by truck were controlled, and just 5 percent of maritime container freight was subdued to security scans at the port of entry (Jones and Seghetti 2015, 25).

Rapid Inspection, while other new programs were implemented, as in the case of FAST, Fast and Secure Trade and its related initiative, and C-TPAT, Customs-Trade Partnerships Against Terrorism (Lee et al. 2013, 70-71).

"When the freight can't wait, go FAST, " reads the reference guide on the program prepared by the US Border and Custom Protection. FAST is a security initiative subscribed by NAFTA's signatories directed toward commercial trucks. It aims to promote the faster circulation of commercial trucks across the NAFTA signatories' ports of entry by providing information on both the importer and the nature of the freight imported into the United States. The Custom and Border Protection then grants access via the FAST program by running a risk assessment on the importer's company. After having received approval, the importer has access to specific FAST lanes at the port of entry, where the border crossing process is sped up (U.S. Custom and Border Protection 2005). FAST is unique in that it has a specific infrastructural feature: a designated lane at the port of entry that only program participants have access to. Using this lane, they are able to skip some of the security procedures that would usually produce congestion.

On the other hand, the C-TPAT, "is a voluntary supply chain security program open to companies around the world that do business with the United States. To be C-TPAT certified, a company must commit to implement a number of security procedures that address issues ranging from conveyance security to encouraging suppliers to strengthen their security" (Lee et al. 2013, 70). According to the proponents of the program, companies that comply with C-TPAT are four to six time less likely to undergo a security or compliance examination, thus expediting their crossing into the United States. In order to access a FAST lane, an importer's cargo must possess a C-TPAT certification. As with FAST, the C-TPAT membership guarantees quicker border crossing in exchange for providing the state with information on the importing process.

The C-TPAT partnership differs from traditional security programs due to its focus on the securitization of the commodity chain rather than a territorialized concept of security. Considering the nature of "global spaces of flow", Deborah Cowen argues that the "disruption" of trade circulation is the most frightening threat to the circuits of trade circulation across the world (Cowen 2014). In order to prevent frictions in the "seamless" flow of commodities, governments have been charged with the task of creating a security environment in which disruptions of the commodity chains are unlikely to occur within the system of logistics in which they circulate. According to Cowen, the de-territorialization of security is particularly clear in the case of borders, which cease to represent a territorial marker of sovereignty and become a part of the network of security built by the state in order to accommodate the circulation needs of the private sector. Within the system of supply chain security, the C-TPAT represents an effort to privatize the security process by shifting the responsibility of security checks from government officials to corporate agents, which are deemed responsible for the implementation of security measures within the specific commodity chain in which they operate.

For its part, the state contributes to the securitization of the commodity chain by constructing a functional infrastructural environment which guarantees the absence of frictions in the reproduction of circulation. Reflecting on the securitization of the infrastructures of the global port city (Vormann 2015), Vormann has pointed out that post-9/11 policies of securitization in the commodity chain have been optimized to ensure that possible costs coming from time-consuming security checks are externalized through the construction of a dedicated infrastructural environment. If shipping companies, carriers and freight brokers are charged with the task of enforcing and implementing security regulations for the commodity chain, the state builds a transactional architecture which materially separates trade circulation, thus creating a dedicated space for circulation where other sources of frictions are eliminated. If Vormann applies these reflections on the separation of port infrastructures from the overall urban context of the global port city, a similar process is observable on the border environment, where the state dedicates specific infrastructural arrangements—like the FAST lane—in order to create a securitized space of circulation for trans-border trade.

Post 9/11 security measures, therefore, have been developed to further reduce congestion at the ports of entry. Whereas initial security endowments seemed to recast the role of the border as a barrier for circulation (Cowen 2014, 76), the state soon receded from its initial positions and undertook a circulation policy which saw the infrastructural element as its centerpiece. While the possible frictions to circulation created by security checks were overcome by entrusting the process to the private sector, the state contributed to the construction of a separated space of circulation for trade by investing into a dedicated infrastructural environment.

Conclusion

Through the construction and managing of border infrastructures, the U.S. state regulates trans-border circulation, thus reproducing different sets of geographical scales across the border space. Looking at the history of NAFTA's trans-border circulation management reveals how the United States has proven to be an essential actor in the enforcement of free trade policies of circulation. In the context of free trade policies, where national-based constraints against trade circulation cease to represent a major obstacle to frictionless circulation, the role of the state is expressed in the form of specific territorial arrangements: the construction of a functional infrastructural environment for the easing of circulation through the management of infrastructural congestion. NAFTA's circulation policies, therefore, are an excellent case to examine the state's role in managing circulation. If the absence of nationally-based rules of trade is what characterizes the contemporary organization of the international economy, the state's regulatory focus shifts to the growing needs of global circulation, thus producing spatial modifications in the form of infrastructural arrangements.

U.S. policy on its southwestern border shows that the state's preferred tool for the regulation of circulation revolves around the modification of space, therefore underlining the function of territory as a strategic device for the implementation of the global scale. Territorially-enforced frictionless circulation, nonetheless, is not applied *erga omnes*: the state targets the trade sector with policies which encourage the removal of barriers against circulation. For the rest of the "trans-border subjects" the border continues to represent a barrier for all forms of circulations whose nature of licit/good circulation is not sanctioned by the state. It is not by chance, as Peter Andreas underlines (Andreas, 2009), that NAFTA's trade liberalization coincided with the exacerbation of the security measures against immigrants and all those subjects which did not take part in the reproduction of capitalist globalization. If anything, NAFTA's trans-border circulation policies reinforce the notion of a border which is still able to create "geographies and choreographies of inclusion/exclusion and domination/subordination which empower some actors, alliances and organizations at the expense of others, according to criteria such as class, gender, race/ethnicity and nationality." (Brenner 2001, 608) Further research in this direction may focus on the effects that the creation of a technostructure for the exclusive circulation of the trans-border trade community had on the overall border social environment.

Circulation, as a structure-dependent phenomenon, sheds a new light on the nature of contemporary economic interactions. The reproduction of its scale of reference, either global or sub-global, will always depend on the kinds of spatial arrangements which are realized by the state upon space. The ways in which the state treats territory, therefore, remains central for every investigation into the organization of capitalist economies in all of its possible scalar displacements. In this regard, infrastructures, as the material expression of policies of circulation, are crucial for those who are interested in the ways in which the state regulates capitalism and its spatial needs.

Works Cited

Alexander, Klint W. and Bryan J. Soukup (2010). Obama's First Trade War: The US-Mexico Cross-Border Trucking Dispute and the Implications of Strategic Cross-Sector Retaliation on US Compliance under NAFTA. *Berkeley Journal of Interantional Law*, 28, 313–42.

Andreas, Peter (2009). *Border Games: Policing the U.S.-Mexico Divide.* Ithaca, NY: Cornell University Press.

Austin, Rose and David Davidson (2010). "Atlas of the Land Entry Ports at the U.S. - Mexico Border". *Border Polic Research Institute Publications*, 30.

Barry, E. and Mark Ojah (2001). *NAFTA in the Next Ten Years: Issues and Challenges in Transportation.* Paper presented at the NAFTA in the New Millennium Symposium, May 24–25, in Edmonton, Alberta.

Boedeltje, Freerk (2012). *Opportunities for Regional Collaboration on the Border: Sharing the European border experience with the San Diego/Tijuana region.* San Diego, CA: Institute for Regional Studies of the Californias, San Diego State University.

Boske, Leigh B., and Robert Harrison(1995). *U.S.-Mexico Trade and Transportation: Corridors, Logistics Practices, and Multimodal Partnerships,* Policy Research Project Report Number 113. Austin, TX: Lyndon B. Johnson School of Public Affairs.

Boutros, Alexandra, and Will Straw (2010). Introduction. In Alexandra Boutros and William Straw (eds.). *Circulation and the City: Essays on Urban Culture*, 3–20. Montreal: McGill-Queen University Press.

Brenner, Neil (2001). The limits to scale? Methodological reflections on scalar structuration. *Progress in Human Geography*, 25.4, 591–614.

California Department of Transportation and California State Transportation Agency (2014). *California Freight Mobility Plan.* Sacramento, CA: California State Transportation Agency.

Center for Transportation Research (2012). *Laredo District Coahuila/Nuevo León/Tamaulipas Border Master Plan, Final Report.* Austin, TX: Texas Department of Transportation, International Relations Office. 22.03.2018. http://ftp.dot.state.tx.us/pub/txdot-info/iro/lbmp/report.pdf, 31.

Conahan, Frank C. (1991). *U.S.-Mexico Trade: Concerns About the Adequacy of Border Infrastructures*, GAO/NSIAD-91-228. Washington D.C.: US Government Accountability Office.

Cowen, Deborah (2014). *The Deadly Life of Logistics: Mapping Violence in Global Trade.* Minneapolis, MN: University of Minnesota Press.

Davidson, David L., Bryant Hammond and Kathleen Mintz (2010). Atlas of the Land Entry Ports on the Canada-US Border. *Border Policy Research Institute Publications,* 28. 22.03.2018. https://cedar.wwu.edu/bpri_publications/28.

Dicken, Peter (2007). *Global shift: mapping the changing contours of the world economy.* New York, NY: Guilford Press.

Economics Research Associates (2005). *Final Draft Report Real Estate Market Analysis Otay Mesa Community Plan Area, Otay Mesa, CA.* San Diego, CA: The city of San Diego. 22.03.2018. https://www.sandiego.gov/sites/default/files/legacy/planning/community/profiles/otaymesa/cpu/pdf/erareport050921.pdf

Foucault, Michel, Michel Sennelart, François Ewald and Alessandro Fontana (2009). *Security, territory, population: lectures at The Collège de France, 1977-1978.* New York, NY: Picador/Palgrave Macmillan.

Frischmann, Brett M. (2013). *Infrastructure: the social value of shared resources.* Oxford: Oxford University Press.

General Service Administration (2018). *Prospectus: Construction Otay Mesa US Land Port of Entry San Diego CA.* 22.03.2018. https://www.gsa.gov/cdn-static/FY2018_San_Diego_CA_Otay_Mesa_U.S._Land_Port_of_Entry.pdf.

Gray, George E. (1999). *Impact of the North American Free Trade Agreement on Transportation in the Border Areas of the United States: With Emphasis on the California-Mexico Border.* San Jose, CA: Norman Y. Mineta International Institute for Surface Transportation Policy Studies IISTPS.

Harrison, Robert, N. Hutson, J. Prozzi, J. Gonzalez, J. McCray, and J. West (2009). *The Impacts of Port, Rail, and Border Drayage Activity in Texas.* Austin, TX: The University of Texas at Austin, Center for Transportation Research, Report 0-5684-1. 22.03.2018. http://www.utexas.edu/research/ctr/pdf_reports/0_5684_1.pdf.

Harrison, Rob (2000). Harmonizing Truck Transportation: Policy Harmonization and Adjustment in the North American Agricultural and Food Industry. In R.M.A. Loyns (eds.). *Proceedings of the 5th Agricultural and Food Policy - 1999 16804, Farm Foundation, Agricultural and Food Policy Systems Information Workshops.*

College Station, TX: Texas A & M University; Guelph: University of Guelph; Mexico City: El Colegio de México.

Hufbauer, Gary Clyde, Cathleen Cimino, and Tyler Moran (2014). *NAFTA at 20: Misleading Charges and Positive Achievements.* Washington, D.C.: Peterson Institute for International Economics.

Hutton, John (2000). *U.S.-MEXICO BORDER: Better Planning, Coordination Needed to Handle Growing Commercial Traffic*, GAO/NSIAD-00-25. Washington, D.C.: US Government Accountability Office.

Jessop, Bob (1999). Narrating the Future of the National Economy and the National State: Remarks On Remapping Regulation and Reinventing Governance. In George Steinmetz (eds.). *State/culture : state-formation after the cultural turn*, 378–406. Ithaca, NY: Cornell University Press.

Jessop, Bob (2003). The Political Economy of Scale and the Construction of Cross-border Micro-regions. In F. Söderbaum and T. M. Shaw (eds.). *Theories of New Regionalism: A Palgrave Reader*, 179–196. Houndmills: Palgrave Macmillan.

Jones, Vivian C., and Lisa Seghetti (2015). US *Customs and Border Protection: Trade Facilitation, Enforcement, and Security*, CRS 7-5700. Washington, D.C.: Congressional Research Service.

Kennish, Tim (1995). NAFTA and Investment - A Canadian Perspective. In Seymour J. Rubin and Dean C. Alexander (eds.). N*AFTA and Investment*, 1–35. The Hague: Kluwer Law International.

Lakshmanan, T. R., and William P. Anderson (1999). Trade and Transportation Integration: Lessons from North American Experience, Paper Prepared for Presentation at WORLD BANK/UNESCAP Technical Workshop on Transport and Transit Facilitation, April 19-21, in Bangkok, Thailand.

Lee, Erik, Christopher Wilson, Franciso Lara-Valencia, Carlos de la Parra, Rick Van Schoik, Kristopher Patron-Soberano, Eric L. Olson, Andrew Selee (2013). *The State of the Border Report: A Comprehensive Analysis of the U.S.-Mexico Border.* Washington, D.C.: The Wilson Center.

Lefebvre, Henri (2003). Space and the State. In Neil Brenner, Bob Jessop, Martin Jones and Gordon Macleod (eds.). *State/Space: A Reader*, 84–100. Hoboken, NJ: Blackwell Publishing.

Maxwell, Cameron A. and Brian W. Tomlin (2002). *The Making of NAFTA: how the deal was done.* Ithaca, NY: Cornell University Press.

Morales, Isidro (2014). Post-NAFTA North America: Reshaping the Economic and Political Governance of a Changing Region. Houndmills: Palgrave Macmillan.

Newman, David and Anssi Paasi (1998). Fences and Neighbours in the Postmodern World: Boundary Narratives in Political Geography. *Progress in Human Geography*, 22, 2, 186–207.

Norton, Joseph J. (1995). The NAFTA "Process" in Context. In Joseph J. Norton and Thomas L. Bloodworth (eds.). *NAFTA and Beyond: A New Framework for Doing Business in the Americas.* Dordrecht: Martinus Nijhoff Publishers.

Office of the Secretary, Department of Transportation (2000). North American Free Trade Agreement's Land Transportation Standards Subcommittee and Transportation Consultative Group: Annual Plenary Session, Federal Register / Vol. 65, No. 167 / Monday, August 28, 2000 / Notices.

Ohmae, Kenichi (1995). *The End of the Nation State: The Rise Of Regional Economies.* New York, NY: Simon and Schuster.

Ojah, M., J. Villa, W. Stockton, D. Luskin, and R. Harrison (2002). *Truck transportation through border ports-of-entry: Analysis of coordination systems.* College Station, TX: Texas Transportation Institute, Texas A&M University.

Pastor, Robert A. (2011). T*he North American Idea: A Vision of a Continental Future*, New York, NY: Oxford University Press.

Phillips, Keith R., and Carlos Manzanares (2001). Transportation infrastructure and the border economy. In Robert W. Gilmer, Lori L. Taylor, Thomas M. Fullerton, Keith R. Phillips, and Carlos E. Manzanares (eds.). *The Border Economy.* Dallas, TX: Federal Reserve Bank of Dallas.

Potter, Simon V. and Gene Kruger (2007). Canada: Trade Law Aspects Of Transportation. *mondaq.com.* 22.03.2018. www.mondaq.com/canada/x/53618/cycling+rail+road/Trade+Law+Aspects+Of+Transportation.

Richman, Erica (2009). The NAFTA Trucking Provisions and the Teamsters: Why They Need Each Other. *Northwestern Journal of International Law and Business,* 29, 555–576.

Rodrigue, Jean Paul, Claude Comtois and Brian Slack (2006). *The Geography of Transport System.* New York, NY: Routledge.

Scheinberg, Phyllis F. (1996). *Commercial Trucking: Safety and Infrastructure Issues Under the North American Free Trade Agreement,* GAO/RCED-96-61. Washington D.C.: US Government Accountability Office.

Soden, Dennis L. (2006). *At the Cross Roads: US / Mexico Border Counties in Transition.* El Paso, TX: IPED Technical Reports. Paper 27. 22.03.2018. http://digitalcommons.utep.edu/iped_techrep/27.

Sosa, O. (2008). Border Planning in the San Diego-Tijuana Region: Local Planning and National Policy. *Berkeley Planning Journal,* 21.1, 169–185.

St. John, Rachel (2011). *Line in the Sand: A History of Western U.S.-Mexico Border.* Princeton, NJ: Princeton University Press.

Texas Department of Transportation (2015). *Texas-Mexico International Bridges and Border Crossing.* Austin, TX: Texas Department of Transportation. 22.03.2018. https://www.txdot.gov/inside-txdot/forms-publications/publications/international-relations.html.

Turnbow, Curtis F. (1991). *U.S.-Mexico Trade: Concerns About the Inadequacy of the Border Infrastructure,* GAO/NSIAD-91-228. Washington, D.C.: US Government Accountability Office.

U.S. Custom and Border Protection (2005). *FAST Reference Guide: Enhancing the Security and Safety of Trans-Border Shipment.* Washington D.C.: US Custom and Border Protection.

U.S. Department of Commerce (2008). *Draft Report: Improving Economic Outcomes by Reducing Border Delays, Facilitating the Vital Flow of Commerce Across the U.S.-Mexico Border.* Washington, D.C.: US Department of Commerce.

U.S. Department of Transportation, Federal Highway Administration (2017). *World Trade Bridge Crossing Summary.* Washington, D.C.: Federal Highway Administration. 15.03.2018. https://ops.fhwa.dot.gov/freight/freight_analysis/world_trade_brdg/wrld_trd_brdg_ovrvw.htm.

Vadali, Sharada R., Dong Kung Kang, and Karen Fierro (2011). *Border Delays and Economic Impact to the Freight Sector: an Exploration of El Paso Port of Entry.* College Station, TX: Texas Transportation Institute, Texas A&M University.

Villarreal, M. Angeles, and Ian F. Fergusson (2017). *The North American Free Trade Agreement (NAFTA),* CRS Report No. R42965. Washington, D.C.: Congressional Research Service.

Vormann, Boris (2015). *Global Port Cities in North America: Urbanization Processes and Global Production Networks.* New York, NY: Routledge.

II. The Smart City: Grounding the Economy of the Future

The Myth of the Green City: Mapping the Uneven Geographies of E-Mobility

Tobias Kalt

In the aftermath of the 2008 global financial crisis and at a time in which economic and ecological crises intensify, the green economy has emerged as a political-economic strategy for managing crises tendencies through an expanded program of ecological modernization (Wissen 2012). The solution seems to be within reach. The green economy promises triple-win scenarios in decoupling economic growth from resource use and carbon emissions through technological innovation and market mechanisms while offering social benefits through the creation of green jobs (UN Environment Program 2011).

In the contemporary urban age, cities are key to the green economy and are regarded as central terrains for restructuring society's relations with nature, as it is here that over half of the world's population lives that leaves an ever-growing ecological footprint on the planet (Bulkeley and Schroeder 2012, 250). The electrification of urban transport is of central importance in the vision for a sustainable urban planet. The UN is but one institution that has pronounced its goal to increase the share of electric vehicles in cities worldwide to at least 30 percent by 2050 (UN Human Settlements Program 2014, 2). What other public and private actors equally hope for is that the switch to e-mobility and electric vehicle technologies will create *green cities* with social and environmental benefits from reductions in air pollution, carbon emissions, and noise and congestion levels as well as economic gains for automotive and supplier industries (e.g. European Commission 2016).

This chapter critically interrogates the promise of the ecological modernization of urban transport. Far from an equitable and sustainable development model, the neoliberal green city is understood here as the product of a process of uneven development in which environmental and economic benefits accrue in the green city while socio-ecological costs are externalized to the Global South. Yet, in restricting our attention to what happens inside the city, the global spatial relations that create the exploitative conditions for the green city to emerge disappear from view. By analyzing the socio-material processes, networks and actor constellations that produce the green city along with its uneven global geographies, this chapter brings into view the entanglements of the green city with uneven socio-ecological conditions at often distant elsewheres.

San Francisco, as the global frontrunner for e-mobility, serves as an exemplary case in this chapter to study technology-driven urban transformations that follow the principles of the green economy. Using global production networks (GPN) as an analytical lens, San Francisco's constitutive socio-material flows with regard to e-mobility are traced back through the various production stages from consumption to manufacture and extraction. Going backward, as it were, from point of sale to point of extraction serves as a heuristic to map the production networks and their actors around these flows. This directs our attention to the territorial and material dimensions of production and brings into view the uneven distribution of economic value and socio-environmental goods and bads across space. As we will see, these processes are not purely market-based but rely along every step on the active work of states at various levels of government which turn a blind eye on the externalization of social and environmental costs, subsidize related industries, and ensure the seamless flow of intermediates and factors of production. As we set out to excavate San Francisco's e-mobility flows back through the various production stages, we rediscover zones of consumption, manufacture, and extraction which are the essential sites of the green economy as they constitute the obligatory passing points of globalized production.

On Method: The Planetary Urbanization of Nature

With its central focus on city-nature relations, the research perspective of urban political ecology (UPE) offers itself for this type of analysis. Emerging as an extension to the traditional way of doing political ecology that has long exclusively focused on rural transformations, UPE has highlighted the city as a site equally constituted by socio-ecological processes (Heynen 2014, 598). Importantly, UPE's theoretical insights are not limited to the (re)discovery of nature *in* the city. With the intensification of urbanization during the late twentieth century, the production of nature[1] has become inseparably linked to the wider processes of urbanization (Swyngedouw and Kaika 2000). In the urban age, in which the majority of resource consumption, waste, and emission production takes place in cities, the transformation of nature is thus markedly an urban process. Swyngedouw and Kaika (2000) propose to refer to the large-scale transformation of nature into city as "a historical-geographical process of the *urbanization of nature*" (p. 569, own emphasis). In understanding the green city as an instance of the urbanization of nature, city-nature relations move to the center of the analysis and bring into view how the production of nature is implicated in the production of the green city.

A central analytic device of UPE is the notion of metabolism. The origins of this concept reach back to Marx who appropriated the term from biology to describe the transformation of nature through labor, understood as "a process by which man, through his own actions, mediates, regulates and controls the metabolism between himself and nature" (Marx 1867/1976, 283). For Marx, this is a fundamental human condition that under capitalist social relations takes the shape of the enrolment of nature and labor to produce commodities as "metabolized hybrid socio-natures" (Swyngedouw 2006, 109). As a way of studying the city that transcends the society-nature divide, UPE adapted the notion of metabolism to the study of the city, as urbanization is understood as "primarily a particular socio-spatial process of metabolizing nature, of urbanizing the environment" (Swyngedouw 2004, 8). UPE's notion of metabolic flows serves as the entry point for the analysis that excavates the socio-natural flows that produce the green city.

Yet in following the city's metabolic flows, it becomes clear from the outset that circulation is anything but confined to city boundaries. As the cultural theorists Boutros and Straw (2010, 9) point out, circulation "is not something that happens exclusively *in* the city. Rather the city is itself constituted by circulation" (emphasis in original). While UPE has been credited with demonstrating how the "hybrid city" (Swyngedouw 1996) is both

1 The production of nature thesis was developed by Neil Smith (1984/2008). In contrast to common views of nature as external and in opposition to society, Smith contends that under global capitalism nature "is more and more the product of social production" (Smith 1984/2008, 49-50). The production of nature thesis describes "how capitalism and class power serve to make, unmake and remake the natural and built environments" (Castree 2013, 161).

thoroughly social and natural, less progress has been made in tackling the urban-rural divide. UPE research has produced insightful analyses of the city as an *outcome* of the urbanization of nature but has yet largely failed to grasp how the same processes affect spaces beyond the city's boundaries and immediate hinterlands (Angelo and Wachsmuth 2015). The potential in the urbanization of nature thesis to overcome the urban-rural divide has never been fully realized. In enriching UPE with the concept of planetary urbanization that has been developed in critical urban theory by Brenner and Schmid (2011, 2015), this research follows up on the initial but yet underexposed formulations of UPE's research agenda.

The notion behind planetary urbanization signifies that in recent times the magnitude of urbanization has reached planetary scale and the whole world has become urbanized to some degree (Brenner and Schmid 2011, 12). This is not a claim that the city has become the only existing spatial form on the planet. Rather, it suggests that the process of urbanization has "increasingly come to condition all major aspects of planetary social existence and, in turn, […] the fate of human social life—indeed, that of the earth itself—[…] hinge[s] upon the discontinuous dynamics and uneven trajectories of urbanization" (Keil and Brenner 2014, 2). Brenner (2013, 102-104) carves out two interrelated moments in the urbanization process. *Concentrated urbanization* produces 'urban' agglomerations, whereas *extended urbanization* transforms 'rural' areas into the operational landscapes of cities. As products of the capitalist urbanization process, capital, labor, information, and built structures agglomerate in areas with high population densities and manufacturing and service economies ('the city'). These exist alongside their life-supporting, often land-extensive operational landscapes ('the countryside') that supply natural resources to urban agglomerations and absorb their wastes. Concentrated and extended urbanization together weave the urban fabric, a term which "internalizes the city/countryside divide within a singular, unevenly developed process [of] urbanization" (Brenner and Schmid 2015, 11).

In extending UPE with the planetary urbanization thesis, the perspective of the *planetary urbanization of nature* brings into view socio-material processes operating beyond city limits that are crucial to understanding the formation and perpetuation of the green city and that reveal asymmetrical relationships to distant sites that would otherwise remain invisible. Bringing planetary urbanization to UPE thus helps to avoid "methodological cityism" (Angelo and Wachsmuth 2015, 16), bridges the urban-rural divide, and expands the analytic view towards the wider circulatory currents of the urban metabolism that produces the green city as well as its uneven global geographies as instances of the planetary urbanization of nature.

UPE's concept of the urban metabolism, extended to its planetary scope, lends itself to the development of a methodological strategy that consists of tracing the metabolic flows across the urban and the rural that produce the green city. Yet, the urban metabolism concept remains unspecific about the shape, character and direction of these flows as well as their enabling structures. In complementing the approach of tracing the flows with the analytical concept of global production networks (GPN), a methodological framework is developed that is attentive to the *organization* of the production process of the green city's planetary flows.

GPN is an actor-centered network approach to the study of capitalist production through the prism of commodity chains and with emphases on the networked character of the chain and its links, the social actors that constitute the network, and underlying power relations (Coe et al. 2008). Since the urban metabolic flows under capitalist social relations take on the form of the "circulation of commodities" (Swyngedouw 2006, 108), GPN and its interest in tracing the "biographies of commodities" (Hartwick 1998, 424) offers a valuable methodological extension for developing an analytic strategy. In this way, the production of the e-mobility city of San Francisco is analyzed in terms of the GPN that extracts raw materials to manufacture electric cars that are to be used on the streets of San Francisco (*Figure 1 below*).

GPN makes use of the network concept as a methodology to map the social relationships among actors involved in commodity chains (Dicken et al. 2001). The analysis of actor constellations in this article focuses on corporate actors directly involved in goods production as well as state actors facilitating production processes. When examining state actors, the focus is restricted to government actions at national and subnational levels since institutions of global governance or international agreements are beyond the scope of a single production network.

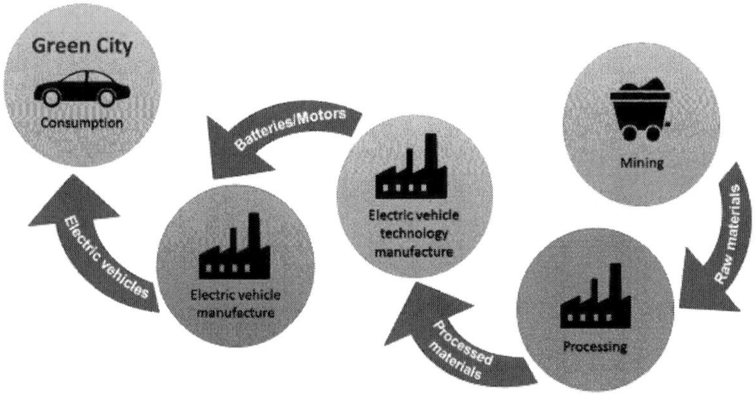

Fig. 1: Urban metabolic flows of the e-mobility city conceived of as part of a commodity chain

Focusing on the networked character of metabolic flows potentially risks ignoring their territorial and material dimensions (Coe et al. 2008). Therefore, this article stresses the spatial dimension of the green city production network in directing attention to its embeddedness in uneven geographies as well as the fundamental grounding of production in the natural environment. A production network may thus be understood as an organizational structure that produces and channels urban flows and that is bound to territories and the natural environment. As the e-mobility commodity chain is very complex, highly dispersed geographically, and to a large degree nontransparent, the goal is not to map the complete production network. Instead, the methodological procedure follows an archaeological strategy that aims to unearth the most important steps in the green city's metabolic production process in order to expose the social logics driving the process. Therefore, the focus lies on the electric car battery as the Achilles' heel of the e-mobility boom and a few of its most relevant raw material inputs (nickel, cobalt, lithium) as well as the most important actors and regions involved in the production process.

Concentrated Urbanization in the Core: Zones of Consumption and of Manufacture

The production of the San Francisco e-mobility city has created a range of urban agglomerations through a process of concentrated urbanization. Zones of consumption of electric cars have been established in the San Francisco Bay Area while zones of manufacture of electric vehicles and related technologies have emerged elsewhere in the US and abroad. By establishing the conditions for the mass deployment of electric vehicles on its city streets, the metropolitan area of San Francisco has been turned into one of the largest zones of consumption for electric vehicles. According to the German American Chamber of Commerce (2013), a quarter of all electric vehicle sales in the US are estimated to take place in the metropolitan areas of San Francisco and Los Angeles.

In this emergence of the green city, and against the rhetoric of free-market restructuring, the state has always been key. The development of a dense network of public and private charging points across San Francisco and the Bay Area has been pursued jointly by local governments and private e-mobility companies. The Silicon Valley has become home to a number of electric automakers and autoparts manufacturers, including the industry-leader Tesla, as well as leading manufacturers of charging equipment. These companies exert their influence on policy-making through public-private partnerships. Of central importance is the Bay Area Climate Collaborative (BACC), a public-private partnership set up in 2009 between the mayors in the Bay Area and a clean-tech advocacy group that includes, among others Tesla. In 2011, the BACC and local governments in the Bay Area jointly set up the *EV Strategic Council* that advises local governments on the development of infrastructure to prepare for an ongoing influx of new electric vehicles. It has since published a number of reports, including an e-mobility policy strategy that was adopted by the Bay Area local governments in 2013 (Association of Bay Area Governments 2013). In addition, the BACC launched the *Bay Area EV Corridor Project* in order to install charging stations along regional transportation corridors and "to establish the greater San Francisco Bay Area as the EV Capital of the U.S." (EV Communities Alliance 2010). Another initiative launched by the Bay Area's Metropolitan Transport Commission awarded 14 million dollars as grants for regional electric vehicle and infrastructure projects with the aim to turn the Bay Area into a "national demonstration model" for electric vehicles (Coté 2010).

Fig. 2: Electric vehicles charging in front of San Francisco City Hall, Source: Felix Kramer (CC BY-SA 2.0)

State and federal governments have also supported the establishment of infrastructural conditions for advancing the mass deployment of electric vehicles in the Bay Area. Some of the measures taken by the California government include loans to electric vehicle supply equipment (EVSE) manufacturers and property owners for installing charging points. Additionally, the California governments installed charging stations at state-owned parking spaces and mandated public agencies to install their own charging points (Alternative Fuels Data Center n.d.). On the federal level, the 2009 American Recovery and Reinvestment Act (Recovery Act) provided direct funding to EVSE manufacturers in the Bay Area to set up charging networks. In addition, the US Department of Energy opened up loan guarantees in 2016 for the creation of charging corridors on national highways between San Francisco and cities in- and outside of the Bay Area (White House Office of the Press Secretary 2016).

In addition to infrastructure development, a range of monetary and non-monetary consumer incentives have been established on the federal and state level that stimulate electric vehicle demand in the city. The US government created a number of large financial incentives, such as the first consumer tax credit for the purchase of new electric vehicles in 2008 that was expanded from 2,500 to 7,500 dollars after the 2008 financial crisis through the Recovery Act. In addition, the Recovery Act launched tax credits for converting a conventional car into an electric car and provided tax credits to businesses and private consumers to reduce the cost of installing charging equipment. Another subsidy for the purchase of fuel-efficient vehicles was offered by the Car Allowance Rebate System, also known as Cash for Clunkers (Consumer Assistance to Recycle and Save Act of 2009, § 1302). On the regional level, California is the US state that offers the widest set of e-mobility consumer incentives. Most notably, the California government offers a tax rebate for the purchase or lease of an electric vehicle and allows electric vehicles to drive solo in the carpool lanes on freeways (Alternative Fuels Data Center n.d.).

In sum, local, state and federal governments have worked with the private sector to turn San Francisco into a major zone of consumption and position the metropolitan area as a focal point in the growing electric vehicle market. The city and the Bay Area reap economic benefits from attracting state and federal level funding and from the development of the Silicon Valley's clean-tech cluster. Furthermore, a number of health and environmental benefits from reductions in air and noise pollution accrue in San Francisco (Maizlish et al. 2013), though they are likely to be unevenly distributed across the city due to the high initial costs of purchasing an electric vehicle and installing home charging equipment (National Bureau of Economic Research 2016). Lastly, electric vehicles are said to have long tailpipes as carbon emissions do not occur at the point of usage but are shifted upstream to electric power plants. While California's energy mix charts a growing share of renewables, it is still made up predominantly of natural gas and nuclear power, thus contributing to carbon emissions and other environmental risks (California Energy Commission 2017).

In following the electric cars that roam the streets of San Francisco outside of the city to their points of origin at the assembly line, the zones of manufacture come into view. The three largest electric automakers Tesla, Nissan and General Motors (GM) together lead the e-mobility market in the US and each operate dealerships in San Francisco (Inside EVs 2018).

In the aftermath of the global financial crisis, processes of concentrated urbanization have led to the emergence of zones of manufacture that produce electric vehicles to be sold in San Francisco and other US cities. Furthermore, battery manufacture for electric vehicle assembly in the US is increasingly shifted from Japan and South Korea to the US and new large-scale and energy-intensive battery manufacturing facilities have been constructed domestically. The US government and a number of state governments heavily nurtured the electric vehicle industry as a way to grow out of the recession and thus laid the groundwork for the emergence of zones of manufacture in the US.

The all-electric automaker Tesla was founded as a start-up in Silicon Valley in 2003 and began mass production of electric vehicles in the Bay Area in 2010. In order to secure the supply of lithium-ion battery cells for its battery packs, Tesla entered into a partnership with the Japanese multinational electronics corporation Panasonic that manufactures lithium-ion cells in Japan through its subsidiary SANYO (Panasonic 2013). In 2014, Tesla and Panasonic jointly invested 5 billion dollars to build the very large-scale lithium-ion battery manufacturing plant, the Gigafactory, in an industrial park in Storey County, Nevada (Tesla 2014b). With a size of more than 530,000 m^2, the Gigafactory is allegedly the largest building in the world by footprint on the ground (Tesla n.d.). The factory is planned to annually reach a battery production capacity of 35 gigawatt hours by 2020 which equates to more than the total worldwide lithium-ion battery supply in 2013 and would allow for an increase in electric vehicle production of up to 500,000 annually (Tesla 2014a).

Next to Tesla, one of the contenders for electric vehicle market leader is the Detroit-based automobile company GM. In the aftermath of the global economic crisis and with rising interest in e-mobility, GM introduced the commercially-successful Chevrolet Volt in 2010 and the more low-cost Chevrolet Bolt in late 2016. GM manufactures both cars at its Detroit/Hamtramck assembly plant in Michigan. The lithium-ion battery cells are supplied by the South Korean batterymaker LG Chem and assembled into battery packs at a newly-constructed plant in Brownstown, Michigan (GM 2009). Since 2013, battery cells for the Chevrolet Volt have seized to be shipped from South Korea and are now produced by LG Chem at a newly-constructed large-scale battery manufacturing plant in Holland, Michigan (GM 2013).

Fig. 3: Aerial view of Tesla's Gigafactory in Nevada, Source: Planet Labs, Inc. (CC BY-SA 4.0)

A third contender in the market is the Japanese company Nissan. The company was among the first automakers to recalibrate its corporate strategy towards e-mobility and in 2010 introduced and mass-marketed the popular Nissan Leaf. While the first units were produced at Nissan's plant in Oppomo, Japan, Nissan retro-fitted its manufacturing plant in Smyrna, Tennessee in 2010 and began to manufacture electric vehicles and assemble battery packs in the US (US Department of Energy 2010). Since 2008, Nissan had sourced lithium-ion cells from the Automotive Energy Supply Corporation, a joint venture of Nissan and the Japanese multinational corporation NEC (Nissan 2008). Yet in 2015, Nissan withdrew from the partnership and is reported to now source lithium-ion batteries from LG Chem's factory in Holland, Michigan (Pfanner and Landers 2015).

Here, too, the state was a central actor. The US federal government and a number of state governments heavily nurtured the electric vehicle and car battery industries in the US through regulations and financial support as a way to grow out of the recession and improve energy security. The Congressional Budget Office (2012) expects the total financial costs of these policies to reach 7.5 billion dollars by 2019. In the aftermath of the financial crisis, the federal government became active in offering direct subsidies and low-interest loans as well as increasing fuel efficiency standards. The Recovery Act included provisions that support research and development on electric vehicle technologies and promote the manufacturing and mass-marketing of electric vehicles (Recovery Act, Title IV, § 1302). For example, funding was awarded to GM to expand car battery production at its facilities in Brownstown, Michigan and to LG Chem to construct its battery plant in Holland, Michigan (US Department of Energy 2011).

Already in 2007, the US Congress passed a direct loans program for electric vehicle manufacturers through the Energy Independence and Security Act of 2007 (§ 136). Among the beneficiaries was Nissan that received low-interest bearing loans to re-tool and expand its manufacturing plant in Smyrna, Tennessee to produce electric cars and battery packs as well as Tesla that also received a loan for opening its manufacturing plant in the Bay Area (Congressional Budget Office 2015, 13). In addition, the US government increased fuel economy standards to induce automakers to establish low-carbon or all-electric vehicles (Corporate Average Fuel Economy Standards 2012).

In addition to these federal programs, state governments established sales mandates for electric vehicles. In 2011, the California Government revived the Zero Emission Vehicle (ZEV) mandate that requires a certain percentage of automakers' sales to be electric vehicles with the aim that only electric vehicles are to be sold by 2040 (California Air Resources Board 2011, 4). Nine other US states have also implemented ZEV programs that are extended with environmental credit trading schemes that allow electric automakers to benefit from the sale of excess environmental credits under ZEV regulatory systems (Wesseling et al. 2015, 94). Furthermore, state governments offer tax exemptions to electric auto- and batterymakers. For example, Tesla received 1.3 billion dollars in tax breaks over 20 years from Nevada in order to build the Gigafactory in Nevada state (Nevada Governor's Office of Economic Development 2014, 7).

In the context of a 32 percent annual growth rate of electric vehicle sales in the US over the past four years, domestic electric vehicle manufacture has been creating substantial economic benefits for the US economy (Rapier 2017). To a lesser extent, economic benefits accrue to auto- and batterymakers in South Korea and Japan, though production is increasingly shifted to the US. Most economic profits and jobs are likely to result from the expansion of car battery manufacture in the US (International Economic Development Council 2013, 12). Tesla's Gigafactory alone is expected to generate a total economic impact of 107 billion dollars and create more than 22,000 jobs over a twenty-year period (Nevada Governor's Office of Economic Development 2014, 8). With regard to environmental impacts, lithium battery manufacturing plants require large amounts of energy due to the use of a so-called dryroom (Dunn et al. 2015, 161). As these factories are located in states with energy mixes dominated by either coal or natural gas (Muyskens et al. 2015), the battery manufacturing process produces significant amounts of carbon emissions.

Operational Landscapes at the Periphery[2]

In order for agglomerations of electric vehicles, charging infrastructures and manufacturing facilities to emerge in San Francisco and the US, operational landscapes must exist that channel the natural resources necessary for electric vehicle production to the zones of manufacture. In tracing the primary raw material inputs for the electric car battery manufacturing process to their points of origins, the zones of extraction and processing that emerge through processes of extended urbanization come into view. Tesla, GM and Nissan all install lithium-based batteries in their electric vehicles obtained from LG Chem and Panasonic. Some of the most important raw material inputs of lithium-ion cells are nickel, cobalt and lithium (Gaines and Nelson 2010, 2).

Multinational mining corporations from the US (Albemarle, FMC), Japan (SMM) and China (Huayou Cobalt) are major suppliers of the battery raw materials for the three US automakers. Nickel is extracted from mines in the Philippines, cobalt in the Democratic Republic of the Congo (DRC) as well as in the Philippines, and lithium in Chile and Argentina. The final stages of the processing of raw materials, and thus a large share of economic value creation, does usually not take place in the countries of origin of the resources but in the home countries of the mining corporations. Nickel is shipped from the Philippines to Japan, cobalt from the DRC to

2 Neil Brenner (2016) coined the term "operational landscapes" to refer to non-urban spaces shaped by the process of extended urbanization (see above).

China, and lithium from Argentina and Chile to the US. Conversely, social and environmental costs associated with extractive activities in terms of environmental pollution, displacements and impairments to livelihoods, and exploitative labor relations remain in the zones of extraction.

In varying contexts, nation-states have taken on crucial roles in establishing and maintaining the conditions for extraction. National governments in the Philippines, Argentina and Chile comprehensively liberalized their mining sectors in the 1990s. In addition, the Philippine government established special economic zones (SEZ) with preferential treatment and employed paramilitaries to repress resistance to mining. In contrast, the DRC government failed to intervene after the collapse of the state-owned mining sector and has since condoned and weakly regulated artisanal cobalt mining. Moreover, national governments in the mining companies' home countries contribute to securing access to strategic resources by either directly subsidizing mining projects (SMM) and mining companies (Albemarle, FMC) or through direct involvement in mining companies (Huayou Cobalt).

Nickel mining in Surigao del Norte, Philippines

Although the global market for nickel is well-established, the growing battery market constitutes an increasingly important driver of nickel demand (USGS 2017, 114). The multinational mining corporation Glencore predicts that "[b]atteries and the onset of the EV revolution could prove to be a transformational event" with nickel demand for batteries expected to multiply three- to fivefold over the next five years (Glencore 2016, 9). Nickel is mined primarily from lateritic nickel ore deposits with cobalt often produced as a by-product. The largest nickel producer worldwide is the Philippines, supplying 22 percent of total global output (USGS 2017, 115).

Whereas LG Chem's nickel suppliers could not be identified, Panasonic receives battery-grade nickel and cobalt from the Japanese mining corporation Sumitomo Metal Mining (SMM 2017). The corporation's largest operations are located in the Philippines, in the mining town of Taganito in Surigao del Norte Province. Nickel is mined in open pits by the Taganito Mining Corporation (TMC), a partnership of the Philippine mining company Nickel Asia and the Japanese Pacific Metal Company. Mined nickel ore is processed on-site into mixed nickel-cobalt sulfides by SMM's subsidiary Taganito HPAL Nickel Corporation (THPAL) before it is shipped to Japan where the refinement of nickel and cobalt into battery-grade materials and thus most economic value creation takes place in SMM's refineries (SMM n.d.).

The Philippine government enabled foreign investments into mining by comprehensively liberalizing the mining sector along with a range of tax exemptions and low tax rates for mining corporations in 1995 (USGS 1995). In addition, the government set up an SEZ at the Taganito mining site in 2009 as a dedicated area with preferential business treatment (Chamber of Mines of the Philippines, n.d.). In the same year, SMM began to invest in TMC and in 2013 opened the THPAL nickel smelting plant in the Taganito SEZ, the largest investment in the Philippine minerals sector at this time (SMM 2013). The project was partly funded with loans from the Japanese government-owned Bank for International Cooperation (Japan Bank for International Cooperation 2012).

Since SMM began nickel mining in Taganito, local residents have complained about environmental pollution from the siltation of marine ecosystems and rivers as well as about health problems, the endangerment of livelihoods due to the pollution of fish stocks, and the destruction of sacred indigenous sites (Reformina 2011). Among the gravest ecological consequences of nickel mining in the Philippines is acid mine drainage that contaminates regional water bodies. A petition filed before the Supreme Court in 2011 accused TMC of polluting water systems in failing to construct proper siltation dams and unsuccessfully demanded an immediate stop of mining operations in the region (ibid.). In addition, the Taganito mine is built on lands inhabited by the indigenous Mamanwas. While TMC agreed to pay a royalty of one per cent of gross revenue to the indigenous communities, the payments did not take place and in response indigenous protestors erected barricades and torched mining equipment (Philippine Indigenous Peoples Links 2009). After the conflict intensified and armed members of the revolutionary New People's Army attacked SMM's facilities (Pacific Strategies and Assessments 2011), the Armed Forces of the Philippines together with TMC increased militarization of the area by training and employing paramilitary groups that have been linked to extrajudicial killings of environmental activists (Holden 2012).

Cobalt mining in Katanga Province, DR Congo

Cobalt's main area of application is battery manufacture. Over the past five years, the battery sector's global demand for cobalt has tripled and is forecasted to at least double again by 2020, mostly attributed to the growth of the electric vehicle market (Frankel et al. 2016). Cobalt is mined from hard rock through industrial or artisanal (i.e. small-scale) operations or as a by-product of nickel and copper mining. The DRC contributes to more than half of the global supply of mined cobalt (USGS 2017, 53), with artisanal mining estimated to contribute to more than 60 percent of the DRC's cobalt production (Tsurukawa 2011, 13).

While Tesla does not disclose its cobalt suppliers, the company claims not to use cobalt of Congolese origin and at least partly covers its cobalt demand through Panasonic from SMM's Taganito mine (Roskill Information Services 2017). LG Chem however has been shown to source its cobalt at least partly from the DRC (Frankel 2016). The batterymaker obtains cathodes from the South Korean component manufacturer L&F Material that sources refined cobalt from the government-linked Huayou Cobalt corporation. Congo Dongfang Mining International (CDM), a fully-owned subsidiary of Huayou Cobalt, is by far the largest buyer of cobalt raw materials extracted by artisanal miners in the DRC's cobalt-rich Katanga province (Frankel 2016). CDM processes low-grade cobalt in the DRC and subsequently ships it to Huayou Cobalt's facilities in China for further refinement (AI 2016, 50-52).

According to a 2010 study, between 110,000 and 150,000 artisanal miners work in the informal mining sector in Katanga and extract the metal by hand-picking cobalt-rich ores (Pact 2010). Artisanal mining in the DRC has significantly grown after the collapse of the state-owned mining company Gécamines in the early 1990s (International Crisis Group 2006, 8). Gécamines used to be the powerhouse of the DRC's economy, employing over 33,000 workers and providing housing, education and health care to its employees and their families (ibid., 8). After its collapse, the DRC government failed to intervene and provide alternative economic opportunities and instead encouraged its citizens to become involved in artisanal mining (Tsurukawa et al. 2011, 15-16). With the passing of the 2002 Mining Code, a governmental agency was established to monitor compliance with safety and health regulations, though evidence suggests that the agency has only poorly performed its task to improve the working conditions of artisanal miners (AI 2016, 7-8; SwedWatch 2007, 30).

The government's failure to absorb the collapse of Gécamines and its reluctance to effectively regulate small-scale cobalt mining in Katanga results in artisanal miners usually working under hazardous conditions without health and safety equipment (AI 2016, 19-27). Mining takes place underground in narrow shafts and long tunnels where exposure to cobalt dust is high, causing fatal lung disease in addition to asthma and damages to the heart and thyroid (Center for Disease Control n.d.). Other negative health effects in artisanal mining areas are linked to contaminated fish stocks and poor hygiene and sanitation in mining camps (Pact 2010, 7). Frequent occupational accidents, resulting in severe injuries and at times deaths, are common in unauthorized mining areas (see the UN-run Radio Okapi 2014, 2015 for recent reports on fatal accidents). In addition to not protecting adult workers, the DRC government fails to protect children under international human rights obligations with the UN reporting in 2012 that 40,000 children are working in the artisanal mines in Katanga (UNICEF 2012).

Mining in the Lithium Triangle in South America

With a share of 39 percent, lithium-ion batteries make up the largest and fastest growing share of demand for lithium with an average annual growth rate of 11 percent (USGS 2017, 100). With the annual lithium demand from Tesla's Gigafactory expected to reach 15,000 to 25,000 tons by 2020, Tesla alone would consume the majority of today's global lithium output of 35,000 tons (USGS 2014, 44.2; USGS 2017, 101). With the rapid increase in lithium demand, estimates are that available global lithium resources may become exhausted in the near future (Wagner 2011). Up to 70 percent of the world's lithium reserves are found in the so-called lithium triangle of Chile, Argentina and Bolivia (USGS 2017, 101).

The world's largest lithium mining corporations, the US multinationals Albemarle Corporation and FMC Corporation along with the Chilean Sociedad Química y Minera de Chile (SQM), all have their major operations in Chile and Argentina and have recently expanded their production capacities. In addition, the lithium boom has attracted a number of new market entrants to the lithium sector in Argentina (USGS 2014, 44.4-44.5).

Albemarle and FMC and new mining projects in Northern Argentina supply lithium to Panasonic and Tesla (Frankel and Whoriskey 2016). Nissan, GM and LG Chem source lithium from FMC as well (ibid.).

Lithium extraction has been underway in Chile and Argentina for several decades. In Chile, Albemarle and SQM have run operations at the Salar de Atacama since 1984 with Albemarle recently tripling its production capacities (Bates 2016). Albemarle transports the mined lithium concentrates to its Chilean processing facility and to its facilities in North Carolina that were re-tooled with a Recovery Act grant to produce battery-grade lithium hydroxide (Albemarle 2012). In Argentina, FMC started lithium mining in the Salar de Hombre Muerto in 1998 and has recently doubled its output after the expansion of its production facilities in 2014 (USGS 2014, 44.4). Mined lithium concentrates are exported to FMC's refinery in North Carolina that scaled up its battery-grade processing capacity in 2009 with a grant from the US Department of Energy (FMC Lithium n.d.).

Under Pinochet's neoliberal government, the extraction of metals and minerals by private companies for export has been aggressively promoted in Chile (Nem Singh 2012, 236-239). While in recent years, lithium mining in Chile has somewhat grown, this expansion has been limited (Sanderson 2016). The Chilean National Lithium Commission, established in 2014, calls for strengthening the state in developing the resource jointly with private companies (Chilean National Lithium Commission 2015). In contrast to Chile's restrictive legal framework and public-private partnership approach, lithium mining in Argentina is firmly in the hands of private companies and investors and has recently experienced a boom (Göbel 2012, 167). Since the 1990s, the Argentinian mining sector has undergone comprehensive liberalization that began with a program of tax benefits and investment assistances for foreign mining companies (ibid., 170). With the 2004 National Mining Plan, the leftist government of the Kirchners opened up the mining sector further under the model of neo-extractivist development[3] (Nacif 2012). The neoliberal government of Macri elected in 2016 continues along the extractivist path and aims to remove capital controls and revoke taxes on mining companies (Jamasmie 2016). In this con-

3 Neo-extractivism refers to a development model that has been embraced by a number of leftist governments in Latin America since the 2000s and that aims to convert economic profits from a renewed resource boom into increases in social spending (Svampa 2015).

text, lithium mining by new foreign market entrants, such as Orocobre, is experiencing an unprecedented boom in Northern Argentina.

Fig. 4: Aerial view of lithium evaporation ponds at Salar de Atacama in Chile, Source: European Space Agency (CC BY-SA 3.0 IGO)

The most severe environmental concerns relate to water resources in one of the world's most arid regions (Wagner 2011). Lithium is mined by pumping large amounts of salt-rich groundwater into vast ponds, where it evaporates yielding brines with high lithium concentration (Friends of the Earth Europe 2011, 12). As a result, groundwater levels may deteriorate and wetlands and meadows are at risk of running dry (ibid., 12-13). In turn, this negatively affects the land available for traditional pasture and the sensitive ecosystem in one of the world's biodiversity hotspots (Critical Ecosystem Partnership Fund n.d.). In response, conflicts between indigenous communities and mining companies have erupted in communities around the Salar de Atacama in Chile (Observatorio de Conflictos Mineros de América Latina 2017). In Argentina, communities around the Salar de Hombre Muerto have accused lithium operations of endangering livelihoods and pastoral farming in contaminating streams used for drinking water, crop irrigation and livestock feeding (Friends of the Earth Europe 2013, 2). In addition, the recent boom of exploration projects in Northern Argentina has caused protests by indigenous communities that fear the destruction of local economies based on salt production from the salt lake (NO a la Mina 2011, 2012).

Conclusion: Islands of Sustainability in Seas of Exploitation

In following the metabolic flows of the e-mobility city of San Francisco beyond city limits, the dynamics of the planetary urbanization of nature have come into view. On the one hand, capital and labor are put together in a process of concentrated urbanization that creates new agglomeration landscapes. In this way, San Francisco has been transformed into a zone of consumption for electric vehicles and a hub for clean-tech innovation while urban industrial zones for electric vehicle and battery manufacture have emerged elsewhere. On the other hand, the operational landscapes of the e-mobility city develop in a process of extended urbanization. Mining operations in rural zones of resource extraction procure the raw material inputs for electric vehicle production. Merging UPE and planetary urbanization has brought into view the urban fabric of the green e-mobility city that reaches far beyond the confines of the city to a range of distant sites around the world—the green city's distant natures. This urban fabric is produced through global production networks that are controlled by powerful multinational corporations in the automotive, battery and mining industries from the US, Japan and South Korea. Crucially, the state, at different levels of government, plays a key role in creating and maintaining the conditions for capital accumulation at every step of the global production network.

As a result, uneven geographies emerge with economic value and socio-environmental costs and benefits unequally distributed along the global commodity chain. The creation of economic value takes place in the capitalist center, namely in the zones of electric vehicle and battery manufacture in the US and with regard to mining corporations that operate from Japan, China and the US. Environmental benefits from reductions in air and noise pollution accumulate in San Francisco due to the mass deployment of electric vehicles.

In contrast, countries in the Global South are mostly relegated to the role of raw material suppliers. The operational landscapes of resource extraction that fuel the urban e-mobility boom are located in the capitalist peripheries with nickel mining in the Philippines, lithium production in Chile and Argentina, and artisanal cobalt mining in the DRC. The socio-environmental costs are externalized into the zones of extraction with the pollution of local ecosystems, displacements and impairments to local livelihoods, poor working conditions and the use of child labor. In addition, carbon emissions linked to the production and use of electric vehicles contribute to climate change that impacts the Global South more severely. This is why the neoliberal green city as a spatial manifestation of the green economy does not lead to the dematerialization of the economy and does not change socially and environmentally harmful patterns of production and consumption. Instead, a mere greening of an "imperial mode of living" (Brand and Wissen 2017) takes place in the green city that consolidates the continued dominance of the Global North and externalizes costs to the Global South. This stands in stark contrast to the dominant narrative of the green city as an environmental, social, and economic win-win situation. Only through a fetishized representation of city-nature relations that occludes the social relations of the production of the green city and its relationships to distant zones of extraction is the green city able to present itself as green and sustainable.

In terms of socio-political implications, progressive politics ought not to miss the green city's distant natures. In other words, urban environmentalists must be conscious that their advocacy for electric cars may mean, to put it in Cook and Swyngedouw's (2014, 20) words, "sustainability here, exploitation elsewhere". Instead of creating islands of sustainability in seas of exploitation, radical politics must understand the neoliberal green city as a moment in the capitalist urbanization of nature and expose the myth of the green city and its hidden relations of exploitation. Since externalization processes are centrally enabled by the state, governments must be held accountable for the distant socio-ecological effects of their policies. What is necessary is a radical transformation of production and consumption patterns towards more democratic and regional modes of development that reduce the exploitation of humans and nature in distant elsewheres.

Works Cited

Albemarle (2012). New Facilities Inauguration in Kings Mountain. 15.02.2017 http://www.albemarle.com/

Alternative Fuels Data Center (n.d.). California Laws and Incentives. US Department of Energy. 08.01.2017 http://www.afdc.energy.gov/laws/

American Recovery and Reinvestment Act of 2009, 26 U.S.C. Title IV, §§ 1121–1144, 1302.

Amnesty International (2016). *"This is what we die for" - Human rights abuses in the Democratic Republic of the Congo power the global trade in cobalt.* Published jointly with African Resource Watch. London: Amnesty International.

Association of Bay Area Governments (2013). *Bay Area Plug-In Electric Vehicle Readiness Plan.* 07.01.2017 http://www.prospectsv.org/

Bates, Jennifer (2016, June 14). An evaluation of the lithium mining environment in South America. *MINING.com.* 18.02.2017

Boutros, Alexandra, and Will Straw (2010). Introduction. In Alexandra Boutros and Will Straw (Eds.) *Circulation and the City: Essays on urban culture*, 3–20. Montreal: University Press.

Brand, Ulrich, and Markus Wissen (2017). *Imperiale Lebensweise: Zur Ausbeutung von Mensch und Natur in Zeiten des globalen Kapitalismus.* München: Oekom.

Brenner, Neil, and Christian Schmid (2011). Planetary Urbanization. In Matthew Gandy (ed.) *Urban Constellations*, 10–14. Berlin: Jovis.

Brenner, Neil, and Christian Schmid (2015). *Combat, Caricature & Critique in the Study of Planetary Urbanization.* Cambridge: Urban Theory Lab.

Brenner, Neil (2013). Theses on Urbanization. *Public Culture*, 25.1, 85–114.

Brenner, Neil (2016). Operational Landscapes. *Kerb: Journal of Landscape Architecture*, 24, 96–97.

Bulkeley, Harriet, and Heike Schroeder (2012). Global cities and the politics of climate change. In Peter Dauvergne (ed.) *Handbook of Global Environmental Politics*, 249–260. Cheltenham: Edward Elgar.

California Air Resources Board (2011). *Advanced Clean Cars – Summary.* 10.02.2017 http://www.arb.ca.gov/

California Energy Commission (2017). Electricity Data: Total System Electric Generation. 03.05.2018 http://www.energy.ca.gov/almanac/electricity_data/

Castree, Noel (2013). A tribute to Neil Robert Smith (18 July 1954 - 29 September 2012). *Progress in Human Geography*, 37.1, 161–163.

Center for Disease Control (n.d.). Workplace Safety & Health Topics: Cobalt. 19.01.2017 http://www.cdc.gov/niosh/topics/cobalt

Chamber of Mines of the Philippines (n.d.). Taganito Mining Corp. 03.02.2017 http://www.chamberofmines.com.ph/members/01taganitomining.html/

Chilean National Lithium Commission (2015). *Litio: Una fuente de energía, una oportunidad para Chile.* 19.02.2017

Coe, Neil, Peter Dicken, and Martin Hess (2008). Global production networks: realizing the potential. *Journal of Economic Geography*, 8, 271–295.

Congressional Budget Office (2012). Effects of Federal Tax Credits for the Purchase of Electric Vehicles. 19.01.2017

Congressional Budget Office (2015). The Advanced Technology Vehicles Manufacturing (ATVM) Loan Program: Status and Issues. 20.01.2017

Consumer Assistance to Recycle and Save Act of 2009, 49 U.S.C. §§ 1301–1302.

Cook, Ian, and Erik Swyngedouw (2014). Cities, Nature and Sustainability. In Ronan Paddison and Eugene McCann (eds.) *Cities and Social Change: Encounters with Contemporary Urbanism*, 168–185. London: Sage.

Corporate Average Fuel Economy Standards (2012). 2017 and Later Model Year Light-Duty Vehicle Greenhouse Gas Emissions and Corporate Average Fuel Economy Standards, 77 Fed. Reg. 62623.

Coté, John (2010, October 27). Electric cars to get boost from Bay Area grants. *San Francisco Chronicle*. 09.01.2017 http://www.sfgate.com/bayarea/

Critical Ecosystem Partnership Fund (n.d.). Tropical Andes. 15.02.2017

Dicken, Peter, Philipp Kelly, Kris Olds, and Henry Wai-Chung Yeung (2001). Chains and networks, territories and scales: towards a relational framework for analysing the global economy. *Global Networks*, 1.2, 89–112.

Dunn, Jennifer, Linda Gaines, Jarod Kelly, Christine James, and Kevin Gallagher (2015). The significance of Li-ion batteries in electric vehicle life-cycle energy and emissions and recycling's role in its reduction. *Energy and Environmental Science*, 8, 158–168.

Energy Independence and Security Act of 2007, 42 U.S.C. § 131–136.

European Commission (2016, July 20). *A European Strategy for low-emission mobility*. Fact sheet, MEMO/16/2497.

EV Communities Alliance (2010, October 19). The Greater Bay Area EV Corridor Project. Presentation by Richard Schorske, CEO EV Communities Alliance at the California Energy Commission. 07.01.2017 http://www.energy.ca.gov/

FMC Lithium (n.d.). FMC Lithium's Facility in Bessemer City, NC, USA. 15.02.2017

Frankel, Todd, and Peter Whoriskey (2016, December 19). Tossed aside in the 'white gold' rush. *The Washington Post*. 15.02.2017 https://www.washington post.com

Frankel, Todd (2016, September 30). Companies respond to questions about their cobalt supply chains. *The Washington Post*. 19.01.2017

Frankel, Todd, Michael Chavez, and Jorge Ribas (2016, September 30). The Cobalt Pipeline - Tracing the path from deadly hand-dug mines in Congo to consumers' phones and laptops. *The Washington Post*. 19.01.2017 http://www.washingtonpost.com/

Friends of the Earth Europe (2011). *Under Pressure. How our material consumption threatens the planet's water resources*. Vienna: GLOBAL 2000.

Friends of the Earth Europe (2013). *Factsheet: Lithium*. Vienna: GLOBAL 2000.

Gaines, Linda, and Paul Nelson (2010). *Lithium-ion batteries: examining material demand and recycling issues.* Argonne National Laboratory. US Department of Energy. 12.01.2017

General Motors (2009, January 12). GM chooses LG Chem to supply Chevy Volt's lithium-ion batteries and will build the packs themselves. [Press release] 19.01.2017

General Motors (2013, May 7). LG Chem Holland plant to start production this summer. [Press release] 19.01.2017 http://gm-volt.com/2009/01/12/

German American Chambers of Commerce (2013). E-Mobility an der Westküste. 08.01.2017 http://www.gaccwest.com/industrien/e-mobility/

Glencore (2016). Nickel Market Developments – September 2016. [Presentation] 25.01.2017 http://www.glencore.com/

Göbel, Barbara (2012). Lithium – das neue Öl der Anden? Sozio-ökologische Konfliktdynamiken im Lithiumbergbau Argentiniens. In Hans-Jürgen Burchardt, Kristina Dietz, and Rainer Öhlschläger (eds.) *Umwelt und Entwicklung im 21. Jahrhundert*, 165–180. Baden-Baden: Nomos.

Hartwick, Elaine (1998) Geographies of Consumption: A Commodity-Chain Approach. *Environment and Planning D: Society and Space*, 16.4, 423–437.

Heynen, Nikolas (2014). Urban Political Ecology I - The Urban Century. *Progress in Human Geography,* 38.4, 598–604.

Holden, William (2012). A Neoliberal Landscape of Terror: Extrajudicial Killings in the Philippines. *ACME: An International Journal for Critical Geographies,* 11.1, 145–176.

Inside EVs (2018). Monthly Plug-In Sales Scorecard. 20.05.2018 http://insideevs.com/monthly-plug-in-sales-scorecard/

International Crisis Group (2006). *Katanga: The Congo's forgotten crisis.* 21.01.2017 http://www.crisisgroup.org/africa/central-africa/

International Economic Development Council (2013). *Creating the Clean Energy Economy. Analysis of the Electric Vehicle Industry.* 23.01.2017 http://www.iedconline.org/

Jamasmie, Jennifer (2016, February 12). Argentina's new government scraps mining taxes. *MINING.com.* 18.02.2017 http://www.mining.com/

Japan Bank for International Cooperation (2012). Loans for Taganito Nickel/Cobalt Project in the Philippines. [Press release]. 03.02.2017 http://www.jbic.go.jp/en/information/press/

Keil, Roger, and Neil Brenner (2014). From global cities to globalized urbanization. *Glocalism: Journal of culture, politics and innovation*, 3, 1–17.

Maizlish, Neil, James Woodcock, Sean Co, Bart Ostro, Amir Fanai, and David Fairley (2013). Health Cobenefits and Transportation-Related Reductions in Greenhouse Gas Emissions in the San Francisco Bay Area. *Journal of Public Health*, 103.4, 703–709.

Marx, Karl (1976 [1867]). *Capital, Volume I.* New York, NY: Vintage.

Muyskens, John, Dan Keating, and Samuel Granados (2015, July 30). Mapping how the United States generates its electricity. *The Washington Post.* 23.03.2017

Nacif, Federico (2012). El litio en Argentina: de insumo estratégico a commodity. *Herramienta* 54. 27.02.2017 http://www.herramienta.com.ar/

National Bureau of Economic Research (2016). Distributional effects of air pollution from electric vehicle adoption. Working Paper 22862. 23.03.2017 http://www.nber.org/papers/

Nem Singh, Jewellord (2012). Who Owns the Minerals? Repoliticizing Neoliberal Governance in Brazil and Chile. *Journal of Developing Societies*, 28.2, 229–256.

Nevada Governor's Office of Economic Development (2014). *Economic Impact of Tesla on Washoe and Storey Counties.* 24.01.2017 http://www.diversify nevada.com/

Nissan (2008, May 19). Nissan and NEC joint venture – AESC – starts operations. [Press release] 18.01.2017

NO a la Mina (2011, July 22). Piquete contra la megaminería en Jujuy y Salta. 19.02.2017

NO a la Mina (2012, May 2). La Mesa de Salinas Grandes lucha por el cumplimiento de sus derechos. 19.02.2017 mineria-argentina/

Observatorio de Conflictos Mineros de América Latina (2017, February 7). Declaración Pública "Todos por el Salar". 19.02.2017 http://www.conflictosmineros.net/noticias/9-chile/

Pacific Strategies and Assessments (2011). *Philippines Communist Insurgency Report January to December 2011.* Manila: Pacific Strategies and Assessments.

Pact (2010). *PROMINES Study: Artisanal mining in the Democratic Republic of the Congo.* Washington DC/Kinshasa: Pact.

Panasonic (2013, October 30). Panasonic and Tesla reach agreement to expand supply of automotive-grade battery cells. [Press release] 19.01.2017 http://news.panasonic.com/global/press/

Pfanner, Eric, and Peter Landers (2015, July 16). Nissan Considers Shift to LG Chem Batteries. *The Wallstreet Journal.* 18.01.2017 http://www.wsj.com/

Philippine Indigenous Peoples Links (2009, February 15). 400 Mamanwa communities installed human barricade to demand royalty fees promised. 27.01.2017 https://web.archive.org/web/20120829080303/http://www.piplinks.org/fees

Radio Okapi (2014). Katanga: 15 creuseurs artisanaux morts brûlés dans une galerie souterraine à Kolwezi. 21.01.2017

Radio Okapi (2015). RDC: 13 creuseurs meurent à la recherche du cobalt au Haut-Katanga. 21.01.2017

Rapier, Robert (2017, February 5). US Electric Vehicle Sales Soared in 2016. Forbes. 20.03.2017 http://www.forbes.com/sites/rrapier/

Reformina, Ina (2011, May 30). Surigao tribesmen seek writ of kalikasan. *ABS CBN News.* 02.02.2017

Roskill Information Services (2017, January 11). Cobalt, Nickel and Lithium: Tesla starts Gigafactory lithium-ion battery production. 20.03.2017

Smith, Neil (2008 [1984]). *Uneven Development: Nature, Capital and the Production of Space*. Oxford: Blackwell Publishers.

Sumitomo Metal Mining (2013). Ceremony Held to Mark Opening of Newly Completed Plant Under Taganito Project in the Philippines. [Press release]. 27.01.2017 http://www.smm.co.jp/E/news/release/

Sumitomo Metal Mining (2017). Increased Production of Cathode Material for Rechargeable Batteries. 22.07.2018 http://www.smm.co.jp/E/news/release/

Sumitomo Metal Mining (n.d.). Glossary Taganito HPAL Nickel Corporation (THPAL). 26.01.2017 http://www.smm.co.jp/E/glossary/

Svampa, Maristella (2015). Commodities Consensus: Neoextractivism and Enclosure of the Commons in Latin America. *South Atlantic Quarterly*, 114.1, 65–82.

SwedWatch (2007). *Powering the Mobile World: Cobalt production for batteries in the DR Congo and Zambia*. Stockholm: SwedWatch.

Swyngedouw, Erik, and Maria Kaika (2000). The Environment of the City... or the Urbanization of Nature. In Gary Bridge and Sophie Watson (eds.) *A Companion to the City*, 567–580. Oxford: Blackwell.

Swyngedouw, Erik (1996). The City as a Hybrid: On Nature, Society and Cyborg Urbanization. *Capitalism Nature Socialism*, 7.2, 65–80.

Swyngedouw, Erik (2004). *Social Power and the Urbanization of Water: Flows of Power*. New York, NY: Oxford University Press.

Swyngedouw, Erik (2006). Circulations and Metabolisms: (Hybrid) Natures and (Cyborg) Cities. *Science as Culture*, 15.2, 105–121.

Teaford, Jon (1993). The Making of the Rust Belt. In *Cities of the Heartland: The Rise and Fall of the Industrial Midwest*, 211–252. Bloomington, IN: Indiana University Press.

Tesla (2014a, February 26). Gigafactory. 18.01.2017 http://www.tesla.com/gigafactory/

Tesla (2014b, September 4). Nevada Selected As Official Site for Tesla Battery Gigafactory. [Press release]. 18.01.2017 http://www.tesla.com/blog/

Tesla (n.d.). Tesla Press Information. 18.01.2017 http://www.tesla.com/presskit/

Tsurukawa, Nicolas, Siddharth Prakash, and Andreas Manhart (2011). *Social impacts of artisanal cobalt mining in Katanga, DRC*. Freiburg: Öko-Institut.

UN Environment Program (2011). *Towards a Green Economy: Pathways to Sustainable Development and Poverty Eradication. A Synthesis for Policy Makers*. New York, NY: UNEP.

UN Human Settlements Program (2014). *Transport Action Plan. Urban Electric Mobility Initiative*. Nairobi: UN-Habitat.

UNICEF (2012, June 13). In DR Congo, UNICEF supports efforts to help child labourers return to school. 21.01.2017 http://www.unicef.org/childsurvival/

US Department of Energy (2010, January 28). Secretary Chu Announces Closing of $1.4 Billion Loan to Nissan. 19.01.2017

US Department of Energy (2011). Recovery Act awards for electric drive vehicle battery and component manufacturing initiative. 19.01.2017 www.energy.gov/articles/

US Geological Survey (1995). The Mineral Industry of the Philippines. 26.01.2017

US Geological Survey (2014). *Minerals Yearbook 2014. Volume I – Metals and Minerals*. 18.01.2017 http://minerals.usgs.gov/minerals/pubs/

US Geological Survey (2017). Mineral Commodity Summaries. 26.02.2017

Wagner, Thomas Cherico (2011). The Lithium future - resources, recycling, and the environment. *Conservation Letters*, 4.3, 202–206.

Wesseling, Joeri, Jacco Farla, and Marko Hekkert (2015). Exploring car manufacturers' responses to technology-forcing regulation: The case of California's ZEV mandate. *Environmental Innovation and Societal Transitions*, 16, 87–105.

White House Office of the Press Secretary (2016, July 21). Obama Administration Announces Federal and Private Sector Actions to Accelerate Electric Vehicle Adoption in the United States [Press release]. 25.03.2017

Wissen, Markus (2012). Post-neoliberale Hegemonie? Zur Rolle des Green-Economy-Konzepts in der Vielfachkrise. *Kurswechsel. Zeitschrift für gesellschafts-, wirtschafts- und umweltpolitische Alternativen*, 2, 28–36.

Wübekke, Jost (2012). China's Mineral and Metals Industry: On the Path towards Sustainable Development? *Pacific Geographies*, 38, 18–21.

Disrupting Regulation? State Capacities in the Digital Platform Economy

Jonas Pentzien

The rise of digital platforms for sharing, swapping, or renting goods and services has transformed the ways in which people, capital, and labor circulate in post-industrial cities. Instead of having to hail a cab in the streets of New York City, a simple click on your phone will now connect you to the nearest Uber driver, who earns an income by taking you home in their private car. Instead of spending a vacation in Berlin in a corporate hotel chain, Airbnb lets you "live like a local" (Benner 2016a) by connecting you to hosts renting out their private apartments.

This reorganization of urban circulation, however, is heavily contested. In public debate, these intermediary platforms—creating value not by producing goods and services themselves, but by bringing together supply and demand from consumer to consumer—are increasingly criticized for skimming off rents from transactions, for bypassing existing regulations, and, in more global terms, for turning *access* to capital and labor into a commodity, thereby promoting a particularly extractive version of digital capitalism (Morozov and Bria 2018; Slee 2016).

Short-term rental platforms have come under particular scrutiny. In recent years, a variety of studies have emphasized Airbnb's role in cutting into limited housing supplies in these post-industrial cities, leading to an increase in median long-term rents and propelling gentrification (Wachsmuth et al. 2018; Barron et al. 2017). In cities with a high influx of tourists, this has sparked a polarized debate on how governments should respond to this platform-driven reorganization of the short-term rental market. Housing authorities in New York City, Berlin, and Barcelona have pioneered an especially straightforward stance, arguing that short-term rental platforms create incentives to convert apartments into permanent vacation rentals, which leads to a removal of rental flats from the housing market. In response, all three governments have pushed for stronger regulation to curb the purported negative impacts and externalities associated with the business model these digital intermediaries employ. Airbnb, however, strongly rejects this assessment, arguing instead that the number of rentals listed on their platform is so marginal that it cannot be seen as negatively impacting the availability of affordable housing (GEWOS 2016, 4).

In Berlin, this controversy reached an early high point when the government's *Zweckentfremdungsgesetz* came fully into force in May 2016. Prohibiting almost all rentals shorter than two months (ZwVbVO 2014, 1292), the law challenged the very foundations of Airbnb's business model, prompting *The Atlantic* to call Berlin "the City with the World's Toughest Anti-Airbnb Laws" (O'Sullivan 2016).[1] In New York City, an updated version of the multiple dwelling law passed in 2016 declared all short-term rentals in buildings with three or more units of fewer than 30 days illegal unless the owner is present (Wachsmuth et al. 2018, 14). And in Barcelona, all hosts now have to register individually with the city council before receiving an allowance to advertise their property on Airbnb (Airbnb 2018).

A closer look at data comparing listings on Airbnb before and after these laws were implemented, however, reveals a more complex picture. While Berlin's regulations may have been some of the world's toughest on paper, a recent study has argued that "any deterrent effect of the ban has been short-term and has had little lasting effect on the behavior of Airbnb hosts" (Karat Studio 2016). *Der Spiegel* went even further, provocatively characterizing the ban as a "rubber paragraph" with no real chance of ever properly being put into practice (Zeiher 2016). In New York, the impact of the city's regulatory framework has been similarly ambivalent: while on paper the legislation imposes fines of up to 7,500 US dollars on hosts advertising illegal short-term rentals, the city only issued them on 139 out of more than 23,000 thousand potentially illegal listings in the first months after the law was passed (Walker 2017). In sum, local governments were quickly confronted with serious obstacles in trying to enforce these new or updated rules, which called into question their general capability of successfully regulating these newly emerging digital platforms.

What is the take-away from the problems regulators face when addressing digital platforms for sharing, swapping, or renting goods and services?

---

1 Berlin once more revised its regulatory framework in May 2018, virtually legalizing short-term rentals under the condition that hosts first register with the city and then display a personalized number when advertising on platforms. In order to allow for a substantial comparison of the three cases at hand, this chapter focuses only on the enforcement problems associated with the stronger version of Berlin's framework in effect between 2014 and 2018.

Are these reorganized forms of circulation entirely overpowering, making it impossible for governments to address their negative impact through regulatory frameworks? Indeed, recent studies explain such regulatory problems by pointing towards the legal uncertainty digital platforms create and the ways in which they leverage technology in order to avoid cooperating with the authorities. Katz, for example, claims that because platforms differ substantially from traditional service providers "[they do] not neatly fit into existing regulatory frameworks" (2015, 1069). Sundararajan posits that precisely because the so-called 'sharing economy'—one of many umbrella terms frequently used in public debate in order to characterize platform-based business models—creates innovative "new ways of providing traditional services," it would be neither "possible nor economically viable to adopt existing rules and apply them to a new economy" (2016, 146). Pointing towards the impact of technological developments, Kenney and Zysman argue that "in a platform economy, government decisions may be constrained by the 'facts' in the software" (2016). Building on this, Morozov and Bria claim that because local governments are incapable of gaining access to the data needed in order to adequately regulate digital platforms and the transactions they facilitate, it becomes "rather difficult for cities to experiment with non-neoliberal political and economic agendas" (2018, 4).

Taken together, the assumption that the techno-legal structure of this "new digital economy" built around intermediary platforms (Sundararajan 2016, 146) increasingly diminishes state capacities is becoming more and more ubiquitous. Mirroring ultra-globalist arguments, the state and its regulatory instruments are framed as incapable of answering the challenges associated with today's globalized economy—or, put in Silicon Valley's terminology, as simply failing or being "disrupted" (Cortez 2014). These arguments often go hand in hand with the normative claim that governments *should* not intervene in this emerging platform economy in the first place as this would only impede its economic potential.[2] Yet, if these regu-

2 A study commissioned by Airbnb in 2017 claimed that the platform generated $3.5 billion in total economic activity for New York in 2016 of which $580 million went straight to the hosts (those who advertise their apartment or room on Airbnb) and $2.9 billion to local businesses. The study also argued that seven percent of guests (those who rent an apartment or room) said they "would not have taken the trip without Airbnb and 39 percent said they would have stayed shorter," implying that the rise of short-term rental platforms creates growth beyond that generated by the existing hotel industry (HR&A 2017). An independently commissioned study on Airbnb's impact on the hotel industry in Aus-

latory problems indeed stem from the techno-legal structure of digital platforms is as of now insufficiently understood. As a result, the relation between the normative stance against regulation and the techno-legal obstacles that purportedly make regulations fail remains blurry. Furthermore, the focus on techno-legal-dimensions neglects the political dimensions of regulation. Who advocates for or against regulations of digital platforms? What type of support do these supposedly failing frameworks have in the relevant political institutions? As of now, little research has been done on identifying the interest groups that organize in order to establish or prevent strong regulatory frameworks from being implemented. As a result, we have an insufficient understanding of who actually wins and who loses in these conflicts surrounding the regulation of digital platforms.

This chapter aims to rectify some of these shortcomings. By taking a closer look at the frameworks New York City, Barcelona, and Berlin have implemented in order to regulate the short-term rental market and the problems encountered in their respective enforcement campaigns, it evaluates the impact digital platforms with a consumer-to-consumer (C2C) business model have on state capacities. Based on a comparison of platform-related state activity in these three global cities, it puts forth the claim that the state's regulatory capacity has indeed been challenged by the rise of such digital intermediaries, but not disappeared. To the contrary, the chapter demonstrates that in spite of the disruptive traits digital platforms evince, regulations in New York, Berlin and Barcelona have come to reinforce contradictions between platforms (which cannot maintain illegalization forever while profiting from it) and consumers (who have a strong interest in the services offered, but are kept from engaging them to the fullest extent), thereby curtailing the growth potential of digital platforms in the short-term rental market. As a result, platforms are increasingly driven to strike deals with cities in order to partially protect their market position.

Building on this, the chapter provides an alternative to the prevalent 'regulations fail'-stance: instead of explaining regulatory problems as deriving from the techno-legal structure of digital platforms, it traces them to

tin, TX partly confirmed these notions, showing that a one percent increase in platform listings correlates only with a 0.05 decrease in hotel revenues (Zervas, Proserpio and Byers 2016). To be sure, the results of studies commissioned by Airbnb should not necessarily be taken at face value. Yet, they illustrate well the strategies the platform uses in order to publically portray itself as a motor of growth.

the contradictions of post-Fordist flexibilization. By taking this perspective, the chapter makes visible that the emergence of platforms provides governments with increasing legitimacy to further unravel the welfare state, while simultaneously forcing them to address the negative implications of this shift, given that platforms create a financial offset only for those who already own goods that can be rented out. While it might therefore initially seem as if digital platforms are indeed fundamentally challenging state capacities, the chapter provides evidence to the contrary by emphasizing the genuinely *political* dimensions of this purported contradiction. Governments, the chapter shows, are not disrupted by the emergence of digital platforms, but actively shape and facilitate the specific ways in which people, capital, and labor circulate in the platform economy.

The Three Types of Disruption of Digital Platforms

Digital platforms with a C2C business model such as Airbnb exhibit three main traits that potentially undermine quick-fixes and simple regulatory measures on the part of the state: (1) they leverage digital technology in order to position themselves as intermediaries that are capable of facilitating transactions on a global scale (the *technological* dimension); (2) they trigger legal and institutional uncertainty by translating services formerly provided by formalized businesses into the private realm (the *legal* dimension); and (3) they bring with them newly constituted interest groups that actively promote or oppose the platform-based reorganization of circulation (the *interest group* dimension).

1. The rise of digital platforms is inextricably connected to the diffusion of smartphones, advances in cloud computing, algorithm-based matching and globally improved availability of high-speed internet connections (Kenney and Zysman 2016). Taken together, these developments created the necessary (technological) preconditions that made it possible for platforms to lower transaction costs, attract consumers (by way of their competitive prices) and through that enclose parts of existing markets by integrating supply and demand into the platform. The platform-internal markets created in these processes now operate outside the (regulatory) constraints that apply to the non-platform-based parts of existing markets—while simultaneously facilitating the exchange of

comparable goods and services. In the short-term rental market, Airbnb was first to attain a critical mass of consumers and use the ensuing network effects to solidify its role as the major competitor to brick-and-mortar hotel chains. Easy access to venture capital in early stages, as well as later capital injections by investment banks such as Morgan Stanley and JP Morgan Chase & Co allowed the platform to scale up quickly and establish itself as the go-to option for C2C-driven short-term rentals (Crunchbase 2018). As Airbnb's business model is based on connecting hosts and renters while skimming off transaction fees, the platform presents itself as a technology company, not a hotel or hospitality service. This is the basis for Airbnb's argument that it should not be subjected to regulations directed at traditional service providers (Miller 2016, 179).

2. The disruptive character of digital platforms stems from the legal and institutional uncertainty they create. While traditional service providers (like brick-and-mortar hotels) are located within the confines of business regulation, the exchanges facilitated by C2C-platforms (such as Airbnb) are located primarily in "non-commercial spaces that are quite often the most intimate of private spaces: homes and apartments located in neighborhoods" (ibid., 167). This leads to an erosion of the distinctions between the commercial and personal, creating a conflict between different sets of civic rights. Where registered businesses (such as hotel chains) are legally forced to share information with regulators, uncertainty persists about the conditions under which providers on platforms have to fulfill similar requirements (such as handing out data or paying income tax). This begs the question of who, ultimately, holds responsibility for providing information about transactions facilitated by platforms. Is the intermediary obliged to give out information (because these services would not have been offered had the platform not existed)? Alternatively, are providers required to register as businesses because they provide services similar to those offered by hotels? If yes, do the privacy rights of those providing services on digital platforms not outweigh the regulator's concerns about possible negative externalities? Furthermore, as laws are passed not only on the city scale, but also on the federal and transnational level, this legal uncertainty is enhanced by the multiple political scales implicated in regulating the platform economy. Institutional overlap can create uncertainty over jurisdiction,

as opposing interests might translate into contradictory laws that are nevertheless equally applicable in the same context.

3. Finally, the disruptive character of digital platforms stems from new interest groups that have emerged in tandem with the reorganization of circulation that these platforms have set in motion. Consistently high demand for C2C-driven transactions in the short-term rental market in spite of illegalization in places like New York is, as Miller claims, indicative of a widespread "desire to monetize under-utilized existing uses" (2016, 157). This desire has been shaped largely by the financial crisis of 2008, which provided the necessary disruption to catalyze this reorganization of circulation. Put simply, in the absence of well-paying jobs, platforms such as Airbnb created an environment in which a certain part of the population—in this case, apartment owners—could generate income through the economic activation of their idle capacity. As a result, economic dependency on digital platforms has brought about a change in how and *by whom* controversies surrounding short-term rentals are mediated.

Which of these potentially disruptive traits of digital platforms serve to explain the regulatory problems seen in New York City, Berlin and Barcelona? Is the techno-legal structure—a combination of the first two of these traits—of platforms really the deciding factor, as Katz and Sundararajan lead us to believe? Or do regulatory frameworks fail because of the particular configuration of interest groups in a given context? The chapter answers these questions by analyzing if, and to what extent, each of these three factors has come to affect state capacities.

Regulating Against the Odds? Technological Specificity and the Disruption of State Capacities

The technology employed by digital platforms undoubtedly affects the enforcement of regulatory frameworks. Two aspects are central here: first, the business model of intermediary platforms is predicated on a technology-enabled globe-spanning decentralization of services offered in a particular market (Botsman and Rogers 2010). Where regulators could simply inspect the premise of a brick-and-mortar hotel in person to evaluate its compliance with existing regulatory frameworks, the platform-enabled tendency of decentralizing the provision of services on a large scale makes it much more difficult and time consuming for authorities to ensure compliance. In New York, where more than 48,000 flats and rooms are offered on Airbnb alone (Inside Airbnb 2018), housing authorities would have a hard time going from door to door in order to inspect each listing advertised on the platform (Walker 2011). Thus, a high degree of decentrally-provided services makes enforcing regulation costlier, as cities would need to contract hundreds of additional investigators to inspect the platforms' listings. While it is *theoretically* possible to ensure compliance, doing so would require a significant increase in spending on the part of the state.

Second, in the cases where intermediary platforms legally operate from a country other than the one in which the regulation is supposed to apply, platforms are not obligated to adhere to a regulators' request for information on the services exchanged through the platform. This constitutes a problem for the regulatory frameworks of Berlin and Barcelona, as Airbnb's European head office is located in Ireland (Worstall 2013). Put simply, while the platform's service can transcend national borders, Berlin and Barcelona's regulatory frameworks cannot.

Taken together, digital intermediaries affect the possibilities for enforcing regulation because their emergence has changed how information circulates between market and state. This is problematic, as the governance of complex systems depends primarily "on good, trustworthy information" (Dietz 2003, 1908). Enforcement campaigns are therefore more likely to encounter problems when it is unfeasible to inspect each service provider individually, as well as when the intermediary—who holds relevant information for the regulatory process—is out of the regulator's jurisdiction and unwilling to cooperate. Consequently, the question of how to attain information on transactions has become crucial for governments trying to regulate these reorganized forms of circulation made possible by the rise of digital platforms.

In the absence of voluntary cooperation, many cities now include a provision in their legislation allowing them to force platforms to hand over data. New York City's former attorney general Schneiderman set a precedent by subpoenaing Airbnb in order to force the company to release personalized user information to the regulators (Schneiderman 2014). Berlin took similar steps: while the initial ordinance issued in 2014 did not include a clause determining responsibilities of the platforms, an updated version issued in 2016 set legal conditions under which the district exchanges were allowed to force platforms to hand over information (ZwVbVO 2016). In order to request data, Berlin's district exchanges had to prove that enforced compliance is the only way to attain the desired information—or that it would constitute a "disproportionate investment" to pursue other options (ibid.). Yet, the case of New York shows that intermediary digital platforms can leverage their technological infrastructure in order to also complicate such legal altercations. Shortly before querying the data and handing it over to the attorney general, Airbnb New York simply 'cleaned up' its listings by removing a majority of the commercial offers. Yet, immediately after the attorney general's request was fulfilled, these listings were allowed back on the platform—thus making the legal possibility of enforcing data access toothless (Cox and Slee 2016).

Barcelona has taken a different approach. The Catalonian capital forces individuals who want to advertise their services on Airbnb to register with the city in advance and, if accepted into the Catalonia Tourism Register, to make their registration number visible in the platform listing itself. This allows regulators to determine if listings on Airbnb are illegal by simply browsing the platform. When illegal listings are posted, the city can fine Airbnb directly for advertising illegal activity. In 2016, Barcelona's government did just that, imposing a fine of 600,000 euros on the platform for continuing to advertise unlicensed flats (Rodero 2017).

For New York and Berlin—neither of which yet operate a similar tourism register[3]—the crucial question has become how to regulate in the absence of information provided by the platforms. Both cities have answered this by primarily enforcing regulation on providers. However, doing so has its own limitations as existing legislation precludes the regulatory body from scouting for information based on *agent provocateur* approaches. This means that the authorities cannot themselves rent an apartment, determine if it violates existing regulation and then fine the provider. For privacy reasons, an investigation can be opened up exclusively based on information provided from third parties. Additionally, providers can simply

3 The stronger version of Berlin's framework in effect between 2014 and 2018 has abstained from enforcing individual registration. The newly revised regulatory framework implemented in 2018, however, has taken inspiration from Barcelona's approach and forces providers to first register with the city and then display a personal number when advertising on a short-term rental platform (rbb 2018). Nevertheless, it is unclear as of now how quickly these new rules will be implemented and enforced.

anonymize their profile by using a fake name, providing pictures of an entirely different flat or by turning off reviews, thereby making it next to impossible to determine misuse based on publicly available user profiles.

In order to sidestep these problems, the authorities in New York City and Berlin have created online denunciation tools and opened special phone lines through which individuals can anonymously report purported violators (Senate Department for Housing Berlin 2017; Griswold 2017). Any denunciation received through these channels creates 'reasonable suspicion,' allowing the regulator to open a case against the purported violator. In only two years, Berlin's district exchanges have received more than 10,000 anonymous denunciations, confirming the public's willingness to actively participate in the enforcement of the regulatory framework. In New York City, the Office of Special Enforcement has completed more than 2,500 inspections in response to 1,280 complaints (Griswold 2017).

Does the technological structure of short-term rental platforms then indeed disrupt regulation? While the cost-efficiency-related limitations outlined above imply that this is the case, there is another side to this story that counters this assumption. Most importantly, Airbnb's conscious strategy of foregoing legalization until city laws are changed in their favor (Hill 2016) has created a contradictory situation that negatively affects the platform's scaling potential. On one hand, providing services declared illegal offers benefits: as soon as platform-based business models in the short-term rental market are 'daylighted,' other actors—including, for example, the disrupted traditional hotel industry—could themselves enter the market and offer services similar to those that are currently provided exclusively by short-term rental platforms (Miller 2016). In a rather ironic twist, the incumbent would then turn into a competitor to the disruptive platforms. Remaining in the 'shadows' thus makes possible a platform's success in the first place, as it allows for enclosing parts of the existing markets which are then inaccessible to the established actors.

On the other hand, illegality cannot be maintained indefinitely, as continuing illegalization renders the initially lowered entry barriers null. Seeing that regulators are continuously scouting platforms for publicly available information, factors beneficial *within* the platform's logic, like a large amount of positive reviews, a status as a 'Power Host,' or particularly informative pictures, provide the regulator with concrete data that can be used against the provider. Continuing illegalization thus turns providers away from platforms, as well-rated profiles can become too great a risk.

Seeing that Airbnb's business model is predicated on facilitating as many exchanges as possible, uncertainty among providers can lead to serious trust-related issues. The fact that Airbnb continues to strike more and more deals with local governments (Woolf 2016) is indicative of the company's desire to end the current state of uncertainty.

In sum, the technological structure of platforms raises enforcement costs, as the decentralization of service provision associated with digital platforms complicates the process of ensuring compliance. Yet the analysis shows that the particularities of the regulatory framework at hand matter. While New York City and Berlin aim at (and struggle with) fining individual service providers, Barcelona's framework—which forces hosts to register with the Catalan Tourist Office—allows for fining the platform directly. Thus, Barcelona's framework gives the regulatory body leverage and creates incentives for platforms to reign in activity declared as illegal themselves. Furthermore, all three regulatory frameworks come to reinforce contradictions between platforms (who cannot maintain illegalization forever but benefit from it) and consumers (who have a strong interest in the services offered but are kept from engaging them fully) that might curtail the platform's growth potential in the long run. Considering these aspects, the technological structure of platforms alone cannot explain current regulatory problems.

Regulating Against the Law? Legal Uncertainty and the Disruption of State Capacities

Besides the role of technology, legal uncertainty associated with the emergence of intermediary digital platforms has also supposedly come to affect the enforcement of regulatory frameworks. In the early stages of implementation, organized opposition to New York's multiple dwelling law and Berlin's *Zweckentfremdungsgesetz* came from real estate companies professionally operating short-term rentals in both cities. These companies opposed the newly implemented regulations for economic reasons, as they were seen as threatening a particularly promising stream of revenue. For example, it was argued in a leaked memo from 2015 that property owners are capable of *doubling* their income by renting out to tourists instead of local people (Hill 2016, 4). While Berlin's initial ordinance (2014) gave these professional providers a two-year grace period for inventory keeping, the law's full implementation in May 2016 declared *any* unapproved rental illegal and thus pulled the switch on their business activities entirely. As a result, a lobbying group of professional vacation rental companies counter-sued Berlin's law by arguing that the new regulations not only disproportionally limit the freedom of property, but also curtail the freedom of choosing one's profession. The plaintiffs were successful in Berlin's administrative court. As a result of the court's ruling, companies who have operated vacation rentals before the law came into force are now exempted from the law, legalizing thousands of the listings previously deemed illegal (Apartment Allianz 2018). A second court ruling built on this and further exempted all owners of registered secondary homes. These cases severely affected the government's capacity to enforce the new regulations, primarily because they created new loopholes enabling providers to avoid being targeted by the city's regulators. Since these court rulings were publicized, Berlin's district exchanges, for example, have received hundreds of exemption requests from individuals asking to establish vacation rentals in newly declared secondary homes, making enforcement even more costly (Homesharing 2017c).

The legal uncertainty associated with digital platforms, however, not only has speculative implications for enforcement (*how might the law be affected by further court rulings?*), but also political ones. This has been particularly visible in Berlin, where the various district exchanges and not the Senate Department itself are tasked with implementing and enforcing the law. Because of this, the districts can use enforcement as leverage. In Berlin, a variety of districts initially abstained from enforcing the law, arguing that absolute legal certainty would have to be reached beforehand (Aulich 2016). However, as the legal basis for the law (that the provision of affordable housing is endangered) can always only be demonstrated temporarily, such legal certainty is inherently unattainable. The decision of the districts against enforcement thus constitutes not only a precautionary measure taken to protect the district from possible claims for compensation, but also a political bargaining tool. On one hand, the city's administrative law determines such instances of non-enforcement illegal. But on the other, forcing districts to enforce the law would have run counter to the government's interest in framing the "World's Toughest Anti-Airbnb Law" (O'Sullivan 2016) as a success. As a result, the districts tasked with enforcing the law were able to use their decisive position to actively undermine the new legislation.

In New York City, legal uncertainty has similarly been used as a political bargaining chip. In order to oppose the city's strong regulatory framework, Airbnb sued against the 2016 law, claiming that the fines set by the city would have drastically impaired its revenue (Benner 2016b). Yet, the platform simultaneously offered to drop the lawsuit under the circumstances that the city would enforce the law against *hosts* only and not directly against Airbnb, as the city had previously done in 2015. While this agreement was initially framed as a success by both the city and the platform, it required New York City to virtually sign away its capacity to force the platform to take responsibility for listings declared illegal itself, thereby—in a rather ironic twist—reinforcing the technology-related problems of needing to fine providers instead of platforms outlined in the previous chapter.

In sum, legal uncertainty has proven to affect the state's regulatory capacity in multiple ways. In Berlin, two counterclaims not only severely limited the scope of the law but, more importantly, also made visible how quickly regulations directed at digital intermediary platforms can partly be declared unconstitutional given that they restrict individual rights (such as the right to property and the right to freely choose one's profession). In New York, Airbnb strategically *created* legal uncertainty (by countersuing the city's law) in order to negotiate for preferential treatment that would protect the organization from being fined directly.

Regulating the Contradictions of Post-Fordist Flexibilization? Interest Groups and the Disruption of State Capacities

These techno-legal conflicts over how to regulate digital platforms make clear that success or failure of regulatory frameworks in the platform economy largely depends on the interest groups involved in the enforcement process and the resources these groups have access to. Conflict between such interest groups, however, has not only arisen between platforms, districts and cities, but at times also *within* city governments.

While Berlin's Senate Department for Urban Development and Housing (which proposes to ban the forms of circulation made possible by digital platforms), for example, frames short-term rental platforms primarily as a *social problem*, the Senate Department for Economics, Energy and Public Enterprises (which proposes to grow and support these forms of circulation) emphasizes its *economic potential*. This conflict became especially visible in a study on the economic impact of the 'sharing economy' in Berlin commissioned by the Senate Department for Economics at the tail end of 2014 (2016, 4).[4] According to this study, Berlin was not only already on its way towards becoming an "international Sharing City role model" (ibid., 29), but also had the "best preconditions" for further integrating such "new forms of economic activity into the agenda of the city" thanks to the diversity of "people, platforms and businesses" already present (ibid.). Short-term rental platforms were framed as some of the "most valuable 'mineral resources' waiting to be lifted" (ibid.) and it was argued that the city should immediately begin to initiate an "open discourse with the actors [in order to develop] forward-looking and strategically oriented policy" (ibid.). In its conclusion, the report claimed that the "[current] dynamic does not allow for any time-consuming work on the perfect agenda" and that, instead, platforms and the city should work in tandem to help the sharing economy quickly realize its growth potential. The report laid out a vision of how to structure platform-enabled circulation in urban spaces fundamentally opposed to the one put forth by the Senate Department for Urban Development and Housing, which had then just implemented the *Zweckentfremdungsgesetz* precisely in order to maintain its ability to shape the development of the new platform-internal market.

The same government limiting the rise of this market through the "World's Toughest Anti-Airbnb Law" (O'Sullivan 2016) while concurrently praising its economic potential undoubtedly stoked uncertainty around the aims of this new legislation. Did the city want to alleviate the harm it claims short-term rental platforms inflict? Or was it interested in harvesting

4 The term 'sharing economy' is strongly contested. On one hand, many platforms promote its use because they have an (economic) self-interest in being associated with the positively connoted practice of sharing. On the other hand, a variety of scholars—most prominently among them Belk (2014)—have criticized the term as an analytically lacking misnomer that incorporates too many heterogeneous types of transactions (such as monetary as well as non-monetary ones). Taking up this criticism, the chapter employs the term 'sharing' not in order to describe the practices facilitated by digital platforms such as Airbnb, but only in order to make visible the role this persisting idea of platform-based 'sharing' plays in regard to the regulatory problems analyzed here.

the economic resources associated with them? Based on the concurrent expression of opposing perspectives within the Senate Department, it seems the government was intent on doing *both at the same time*. While this approach to regulating platforms—unfolding in a similar fashion in New York and Barcelona—might appear rather contradictory on first sight, it becomes intelligible when contextualized with the emergence of what Morozov and Bria call processes of 'post-Fordist flexibilization' (2018).

Viewed through this analytical lens, one of the most important attributes of digital intermediaries such as Airbnb is the shift in labor relations they reinforce—away from Fordist employment, towards extreme flexibility, short-term gigs and self-employment. These flexibilized work arrangements were able to establish themselves, among other factors (see Jessop 1991), because after the financial crisis of 2008 the comparatively more stable jobs associated with Fordism were increasingly more difficult to come by. For those who chose to or were forced to switch from Fordist to platform-based employment in the context of the crisis, the rise of platforms has primarily brought with it a fall in real income—while simultaneously facilitating higher surplus extraction possibilities for those owning the technological infrastructure.

Yet, it is not only the platforms that have benefitted in this process: seeing that digital platforms for sharing goods and services have kept those individuals with access to idle capacity off welfare and unemployment registers in times of severe economic crisis, their rise also implied savings on the part of the state (as individuals depended less on welfare provision). As these platforms have also contributed to lowering the prices of goods and services on the demand side (such as in transportation), the falling real incomes and cutbacks in welfare provision were further concealed (Morozov and Bria 2018, 16).

Nevertheless, this process of countering job loss not with state-run welfare programs but with a system that incentivizes self-employment based on the activation of idle capacity also increasingly poses a problem for post-industrial cities, as it provides no solution for those individuals who *lack* access to idle capacity and can therefore not create supplemental income. In this context, the purportedly contradictory stances within local governments that unfold simultaneously in current processes of economic restructuring become intelligible: on one hand, the rise of platform based employment creates the possibility for governments to save welfare costs. Because of this, cities have an interest in supporting such platforms. On the other hand, local governments need to somehow address the negative social implications of this shift—such as rising real-estate prices, housing shortages and displacements *qua* gentrification. These persisting contradictions make the enforcement of bans more difficult, as they undermine and ultimately diminish the legitimacy of the law's enforcement campaign in the eye of the public (which has already been made dependent on alternative means of income in order to account for an increasingly reduced welfare system).

In Europe, conflicts of interests surrounding short-term rental platforms on the city-scale are also mirrored in the relation between city and nation state, as well as city and European Commission. Regarding the city-state-relation, an early 2017 guideline published by Germany's Federal Ministry for Economic Affairs and Energy emphasized the need to give intermediary platforms a "degree of freedom to experiment with new services" in order to untangle the "confusing mix of policy" currently surrounding for-profit platforms (Heide 2017). A similar dissatisfaction with strong regulation was voiced by the European Commission, which, in its *Agenda for the Sharing Economy,* outright condemned the idea of bans:

> "Bans […] constitute a measure of last resort. They should only be applied if and where no less restrictive requirements to attain a legitimate public interest objective can be used. For example, banning short-term letting of apartments appears generally difficult to justify when the short-term rental use of properties can be limited to a maximum number of days per year. This would allow citizens to share their properties on an occasional basis without withdrawing the property from the long-term rental market" (European Commission 2016, 4).

Referring directly to platforms in the short-term rental market, the European Commission made its objection to bans clear and instead stressed that governments "should proactively support the innovation, competitiveness and growth opportunities offered by modernization of the economy" (ibid.). Platforms quickly changed their strategy accordingly: in addition to negotiating with city governments such as Barcelona's and Berlin's, Airbnb has also started to invest more into lobbying the European Commission directly. Leading a 47-company effort to convince European Union leaders that the sharing economy helps growth, Airbnb published a statement urging member states to "support the objectives [of the European Commission] and continue to seek to ensure that local and national laws do not unnecessarily limit the development of the collaborative economy to the detriment of Europeans" (Hern 2016). While the possible outcomes of such supra-national lobbying efforts are uncertain at the moment, a look at comparable cases in the US in which overlapping jurisdictions also reinforced legal uncertainty makes visible potential implications: fed up with the city of Boise banning its services entirely, gig work platform Uber decided to lobby the Idaho Legislature directly, which, in turn, decided to "pass a statue preempting all local government regulation of transportation network companies," thereby preventing Boise from having any regulatory power over gig work platforms in its jurisdiction (Miller 2016, 156ff.). By using capital to lobby every level of government implicated in the writing of regulation, Airbnb aims to do something similar: subvert undesired strong local frameworks by pitting overlapping but politically opposed jurisdictions against each other.

The contradictions of post-Fordist flexibilization have also become visible in the increasing alignment of the interests of providers (those listing their apartment online in order to create additional income) with those of profit-seeking platforms like Airbnb. Prime examples for this development have been the so-called Home Sharing Clubs in which hosts and guests unite and organize in order to push back against governmental intervention. These Home Sharers claim to differ from professional providers in so far as that they "temporarily rent [only their] private home to tourists" (Homesharing 2017a). Countering strong regulatory frameworks, they posit that temporarily subletting one's own apartment should be exempted from governmental regulations, as living space is not removed permanently from the housing market.

On the surface level, the interests of short-term rental platforms and these self-proclaimed Home Sharers align: both profit from the exchanges facilitated through intermediary digital infrastructures and both consequently have an interest in legalizing the business model by changing regulatory frameworks in their favor. That Airbnb in particular showed a sudden interest in bottom-up community organizing activities therefore comes as no surprise: faced with a political and legal deadlock in many global cities such as New York City, Berlin, and Barcelona, these clubs are meant to add another layer to its lobbying campaign against bans. Through its globe-spanning *Citizen* program, Airbnb now actively supports more than 100 of such clubs with the desire of helping "hosts come together to advocate for fair [...] laws in their communities" (Airbnb 2015) and to push the company's agenda to politicians more effectively.

But how *exactly* does community organizing benefit a company worth more than 25,5 billion US dollars? Seibel, one of Airbnb's strategic advisors, boils this strategy down by arguing that

> "at the end of the day, do people like using Airbnb? Do millions and millions and millions of people want Airbnb? Yes, […] everything else is a solvable problem. It's solvable with the application of smart people, time, and money" (quoted after Gallagher 2017, 137).

Seibel's assessment helps to make sense of the company's interest in community organizing: while the shift in public opinion brought forth by the legal push-back against short-term rental platforms limited the company's capacity for associating its business model with positively-connoted notions of "true sharing" (Belk 2014), individuals economically or socially benefitting from and organizing in order to *support* the platform are seen as capable of providing legitimacy to the transactions facilitated by the platform. Home Sharing Clubs now constitute focal points for Airbnb at which the very "people, time, and money" needed to create public support for the platform's business model come together as "powerful people-to-people based political advocacy bloc[s]" (Airbnb 2015) that can potentially 'solve' the problem of restrictive regulatory frameworks.

On the ground, Home Sharing Clubs seek to counter strong regulatory frameworks with affective and inclusive imagery. Through its *Citizen* program, Airbnb finances videos published by these clubs that offer detailed descriptions of the negative effects regulations in New York, Berlin and Barcelona have on their livelihood. Through this, the company aims at solidifying the differentiation between 'good' sharers—those who only temporarily rent out their own apartment in order to create an additional income—and 'bad' sharers—those using Airbnb professionally. While the practice of Home Sharing is presented by Airbnb as an example of 'good sharing' that is rooted in a societal *common sense* ("why would anyone be negatively affected by me renting out my own apartment?"), strong regulatory frameworks are depicted as an overreaching intrusion into an individuals' freedom of property—strategically incorporating the legal problems of the regulations described above into the group's campaign (Homesharing 2017b).

However, evaluating these clubs as a mere lobbying tool reduces complexity in a problematic way: Yes, Home Sharers irrefutably *are* economically supported by Airbnb and constitute part of the platform's campaign against strong regulatory frameworks. Equally interesting, though, is that the (economic) self-interest of the consumers organizing in the group at the same time also points *beyond* the interests of any particular company. While the specific platform at hand (in this case Airbnb) is not of indispensable relevancy to Home Sharers, the possibilities that have been opened up by the platform are. As argued by both Hamari et al. (2016) and Schor (2017), the majority of providers do not offer their apartment on short-term rental platforms because they ideologically support the specificity of a platform's business model, but because the platforms offer an outlet for creating additional income without having to invest beforehand. The regulatory frameworks implemented in New York, Berlin and Barcelona therefore not only bring to the fore contradictions within and among governments (as demonstrated earlier), but also between governments trying to address the negative outcomes of a cutback of welfare associated with digital platforms and individuals with access to property benefitting from these new intermediary structures. As a result, strong regulatory frameworks create a situation in which individuals negatively affected by the global financial crisis are driven to strongly support the freedom of the market and their right to property, while local governments are driven to increasingly emphasize the protection of the common good of housing.

Again, these developments need to be contextualized with the last decades of economic restructuring in which homeownership in particular, as Morozov and Bria argue, has served as a central building block. While renting—particularly in the US—is frequently framed by the government as undesirable and a sign of dependency, investing in privately-owned housing is characterized as a source of wealth. This framing has been central to the overall restructuring of society, as it helped to "decouple workers' loyalty from previous institutions of solidarity and support, such as trade unions, and instead tie it to the performance of stock markets and central banks" (2018). Short-term rental platforms follow this logic to its conclusion: they allow those who already own property to earn a supplemental income, creating a genuine bond between platform and provider. As a result, cities trying to implement strong regulatory frameworks are trapped in a catch-22: confronting the forms of circulation associated with digital platforms creates frustration on the part of those who feel they have a right to freely use their property, while not confronting them alienates those who do not own property or are affected by the negative externalities these platforms exert.

This catch-22 affects government capacity to enforce regulation in two ways: First, it creates problems of legitimacy because Home Sharing *aligns* with the rationality underlying post-Fordist flexibilization. 'Home Sharers' can seamlessly frame sharing one's own apartment as *common sense,* as this practice is consistent with the discourses that propelled this process of economic restructuring in the first place. Second, it creates problems of legitimacy because the forms of circulation facilitated by the rise of short-term rental platforms are also complementary with the *state's own rationality*. Miller boils this down succinctly by arguing that bans directed at the transactions facilitated by platforms such as Airbnb are to a certain extent counterintuitive, as "most state and local governments would *naturally* seek to encourage the sharing economy because it permits jurisdictionally-bound entities to grow their economies while adding little in the way of infrastructure costs" (2016, 172).

Consequently, the forms of circulation associated with sharing gain relevancy in spite of political resistance precisely because they are not opposed to but ultimately *complementary* with the rationality of today's smart economy (see also Vormann and Lammert 2018, in this volume). Cities such as New York, Berlin and Barcelona find themselves in the contradictory situation wherein addressing the platform economy's purported negative impacts and externalities is at odds with their own post-Fordist rationalities. The paradox that derives from this and ultimately complicates enforcement of bans in the platform economy is that the stronger the regulatory framework with which the government intends to limit the rise of platforms, the more this gap between post-Fordist discourse and governmental intervention becomes apparent. Moreover, the stronger this gap is politicized by, for example, Home Sharers with a self-interest in normalizing these forms of circulation, the less the government is capable of justifying the use of strong enforcement.

Thus, ruptures in post-Fordist rationality are not necessarily elicited only by 'local resistances' that push back against a seemingly inexorable 'global project' implemented through state policy. To the contrary, in New York City, Berlin and Barcelona, pushback against economic restructuring associated with the rise of platforms expresses itself—as counter-intuitive as this may sound—also through regulations. Consequently, studying the contradictions of post-Fordism that the emergence of digital platforms have come to reinforce allows us to see how even the state—usually characterized as an institution at the forefront of putting post-Fordist transformations into practice (Jessop 2014)—can temporarily become the central actor that enforces pushback against both increasing economic restructuring *and* the interest of 'local resistances' promoting sharing (such as the Home Sharing Clubs).

How concretely does this alignment between consumer-entrepreneurs and proponents of economic restructuring complicate the enforcement of regulation? Miller's claim that "an effort to force compliance would (...) require intimate enforcement" (ibid., 168) detrimental to the city's own interests provides an interesting starting point for answering this question: does New York City really want to use police force to violently remove renters on vacation from their Airbnb apartments? Persecuting an Italian tourist who rents an apartment in Brooklyn for a weekend with force is ultimately as difficult to justify *within* the discourse of the smart economy as it is to justify persecuting a Home Sharer who rents out his apartment in order to be able to pay their rent. Put simply, the force needed in order to ensure compliance stands in conflict with the rationality the smart economy is based upon. Consequently, the rise of digital platforms brings limits of liberal forms of governing to the fore: without a "rationalization of a pragmatics of guidance," as Lemke calls it (2000, 7), the state is incapable of establishing a perception of consumers as *pursuable violators.*

The table below summarizes this double-sided nature of regulating intermediary digital platforms outlined in the last three chapters.

	Regulation Fails	**Regulation Works**
Techno-Legal Structure	– Decentralization of service provision increases enforcement costs – Jurisdictional boundaries impede the regulation of globally operating platforms – Conflicts between individual and collective rights restrict platform-related state capacities	– Possibility of being fined discourages providers from fully engaging platform-based business models – Legal uncertainty creates leverage for governments to strike beneficial agreements with platform organizations
Interest Groups	– Post-Fordist flexibilization increases individual dependency on digital platforms – Alignment between consumer-entrepreneurs and platform organizations weakens public legitimacy of regulations	– Given intra- and interinstitutional support, governments can fine platforms directly and thereby specify operating conditions

Table 1: Double-sided nature of regulating intermediary digital platforms

Conclusion

What do we learn from this analysis? Have the disruptive traits of digital platforms indeed rendered the state incapable of enforcing strong regulatory frameworks directed at them? Are Sundararajan, Katz, and Morozov and Bria right in claiming that regulations directed at short-term rental platforms are bound to fail because their techno-legal structure renders governmental command-and-control regulation obsolete? The answer is ambivalent. On one hand, this chapter has shown that the regulatory frameworks implemented in New York City, Berlin and Barcelona have indeed encountered fundamental problems that can be traced to the techno-legal structure of digital platforms. Enforcing regulation in markets with a high degree of decentralization is costlier than enforcement in traditional markets. Persisting legal uncertainty undermines the credibility of these frameworks. Finally, the alignment of interests between commercial platforms and consumer-entrepreneurs has made it difficult for cities to justify strong regulatory frameworks.

Still, this is just one side of the story. This chapter has also illuminated *limits* of the 'regulations fail'-stance. Indeed, the impact of short-term rental platforms on governmental regulation is more complex than initially discernible, as the specificity of the state-market relations outlined here also causes (economic) problems for platforms. Concerning the techno-legal structure, this chapter has shown that it is indeed possible to curb illegal listings by enforcing registration given that interests align within the regulatory body and that enforcement campaigns are sufficiently funded—as is the case in Barcelona. Furthermore, the chapter has demonstrated that all three regulatory frameworks put short-term rental platforms in a contradictory situation in which continued illegalization of their core services with the highest profit margin (the subletting of entire flats) contradicts their long-term business strategy (normalizing sharing through attracting more providers). Consequently, the cases studied here show that platforms depend on legalization in order to allow consumers to use their platforms fully while simultaneously benefitting from ongoing illegality.

What then explains the problems of enforcing regulations in the digital sphere? What do these findings tell us about the state-market relations of the platform economy on a more general level? First, the cases studied here show that profit-oriented platforms with a C2C business model are engaged with the state in a mutually dependent relationship. The initial absence of platform-specific regulation, as well as the subsequent implementation of strong regulatory frameworks have both, counterintuitively, benefitted short-term rental platforms. Meanwhile, the state's political legitimacy has come to depend on the platforms as well. On one hand, for-profit platforms with a C2C business model portray themselves as providing many opportunities for economic development. Independently of the actual growth platforms such as Airbnb ultimately generate, the reiterated claim that they do so (or *might* do so in the future) increasingly forces 'entrepreneurially'-oriented urban policymakers, using Harvey's terminology, to treat this notion as gospel (1989). As a result, a government's entrepreneurial capability is called into question as soon as it fails to deliver or realize these development possibilities through the activities of firms and markets within its borders. This became especially apparent in the case of Berlin, where the Senate Department for Economics, Energy and Public Enterprises, the federal government and the European Commission have all urged the local government not to stifle the (economic) potential of platforms. Investing in platforms and daylighting their activities as quickly as possible—and thereby reinforcing the common sense of sharing inscribed in the smart economy—were framed by these institutions as the only means of fulfilling the state's entrepreneurial role. The legitimacy of the local government (in the eyes of other institutions) has thus come to depend on translating the economic promise associated with the rise of for-profit platforms into *actual* growth.

On the other hand, for-profit platforms threaten the provision of common goods. If the state fails to curb the negative impacts and externalities of the platform economy, its capability of protecting and furthering the provision of a common good (such as affordable housing) is similarly called into question. Subsequently, the state's legitimacy depends not only on realizing the economic potential of the platform economy, but on doing so *without endangering the common good* it is supposed to protect and further. In relation to the for-profit subset of the platform economy, the state is thus forced to constantly mediate trade-offs between furthering economic restructuring (by emphasizing the potential of platforms) and protecting the common good (by implementing regulations), knowing that both strategies potentially contradict one another.

Second, the cases studied here make visible the extent to which processes of governmental downscaling have rendered city-regions the most prominent scale of negotiating and implementing platform-related trade-offs. Although multiple levels of government have a stake in the emerging platform economy, responsibility for shaping its evolution and regulating its negative impacts and externalities has mostly been delegated to the city-scale. This is due to the specificity of these platforms. As this reorganization of circulation in urban spaces primarily relates to daily life activities and is generally embedded in local markets (given the transport cost involved in sharing one's goods)—Airbnb encourages the subletting of one's own apartment; Uber and TaskRabbit encourage the allocation of one's manual labor—the impact of these platforms is also primarily felt on the city-scale. Yet, these reorganized forms of circulation facilitated by for-profit platforms at the same time also hold relevancy *beyond* the city-scale: the more individual consumers treat temporary access to capital as a commodity, the more the federal entrepreneurial state is also expected to simplify the use and exchange of this commodity—and to further realize its growth potential. In this self-reinforcing process, platform-based work arrangements are increasingly established as a central building block of labor relations in the smart economy. Platform-related processes of economic restructuring are thus on one hand mediated foremost on the local scale, in spite of them, on the other, also having strong implications for the ways in which labor relations on a more general scale are reconfigured politically.

This makes the necessity of better understanding the problems cities face in mediating opposing approaches to this reorganization of circulation all the more apparent. Both governmental responses to the rise of digital platforms identified here—furthering economic restructuring (by emphasizing their economic potential) and protecting the common good (by implementing strong regulatory frameworks)—are not easily reconciled, as they come with their own respective normative assumptions, policymaking dynamics, interest groups and varying public acceptances. The contradictions between these agendas therefore leave cities with the impossible task of consolidating a purportedly 'global' rationality of growth and welfare cuts on one hand and 'local' notions of (social) sustainability aimed at providing a minimum safety net on the other.

Contextualizing the emergence of platforms within the contradictions of post-Fordist flexibilization has shown that the purported failure of the regulatory frameworks implemented in New York, Berlin and Barcelona is therefore related not so much to the techno-legal structure of digital platforms, but to the fact that these regulations stand in opposition to entrepreneurial approaches of urban governance that have been and continue to be promoted within and by the state itself. This analysis of the relationship between digital platforms and state capacities gives further weight to Zimmermann's argument that technology is not inherently problematic, but *socially over-determined* (2018, in this volume). It is insufficient to push back against the rise of the platform economy without interrogating the social and economic foundations that make these forms of circulation so attractive in the first place. Put simply, it is not the techno-legal structure of platforms—as Sundararajan and Katz would like us to believe—that disrupts the regulatory capacity of the state, but the particular social relations in which these technologies are embedded.

What to do then? Clearly, cities cannot overturn decades of policymaking at the national and global level through regulatory frameworks addressing particular exchanges of goods and services facilitated by single platforms such as Airbnb. Employing strong regulatory frameworks will necessarily bring these contradictions to the fore. Yet, strong regulations remain a central tool with which governments can shape the circulation enabled by these platforms. As the rise of digital platforms provides a first glimpse at potential downsides of reconfigured labor relations in the emerging smart economy, these options should be kept on the table. An emancipatory perspective on the platform economy, however, cannot approach these reorganized forms of circulation solely through the lens of regulations and bans. To the contrary, it is indispensable to focus on how digital platforms can be disassociated from the persisting common sense of smartness instead of trying to return to a long-gone pre-platform period. The language of disruption—with its overemphasis on technology-driven change—, however, obscures the socio-economic dimensions of why regulatory frameworks in the platform economy fail and therefore does not provide us with the tools needed to make such alternatives comprehensible.

Works Cited

Airbnb (2015). *Organizing in 100 Cities: The Airbnb Host Movement.* https://www.airbnbcitizen.com/organizing-in-100-cities-the-airbnb-host-movement/ (accessed: August 27, 2018).

Airbnb (2018). *Regulación en Cataluña y Barcelona.* https://es.airbnb.com/help/article/862/catalu-a---barcelona (accessed: August 27, 2018).

Apartment Allianz (2018). *Neuigkeiten.* http://www.apartmentallianz.net/neuigkeiten (accessed: August 27, 2018).

Aulich, Uwe (2016, April 26). Hebeln Berliner Bezirke das Ferienwohnungsverbot aus? *Berliner Zeitung.* https://www.berliner-zeitung.de/23953152 (accessed: August 27, 2018).

Barron, Kyle, Kung, Edward, and Davide Proserpio (2017). The Sharing Economy and Housing Affordability: Evidence from Airbnb. *Working Paper.* https://ssrn.com/abstract=3006832 (accessed: August 27, 2018).

Belk, Russell (2014). You are what you can access: Sharing and collaborative consumption online. *Journal of Business Research*, 67.8, 1595–1600.

Benner, Katie (2016a, April 19). Airbnb Wants Travelers to 'Live Like a Local' With Its App, in: *New York Times.* https://www.nytimes.com/2016/04/20/-technology/airbnb-wants-travelers-to-live-like-a-local-with-its-app.html (accessed: August 27, 2018).

Benner, Katie (2016b, December 3). Airbnb ends fight with New York, in: *New York Times.* https://www.nytimes.com/2016/12/03/technology/airbnb-ends-fight-with-new-york-city-over-fines.html (accessed: August 27, 2018).

Botsman, Rachel, and Roo Rogers (2010). *What's mine is yours: How Collaborative Consumption is changing the way we live*, New York, NY: HarperCollins Publishers.

Cortez, Nathan (2014). Regulating Disruptive Innovation. *Berkeley Technology Law Journal*, 29, 175–228.

Cox, Murray, and Tom Slee (2016). *How Airbnb's Data hid the facts in New York City.* http://insideairbnb.com/reports/how-airbnbs-data-hid-the-facts-in-new-york-city.pdf (accessed: August 27, 2018).

Crunchbase (2018). *List of Investors in Airbnb.* www.crunchbase.com/organization/airbnb (accessed: August 27, 2018).

Dietz, Thomas (2003). The Struggle to Govern the Commons. *Science,* 302, 1907–1912.

Rodero, Sara (2017, June 26). El Ayuntamiento de Barcelona sancionará con 600.000 euros a Airbnb. *El Mundo.* http://www.elmundo.es/cataluna-/2017/06/26/59511198e2704e2b208b45c9.html (accessed: August 27, 2018).

European Commission (2016), *A European Agenda for the Collaborative Economy.* https://www.eesc.europa.eu/resources/docs/com2016-356-final.pdf (accessed: August 27, 2018).

Gallagher, Leigh (2017). *The Airbnb Story: How Three Ordinary Guys Disrupted an Industry, Made Billions . . . and Created Plenty of Controversy*. Boston, MA: Houghton Mifflin Harcourt.

GEWOS (2016). *Airbnb und der Berliner Wohnungsmarkt 2016: Auswirkungen des Airbnb-Angebots auf die Berliner Wohnraumversorgung.* https://www.airbnbcitizen.com/wp-content/uploads/sites/59/2016/12/Okt.2016-Studie-GEWOS-Studie-Airbnb-und-Wohnungsmarkt-Berlin.pdf (accessed: August 27, 2018).

Griswold, Aliswon (2017, September 30). New York City is using sheriffs and obscure building code violations to crack down on Airbnb. *Quartz*. https://qz.com/1084108/1084108/ (accessed: August 27, 2018).

Hamari, Juho, Sjöklint, Mimmi, and Antti Ukkonen (2016). The sharing economy: Why people participate in collaborative consumption. *Journal of the Association for Information Science and Technology*, 67.9, 2047–2059.

Harvey, David (1989). From Managerialism to Entrepreneurialism: The Transformation in Urban Governance in Late Capitalism. *Geografiska Annaler. Series B, Human Geography,* 71.1, 3–17.

Heide, Dana (2017, January 18). Germany Plans Sharing Economy Reform. *Handelsblatt.* https://global.handelsblatt.com/companies/germany-plans-sharing-economy-reform-684623 (accessed: August 27, 2018).

Hern, Alex (2016, February 11). Uber and AirbnB call on EU to support 'collaborative economy.' *The Guardian.* https://www.theguardian.com/technology/2016/feb/11/uber-airbnb-eu-support-collaborative-economy (accessed: August 27, 2018).

Hill, Steven (2016). The California Challenge: How (not) to regulate disruptive business models. *Friedrich-Ebert-Foundation Berlin, Working Paper.* https://www4.fh-swf.de/media/downloads/meschedestandort/fachtagung_industrie_4_0/2016_6/downloads_unterlagen/03_Steven_Hill_FINAL_ENGL_print.pdf (accessed: August 27, 2018).

Homesharing (2017a). *Über uns.* http://homesharing.berlin/ueber-uns/ (accessed: August 27, 2018).

Homesharing (2017b). *Persönlich.* http://homesharing.berlin/homesharer-persoenlich/ (accessed: August 27, 2018).

Homesharing (2017c). *Neuigkeiten.* http://homesharing.berlin/category/news/ (accessed: August 27, 2018).

HR&A (2017). *Sharing for a Stronger New York. Analysis of Economic Activity 2016. Findings Report.* https://2sqy5r1jf93u30kwzc1smfqt-wpengine.netdna-ssl.com/wp-content/uploads/2017/05/Airbnb-Economic-Activity-Report-New-York-State-HRA-FINAL-4.5.17-1.pdf (accessed: August 27, 2018).

Inside Airbnb (2018). *How is Airbnb really being used in and affecting your neighborhoods? The Case of Berlin.* http://insideairbnb.com/berlin/ (accessed: August 27, 2018).

Jessop, Bob (1991). The Welfare State in the Transition from Fordism to Post-Fordism. *The Politics of Flexibility: Restructuring State and Industry in Britain, Germany and Scandinavia*, ed. Jessop, 82–104. Cheltenham: Edward Elgar.

Jessop, Bob (2014). Revisiting the Regulation Approach: Critical Reflections on the Contradictions, Dilemmas, Fixes and Crisis Dynamics of Growth Regimes. *Capital & Class*, 37.1, 5–24.

Katz, Vanessa (2015). Regulating the Sharing Economy. *Berkeley Technology Law Journal*, 30.4, 1067–1126.

Karat Studio (2016). *Airbnb Misused. What effect is the partial Airbnb ban having in Berlin? – A look at new data from Airbnb*. http://karat.studio/blog/airbnbmisused (accessed: August 27, 2018).

Kenney, Martin, and John Zysman (2016). The Rise of the Platform Economy. *Issues in Science and Technology*, 32.3, 61–69.

Lemke, Thomas (2000). *Foucault, Governmentality, and Critique*. Presentation given at Rethinking Marxism Conference, University of Amherst. http://www.thomas-lemkeweb.de/publikationen/Foucault,%20Governmentality,%20and%20Critique%20IV-2.pdf (accessed: August 27, 2018).

Miller, Stephen R. (2016). First Principles for Regulating the Sharing Economy. *Harvard Journal on Legislation*, 53, 147–202.

Morozov, Evgeny, and Francesca Bria (2018). *Rethinking the Smart City. Democratizing Urban Technology*. New York, NY: Rosa Luxemburg Foundation.

O'Sullivan, Feargus (2016, December 1). The City with the World's Toughest Anti-Airbnb Laws, in: *The Atlantic City Lab*. https://www.citylab.com/equity/2016/12/berlin-has-the-worlds-toughest-anti-airbnb-laws-are-they-working/509024/ (accessed: August 27, 2018).

rbb (2018, March 22). *Zweckentfremdungsverbot in Berlin - Weltreisende dürfen weiter untervermieten*. https://www.rbb24.de/politik/beitrag/2018/03/berlin-zweckentfremdungsverbot-ferienwohnungen-betreutes-wohnen-leerstand.html (accessed: August 27, 2018).

Schneiderman, Eric T. (2014). *Airbnb in the City*. The Office of the Attorney General of the State of New York. New York. https://ag.ny.gov/pdfs/AIRBNB%20REPORT.pdf (accessed: August 27, 2018).

Schor, Juliet B. (2017). Does the sharing economy increase inequality within the eighty percent? Findings from a qualitative study of platform providers. *Cambridge Journal of Regions, Economy and Society*, 10.2, 263–279.

Senate Department for Economics, Energy and Public Enterprises Berlin (2016). *Potenzialanalyse der Share und Collaborative Economy in Berlin*. http://sharing-berlin.de/potenzialanalyse/ (accessed: August 27, 2018).

Senate Department for Urban Development and Housing Berlin (2016). *Zweckentfremdungsverbot von Wohnraum*. http://www.stadtentwicklung.berlin.de/wohnen/zweckentfremdung_wohnraum/ (accessed: August 27, 2018).

Senate Department for Urban Development and Housing Berlin (2017). *Eine zweckentfremdete Wohnung melden*. https://ssl.stadtentwicklung.berlin.de/wohnen/zweckentfremdung_wohnraum/formular/adresswahl.shtml (accessed: August 27, 2018).

Slee, Tom (2016). *What's Yours Is Mine. Against the Sharing Economy*. New York, NY: OR Books.

Sundararajan, Arun (2016). *The Sharing Economy. The End of Employment and the Rise of Crowd-Based Capitalism*. Cambridge, MA: MIT Press.

Wachsmuth, David, Chaney, David, Kerrigan, Danielle, Shillolo, Andrea, and Robin Basalaev-Binder (2018). *The High Cost of Short-Term Rentals in New York City. A report from the Urban Politics and Governance research group*, School of Urban Planning, McGill University. https://mcgill.ca/newsroom/files/newsroom/channels/attach/airbnb-report.pdf (accessed: August 27, 2018).

Walker, Ameena (2017, May 11). New York's anti-Airbnb law is proving tough to quickly enforce. *Curbed New York*. https://ny.curbed.com/2017/5/11/-15626876/new-york-anti-airbnb-law-enforcement-issues (accessed: August 27, 2018).

Woolf, Nicky (2016, December 3). Airbnb regulation deal with London and Amsterdam marks dramatic policy shift. *The Guardian*. https://www.theguardian.com/technology/2016/dec/03/airbnb-regulation-london-amsterdam-housing (accessed: August 27, 2018).

Worstall, Tim (2013, September 13). What A Surprise, AirBnB Chooses Dublin As European Headquarters, Here Comes The 2% Tax Rate. *Forbes*. https://www.forbes.com/sites/timworstall/2013/09/13/what-a-surprise-airbnb-chooses-dublin-as-european-headqaurters-here-comes-the-2-tax-rate/#275dd20e42a5 (accessed: August 27, 2018).

Zeiher, Christoph (2016, November 11). Berlin kann Zweckentfremdungsverbot nicht durchsetzen. *SPIEGEL ONLINE*. http://www.spiegel.de/reise/aktuell/zweckentfremdungsverbot-verhindert-kaum-airbnb-buchungen-a-1120830.html (accessed: August 27, 2018).

Zervas, Georgios, Proserpio, Davide, and John W. Byers (2016). The Rise of the Sharing Economy: Estimating the Impact of Airbnb on the Hotel Industry. *Boston U. School of Management Research Paper* No. 2013–16.

ZwVbVO (2014). Ausführungsvorschriften über das Verbot der Zweckentfremdung von Wohnraum (AV - ZwVb). *Amtsblatt Für Berlin*, 64.28, 1290–1302.

ZwVbVO (2016). Erste Änderung der Ausführungsvorschriften über das Verbot der Zweckentfremdung von Wohnraum (1. Änderung AV - ZwVb). *Amtsblatt Für Berlin*, 66.35), 2132–2143.

Fear and Loathing on the High Line: Notes from the Spatial Frontline of Spectacle Techno-Capitalism

Jeremy Williams

The current conjuncture of capitalism is seeing rapid changes across many sectors of culture and society. From the purposeful havoc wreaked by the so-called tech industry's aggressive gospel of disruption, to the economic restructuring inherent in a doctrine of neoliberal austerity, to the breakdown of social solidarity and emergence of cultural narcissism, the contemporary moment across Western democracies is defined by a profound sense of flux and change. While the manifestation of these changes can be seen in everything from the decline of print media to ever-increasing wealth inequalities, the spatial manifestations of these changes have been particularly profound. In particular, the realm of public space—in the past often a site of respite from and resistance to broader structural changes foisted upon society—has undergone a creeping yet consistent process of reshaping. This process has resulted in changes not only in the ways in which public space is conceptualized, built and operated, but also the ways in which it is thought about, experienced and understood.

Although public space has always been contested, nuanced and complex, the current regime of Spectacle Techno-Capitalism[1] finds public space at a particular moment of crisis: both measured against normative ideals of what democratic public space could be and should accomplish, as

1 Various terms exist for describing different aspects of the current conjuncture. These include "late capitalism" for analyses grounded in Cultural Studies, the middlebrow commentariat or so-called internet meme culture, as well as "the smart economy" for discussions of dominant trajectories in the current economy, usually referring to more prosaic debates around automation, the future of work and the depressingly disruptive race to the bottom of the precarity-laden gig economy. For my purposes however, I use the term "Spectacle Techno-Capitalism" for the particularities of the current conjuncture's relation with and production of public space, combining as it does the marriage of a Debordian atmosphere of surface-over-substance (Spectacle) with the technological determinism associated with tech culture (Techno) with, well, capitalism (Capitalism).

well as as a subjective experience for those who use it, or live in its vicinity.[2] At the contemporary moment, public space seems frequently to be stale, exclusionary and contradictory, often seemingly operating against the public, rather than allowing for the possibility of the public creatively producing public space itself. In order to investigate this development, we turn our attention to the capital of capitalism—New York City—and arguably the most influential and paradigmatic public space existing in the West today: the High Line.

The High Line is an elevated park on the site of an old goods railway line between Gansevoort Street in the Meatpacking District and the luxury Hudson Yards development near Penn Station in Midtown Manhattan. Opened in stages from 2009 onwards, it snakes through the West side of Manhattan, elevated throughout its entire length.[3] It is designed as an urban walkway, complete with landscaped gardens, gift shops, and pieces of urban theater such as a glass bridge looking out over the intersection of 10th Avenue and West 17th Street. Highly popular with visitors, the High Line can be seen as something of a victim of its own success. It is generally crowded, with the combination of the narrow pathways and large numbers of visitors creating an atmosphere sometimes bordering on the claustrophobic. It is of course worth noting that just because the High Line attracts large numbers of visitors, these may not include large number of residents (or former residents) of the local area.[4] Nevertheless, the park continues to impress most who use it, as a perusal of reviews on sites like Trip Advisor will attest to. City taste-makers[5] are equally effusive, and the park is frequently promoted as one of the essential tourist attractions in

2 See Chapter 1 of Low et al (2003) for a discussion around democratic public space, particularly their "lessons for promoting social and cultural diversity" (ibid, 5-6).

3 Facts about the High Line taken from Friends of the High Line (2017).

4 In a recent demographic study of the park, Reichl (2016) noted that the majority of visitors they observed in the park were white (83.0 percent), and thus more likely to be tourists and out-of-towners when compared to the demographic make-up of both New York City (33.3 percent) and Manhattan (48.0 percent) as a whole.

5 Writing a glowing review of the park in the New York Times upon the opening of its first stage in 2009, architectural critic Nikolai Ouroussoff described the park as "an invaluable and transformative gift" from the project's architects and founders. Note the framing of a public space as a philanthropic donation.

New York.[6] The High Line's effect on the surrounding area has been marked, with the park being flanked throughout much of its length by luxury housing towers, some of them designed by starchitechts such as Zaha Hadid.[7] Walking down off the park at many of the exits finds one confronted with luxury boutiques and artisan coffee shops, many, like the luxury towers, boasting the words High Line in their names.

An aggressive development strategy championed by Mayor Michael Bloomberg (2002-2013) has seen the Meatpacking District and West Chelsea areas which surround much of the park rezoned for extensive luxury residential development, with many local independent businesses having vanished, being replaced by high-end retail stores (Brash 2011; Moss 2017). At the park's north end sits the Hudson Yards developments, an under construction luxury housing complex which prompted the opening in 2015 of New York City's first new subway extension in over a quarter of a century.[8] The park has seen the area transform from one of the poorer in Lower and Midtown Manhattan to one of its most desirable: according to the New York Economic Development Corporation (2011), rents increased an average of 103 percent in the area surrounding the park between 2002 and 2011. This transformative effect, and indeed the perceived desirability among elites of this effect given the park's popularity among administrators from other cities across the country, seems to be a key dynamic at play in the current conjuncture: that of public space being used to upscale or seemingly improve a local area.

Thus, in addition to the park's popularity with the public, this dynamic plays out through the High Line's acting as a kind of poster child for good urbanism among both administrators and establishment/influential urban thinkers, with many cities both in the United States and worldwide actively copying it as a tool for so-called urban renewal. This status has seen an explosion of new public spaces explicitly copying or referencing the High

6 See Dao et al (2017) in Time Out New York for an example of placing of the High Line alongside the Empire State Building, Central Park, etc. as essential attractions for tourists and locals alike. Similar such lists in other publications now will inevitably include the High Line.

7 Zaha Hadid's final apartment building commissioned prior to her death is 520 W 28th Street by Zaha Hadid, parallel to the High Line. Note the inclusion of her name in that of the building.

8 It is worth noting that no new subway stations or extensions have been built to serve the many lower income areas of New York City without subway service during this period.

Line through their re-purposing of old elevated railroads, with numerous such schemes currently either in planning, under construction or recently opened (Gibson 2017).[9] However, this use of the High Line as inspiration extends beyond merely replicating its elevated design atop disused infrastructure: regardless of the particularities of the spaces themselves, new public spaces across the United States are increasingly displaying other characteristics of the High Line including heavy regulation and social control, private elements in both their construction and management, a general sense of being over-designed and in their knock-on gentrification effects on surrounding areas.

The paradigmatic status of the High Line as a public space stems both from its self-conscious self-definition as the show-piece park in capitalism's capital city, situated at the epicenter of the flows and circularities which form the most global of global cities, but also through its inherent characteristics at a time when public space in the United States seems to be on a trajectory where more and more of it is being conceived, designed and operated like the High Line. Even the recent *mea culpa* by Robert Hammond, one of the High Line's initial founders and boosters, that the transformative effect of the park on the surrounding area and its community was not sufficiently taken account of during its planning and design, has not dulled the championing and urbanist clamor for similar types of public space.[10]

Against this backdrop, this case study considers four different but connected dynamics which are at play on the High Line itself. It will first consider the unseen role of government within the space, particularly the seeming contradiction between the High Line's self-mythologization as a benevolent grassroots endeavor and the network of government support which underpins both the construction and operation of the space. In particular, this includes the High Line's philanthropic facade masking the neoliberal political context which is a prerequisite of its development, a context which contrary to myths of free market self-sustainability, requires significant (invisible) government intervention. Secondly, it examines the role of neoliberalization on the space itself, both in terms of its expression of the idea that worth only exists in financial terms, as well as the at-

9 Gibson (2017) identifies 18 such schemes which explicitly reference the High Line in cities including Philadelphia, Chicago and Los Angeles.

10 See interview with Bliss (2017).

tendant implications for the kind of public space(s) which can be produced under such a reductive regime of meaning. Thirdly, it considers the dynamics of social control at play in the space, including spatial hyper-regulation and both operative and design-based securitization. It closes with an examination of the fourth dynamic at play, that of spectacle and performance, both in terms of the park's design as well as how it is used in itself, before concluding with some thoughts as to the democratic and socio-cultural implications for a public space which displays these aforementioned characteristics.

Much critical analysis of the High Line, as much as exists at the park's relatively young stage of completion, focuses on the park as a product of seemingly inevitable forces of contemporary global capitalism (see for example Cataldi et al 2011; Loughran 2014; Reichl 2016; Brash 2017; Lindner and Rosner 2017).[11] While not disputing the pertinence of such analyses, I intend to invert this approach somewhat, finding value in analyzing the contours of public space under the regime of Spectacle Techno-Capitalism from the bottom up: privileging the experiential and the human above the methodological and the structural. Through doing this, I hope to understand both how and why so many of us beyond the socio-economic strata by whom the park was designed by and for whom the park was designed for, experience a sensation of Fear and Loathing on the High Line.

11 Cataldi et al's (2011) photo-heavy paper sees the High Line's image representation as a "supplementary form of neoliberal property accumulation". Loughlan (2014) argues that parks like the High Line becoming more prevalent under neoliberal urbanism need to be analyzed on a "continuum of privilege". In addition to noting the park's disproportionate whiteness, Reichl (2016), argues that this demographic reality makes the park fundamentally undemocratic. Brash (2017) notes that the park's fundamental inequity has potential possibilities as galvanizing for activists for a more equitable park system. Lindner and Rosa's edited 2017 volume Deconstructing the High Line, which includes the abovementioned Brash essay as well and updated version of Loughlan's, also includes a reflection by one of the park's main designers, as well as comparisons with other High Line-esque city park projects in Rotterdam and Sao Paolo.

The Invisible Yet Contradictory Role of Government

The role of government in public spaces under Spectacle Techno-Capitalism is far from simple, with public space also increasingly being at least quasi-private space. Thus, in common with Privately Operated Public Spaces (POPS) such as those found in Business Improvement Districts, or in the plazas in front of many New York City skyscrapers, the ownership, management and operation of parks such as the High Line straddles both the public and the private sector, often in confusing and contradictory ways.[12] Private elements can extend from the design and impetus for the space—for example, the High Line's conception, and elements of its operation and management is controlled by the private sector, couched in a narrative of a philanthropic Trust (Friends of the High Line 2017)—to also the mechanics of a space's operation: witness the security guards at work on the park who are contracted through the Citadel Security Agency (2018), a private company contracted to patrol various public spaces in New York City, with it being unclear as to which public or private authority they are responsible to. While less explicitly non-public than the experience of the aforementioned skyscraper plazas, this non-public, quasi-private element permeates throughout spaces such as the High Line. Such a situation, particularly for visitors who are used to a more formal divide between public and private spaces, can lead to a degree of cognitive dissonance, and lends itself to a questioning of the extent to which public spaces such as the High Line can truly be thought of as public spaces at all.

However, the role of government on the High Line is not limited to confusion regarding to the extent to which the space is public or private: governance on the High Line is itself a contradiction, existing simultaneously both everywhere and nowhere. While the Park aggressively self-mythologizes as a grassroots, community-minded and philanthropic "gift to the City of New York" (Friends of the High Line 2017), this masks the unseen mechanics and actions of government which underpin such a space. This takes a variety of forms including direct input through financial contributions and zoning ordinances, as well as a more complex and confusing approach to the private sector including unseen boosts in property

12 Often built by developers as a planning requirement or, as frequently the case in New York, in exchange for being allowed to add additional floors to a skyscraper. See Kayden 2000.

values and other, difficult to quantify forms of support. The park simultaneously self-mythologizes as a volunteer-led community project, with the veneer of the City Parks Department providing a layer of civic legitimacy, while the actual, activist role of government which underpins the space is largely obscured.

This obscuring of the role of government often takes the form of constant visual reminders of the park's self-narrative while in the space itself: for example one of the golf buggies (sponsor: TD Bank) which uniformed park employees use to travel up and down the High Line bears the legend "Friends Like You Provide 100% of The High Line's Operating Budget". The impression of community-spiritedness and philanthropy is further emphasized in everything from its promotional materials to the friendly and informal uniform of the park's employees and wardens. However, all this obscures the fact that the High Line is not a grassroots endeavor. From 2005 to 2008, the High Line received $73.8 million of its total $86.2 funding from the City of New York, a figure which increased to $122.2 million of a total $243 million income by 2016 (Friends of the High Line accounts 2013, in Halle and Tiso 2014, 156-7). Contrary to the David and Goliath narrative portrayed in the park's official narrativization (immortalized on their website, in their illustrated coffee table book (David and Hammond 2011), in YouTube guided tour videos and on large plaques of narrative text in the space itself), the park is anything but "the park that almost wasn't",[13] a framing which implies that its existence is the result of the sheer force of civic will of an army of local volunteers. A more accurate description would be that the park that was, at least in its initial phases of construction, almost completely dependent upon the City of New York for its funding.

The High Line's dependence on city government was not limited to (significant) financial contributions alone. The majority of the area surrounding the park was rezoned on 25 May 2005 from industrial to residential use, through the establishment of the West Chelsea Special District (City of New York 2005). This conversion of an area of Manhattan from industrial to luxury condo use allowed for both an increase in the city's property tax revenue, as well as providing a boon to developers who were able to erect frequently starchitect-designed towers surrounding the park. A park volunteer on a video tour of the High Line available on YouTube

13 Plaque on display at the High Line photographed by the author, November 2017.

can be found marveling at the increase in luxury lodgings, proclaiming that "beautifully-designed high rises" have "[...] basically brought wealth to the community", before adding that "what's kind of cool [...]" is that the new buildings "were not created by The High Line, they were [instead] created because of The High Line" (Amoeba Films 2012). The volunteer has the manner of a prophet portraying a miracle, consistent with the High Line's self-mythologization as a parable of community-spirited grassroots endeavor, rather than as an economic process with government, frequently invisibly, at its heart.

The city government is not totally invisible though, and part of its contradictory role at the heart of Spectacle Techno-Capitalism is its appearance in providing a form of what I term civic washing, a process which gives an official veneer to an enterprise which, for all its (unseen) governmental support, is also at some level a private one. This patchwork and confusing approach to governance itself sees the park officially owned by the City of New York, but operated by Friends of the High Line, with however some day-to-day management also carried out by New York's Parks Department (Halle and Tiso 2014, 175). This leads to the park being patrolled by private Friends of the High Line wardens, while upon entry one is confronted with the City of New York Parks Department logo, with signs rendered in their corporate look and feel. Thus the government's role in a space like the High Line is somehow inverted: the true role of the public sector in financing the space is obscured, but an *ersatz* role for the state is created, thereby providing a highly visible civic veneer to what is in many ways a private enterprise.

The Financialization of Worth

This contradiction between public and private which underpins the government's role in spaces like the High Line can be framed in structural terms as part of an inevitable broader societal-cultural process of neoliberalization. One particular manifestation of this set of processes has been a crisis of meaning in both government and society, with the resulting vacuum filled by a reductionist view of the human condition which sees *worth* or *value* as measurable only in financial terms. Much of contemporary urbanism (by which I mean the likes of Smart Cities, City Lab, Richard Florida et al, as well as policy and planning professionals trying–to use the terminology of Silicon Valley–to hack cities: in short, the people who actually make decisions about the urban fabric) is awash with cost-benefit analyses, data sets and breathless quantifications of the value of public space within a purely financial frame. Such a situation can be seen in the context of the moves by administrators and politicians towards emphasizing entrepreneurial governance (Harvey 1989, Du Gay 1996), with city services increasingly designed around the generation of economic activity, rather than as services for citizens. While I find varying mileage in understandings of public space which see them purely as a product of the logic of capitalism, I would follow in the footsteps of Mark Fisher's Capitalist Realism (2009) in arguing that there is also a psychological element at play in neoliberalization's' role in shaping contemporary public space. With this in mind, I would argue that for an understanding which foregrounds the potential transcendence of current conditions, public space needs to be viewed as more than simply the product of structural economic forces. However, a viewing of worth in merely economic terms remains the political and policy context through which public spaces like the High Line are justified, built and managed.

Thus, the age of Spectacle Techno-Capitalism is one in which things are no longer seen as good or desirable in their own right or because they are for example beautiful or meaningful, but instead are seen as the means to some other (usually financial) end. Therefore, the stated impetus for and design of new or improved public parks or public plazas rarely takes place in a context where such places are seen as having inherent worth in themselves: instead, they are framed as a means to a nebulous goal such as economic development (with this goal often accompanied by an uncritical lionization of the idea that business is something inherently desirable, regardless of its individual characteristics) or regeneration (aka gentrification, displacement, exclusion and social cleansing). This context found expression in Friends of the High Line's hiring of real estate consultants HR&A (mission statement: "we create and implement real estate strategies to unlock value and establish vital places") to assist with lobbying for the project, with the latter's website proudly boasting that the company demonstrated the "economic rationale for transforming the High Line into a vibrant public park" (HR&A 2018). This economic rationale was also name-checked by then Mayor Bloomberg in the opening ceremony for the park when he stated that that it would "create jobs and economic opportunities for our city" (City of New York 2009), dove-tailing neatly with his frequently stated desire to "run government like a business" (Brash 2011, 75).[14] This focus on economic rationale imposes on public space an elite-defined meaning and purpose which the design and the operation of the spaces then becomes subservient to, the purpose in these cases being the generation of profit.

The purposing of The High Line around the economic imperative also finds expression in the pervasive atmosphere of commerce which pervades the space. Gift shops selling High Line branded coasters, tea towels and teddy bears can be found at several places on the park. Additionally, so-called entrepreneurs seek to further monetize the space by actively naming adjoining businesses after it: one can catch a show in the High Line Ballroom, spend the night in the "vintage chic lodging" of The High Line Hotel, or grab an espresso or "gourmet roast" at Underline Coffee beneath the tracks. This combination of the economic rationale for the creation of a space, and a pervasive atmosphere of commerce inevitably leads to the creation of a certain type of public space, which in turn has a knock-on effect on the way in which these spaces can be experienced, limiting the limit the degree of ambiguity as to the meaning and purpose of such spaces and thus how they feel on the ground. This lack of ambiguity then serves to prevent the the public from being able to creatively produce the meaning(s) and purpose(s) of such spaces themselves, a situation which has inevitable negative democratic and societal side effects.

One such side effect of this state of affairs sees public spaces such as The High Line then only attracting a relatively homogeneous demographic and social mix of visitors. Reichl's (2016) demographic survey of the park by ethnicity (short version: the park is disproportionately visited by white people) is an instructive starting point as to understanding that the racial mix within the park is much less diverse than Manhattan, or of the City of New York as a whole. However, this neglects a broader dive into the predominant social class of the (mainly) white visitors to the park. While not conducting a hard social scientific survey of who were tourists and who were not, my ethnographic fieldwork revealed that a disproportionate number of visitors one sees on any given day belong to a certain socio-

14 Brash (2011) in his book on the Bloomberg mayoralty does a good job of exposing the deeply political (neoliberal) nature of this rhetorically surface-level de-politicization of politics.

economic strata, similar to that identified by Sharon Zukin in her work on (the also quasi-private) terrain of New York's Union Square (Zukin 2010, 125-130): white, often under 40, economically well-off, and seemingly attracted to a particular type of urban cultural experience which the High Line seems to provide. Taken together with the omnipresent adverts for high-end apartments, yoga studios and the like, the question can be asked as to whether spaces like the High Line – in addition to attracting this particular certain socio-economic strata - are also implicitly or explicitly designed for this group as well. If this is the case, are there then democratic implications for the structuring of public space in a society around a particular socio-economic strata? And, what of those who cannot participate in the High Line's particular version of urbanity: those who feel alienated by this focus, or who are unable to use the space because of time or distance reasons? For a democracy to function, do its composite aspects, including public space, need to be arranged around a broad range of realities, needs and preferences? The reality of the experience of the High Line prompts some reflection on these questions.

The Stale Suffocation of Social Control

To walk on The High Line is to walk on one of the most tightly-regulated and socially-controlled spaces in New York City. The atmosphere is one of strict order, social acceptability and total conformity. Visitors entering the park are confronted with a large list of behavioral regulations including the prohibition of alcohol, smoking, large groups, bicycles, skateboards, dogs, and throwing objects, in short many activities which are traditionally enjoyed in public parks. Signs are scattered the length of the park, screaming instructions such as DO NOT GIVE MONEY TO PANHANDLERS and telling the public not to step on lawns. The regulations are enforced by private security guards and teams of park wardens, who patrol up and down the walkway in teams of two, either on foot or on mechanical contraptions which fall somewhere between commodified golf buggies and mini armored personnel carriers (currently, and somewhat surprisingl;y given the current militarization of American civic life, seemingly free of arms for at least the time being). They also hang around in crowds by some of the parks main entrances, forming an atmosphere which cannot fail to re-enforce the impression for those visiting that they are merely guests in a space controlled by some greater authority.

My own appearances in the park have frequently been met with suspicion by security. Because I was not dressed in the sartorial uniform of either upper middle class tourism or of money, my presence, together with attempts to transcend the stifling constraints of the parks interior by climbing on benches, feeling and touching the infrastructure and so on was often met with a combination of wary incomprehension and hostile suspicion. Likewise, my attempts to photograph security guards inevitably led to altercations and confrontations, with their responses being often attempting to hide from the camera or angrily demanding that I cease what I was doing, sometimes simultaneously. Regulation, both explicit (through the numerous prohibitions) and implicit (through the atmosphere of suspicion rendered by the security guards and CCTV) is an integral part of the produced meaning of the High Line. With this in mind, a highly regulated public space—where every visitor is subject to both social control and suspicion by officialdom—likely narrows the potential for human activity to the extent that even my relatively innocuous attempts to resist this paradigm of control, let only undertake more radical activity, became largely impossible. That a network of Closed Circuit Television cameras keeps an ever watchful eye on those using the park, doubtless monitored by faceless individuals in a hidden control center, only enhances a dynamic where resistance becomes simultaneously both impossible and futile.

This situation is an expression of one of the key characteristics of public space at the current conjuncture: that of a distinctive suspicion of and contempt for the public by the authorities who both design and operate such spaces. The myriad rules and regulations governing conduct in said spaces lead to an atmosphere of conformity and social control, one which is further exacerbated through excessive, defensive over-design. This has resulted in a contemporary prevalence of what Aspen (2013) calls "Zombie Urbanism", a kind of design determinism reflecting the cultural preferences of upper middle class professionals married to a broader cultural trend towards infantilization and mistrust of the public, leading to public spaces which instinctively feel stale, controlled and exclusionary. While public parks and the like generally have been subject to local bye-laws and occasional patrols by park wardens, the explicit use of defensive architecture (through phenomenon such as benches designed so the homeless cannot sleep on them), constant monitoring by CCTV and security guards and an increase in the number and scope of prohibited activities to include many of those traditionally associated with park life, sees a reduction in the scope for creative or spontaneous uses of the spaces themselves.

Increased social control through regulation is complemented by increased social control through increased securitization of public space. Whilst trends towards securitization can be identified throughout the neoliberal revolution—and indeed can be seen as an integral part of neoliberal logic if one is to subscribe to a critique of neoliberalism which sees most social change being a logical result of it—attitudes towards public space in the United States became increasingly concerned with security, and an increased cultural atmosphere of fear in the aftermath of 9/11. This has found an expression in the increased presence in contemporary public space of security guards who have a role both in enforcing the numerous rules and regulations—a kind of authority for the purpose of authority identified by Appleton (2016) as a manifestation of the Busybody State—as well as in regulating entry to the space itself. The restrictive atmosphere fostered by the presence of these guards on the High Line is further propagated by specific (rule-based) prohibitions serving to restrict the definition of the public who will feel welcome in such a space: the prohibition on soliciting naturally prohibits those who rely on this activity to make a living from practicing it in the park while, at a more prosaic level, the prohibition of throwing objects also means those who wish to play ball games are not welcome. Indeed, the same could be said for those who wish to drink alcohol, or those who wish to smoke. Either way, a definition of the public which excludes some activities that the public wishes to take part in is an explicit attack on the very idea of the public itself. Additionally, the presence of CCTV performs a similar and slightly more sinister function, with the possibilities for democratic and non-hierarchical experiences inherent in the promise of public space replaced by an Orwellian monitoring and suspicion of all human behavior. Such a dynamic in play between elite and the *hoi polloi*, that of an overt fear and suspicion towards the public by those in control, leads to a kind of social emasculation in an atmosphere of suspicion, fear and control.

The Scripted Spontaneity of the Curated Urban Spectacle

Our fourth and final characteristic common to public space under Spectacle Techno-Capitalism is a spatial consummation with spectacle and performance, a phenomena which finds expression in both depressing spectacle-over-substance urban design and the equally dispiriting behavior of those using the spaces themselves. Firstly, while I have already noted the use of over-design as a tool of defense as part of our discussion of social control, defensive over-design is also wedded to a kind of spectacle-based architectural whimsy which, in a similar manner to that in which Stalinist architecture aimed to make the citizenry feel small, fundamentally seeks to make the public who inhabit such spaces its subjects rather than its masters.

Secondly, the High Line's scripted architectural moments of spontaneity (surprise passageways, socially acceptable public art etc) symbiotically interact with the behavior and attitudes of those who use the park. The prevalence of selfie-taking, where the object of being in public space seems more to document one's presence than to actually truly be experientially present, combines with the spectacle architecture to create an atmosphere which is by turns performative, vacuous and actively conspiring against the possibilities of radical change. The performance of the promenade (interrupted for frequent selfies) interacts with the performance ongoing behind the floor-to-ceiling glass windows of the luxury condominiums which line either side of the High Line to produce a space where spectacle replaces substance, and one-dimensionality replaces the contradictions of the lived condition. Indeed, when I try to imagine a defining image of public space under late capitalism, I think of a conventionally beautiful group of twentysomethings who work in the tech industry, using a selfie-stick in front of a piece of novelty utility-less starchitectural structural ephemera: an Instagram moment stamping on the human and the authentic, potentially forever.

Such a dynamic is re-enforced by the park's increasing popularity as a backdrop for fashion photography, with models, amateur and professional, often to be found posing against the backdrop. Indeed, while walking upon the High Line one Saturday afternoon, I stumbled across two separate pornographic photography shoots taking place: two models occasionally exposing themselves for the cameras as a member of their team frequently glanced around to check for the approach of security guards. The fact that the High Line is now a backdrop for the creation of pornography—probably the ultimate cultural expression of the unreal replacing the authentic—is a particularly apt expression of its importance both at and as the spatial frontline of Spectacle Techno-Capitalism.

On the High Line, this symbiotic performative atmosphere takes place on a space which seeks to explicitly replicate an *ersatz* version of the authentic which, in the words of Sorkin in his musings on the city as theme park, is "at pains to assert its ties to the kind of city life it is in the process of obliterating" (Sorkin 1992, xiv). Such an experience is a natural fit to the preferences of the selfie-taking tech workers who frequent the space, whose moving into the area creates a vicious circle of authentrification (a term coined by Symonds 2011), economically and socially cleansing the area's authentic inhabitants as the specter and spectacle of tech bro disruption haunts and replaces the genuine and lived experience of the real. In such a situation, signifiers of the authentic (for example, the rusted rail viaduct which the High Line is upon itself, or faded former signs of businesses preserved on old buildings) become more important than the genuine experience of a living and working city.

This appeal to the values of a particular social class—predictability, order, safeness—is re-enforced by the (over-) design present in the park. Tastefully arranged flower beds are fenced off and public benches are placed at perfect right-angles to the path. Art—commissioned by Friends of the High Line and thus safe, predictable and in keeping with the High Line's aesthetic—is strategically placed throughout the park, while a glass window allows people to look down at an intersection and watch city life go by. These moments of scripted spontaneity, part of the design determinism of the park's physicality, combine with its homogeneous clientele and rigidly conformist atmosphere to preclude the opportunity for anything unexpected, or for anything which has not been designed by the parks designers. This state of affairs has implications for a democratic public space where the unexpected, and thus challenges to structural forces, are possible.

The tightly-structured (lack of) possibilities for interpretation and creativity are also re-enforced by the physical manifestations of the High Line's aforementioned aggressive program of self-mythologization such as the large textual murals depicting the park's donors and history, framed as a creation by charitably-minded "neighborhood residents," who, along with "tens of thousands of people" created "something wonderful for future generations"[15] (the opinions of the socially-cleansed former residents of the area are strangely absent from this self-mythologization). However, the most mendacious act of self-narrativization can be found in boards which have appeared throughout the length of the park in 2017 recently, written in both English and Spanish. The English language version is worth quoting in full:

> You Are Welcome Here
> To our friends, neighbors, and visitors, we say: you are welcome here. No matter who you are, what you look like, who you love, how much money you have, what your religious beliefs are, or where you are from, the High Line is for you.
>
> Like many, we at Friends of the High Line are concerned about the divisive, hateful speech and actions we are hearing and witnessing across our country. While these feelings are not new for many, we recognize that this is a crucial moment to take a stand for what we believe is right. It is important that we do not become complacent in our mission to cultivate equitable and open public spaces that reflect and celebrate the diversity of our communities.
>
> Friends of the High Line is committed to re-examining and strengthening our continuing efforts to ensure the High Line is a safe and welcoming place for everyone. If you have any suggestions for how we can make this public space better, please send us an e-mail with your thoughts.[16]

The various sleights of hand, inclusivity-washing and downright patronization at work in this public-facing screed are, even by the lamentable standards of the High Line, quite something. The sign does however do an excellent job of demonstrating one of the dominant dynamics of the park, and indeed of public space under Spectacle Techno-Capitalism itself: that of the triumph of the spectacle. While neglecting the external dynamics of gentrification specifically caused by the park, as well as the internal dynamics of exclusion and its appeal to the aesthetic and cultural preferences of a certain socio-economic strata, the sign demonstrates a shallow concern with the appearance of being inclusive at the expense of an authentic attempt to deal with the park's inherently exclusionary nature.

On the High Line, and by extension increasingly in public space under Spectacle Techno-Capitalism more generally, what matters it not that the space is genuinely inclusive (or indeed inclusively genuine): were that to be

15 Text from mural on the High Line. See also Friends of the High Line (2017) for further self-mythologization.

16 Sign on display at the High Line photographed by the author, November 2017.

the case, the space would be set up specifically with this goal, or at least be set up in a less exclusionary and socially-controlled manner. Instead, what matters is the performance of inclusivity, the ability for both those in charge of the park to proclaim inclusivity in a space which is anything but, and also for the largely white, upper middle class clientele of the space to bask in the moral righteousness of participating in a space where this surface-level message is prominent, but where no further substance beneath or beyond this—for example, the serious business of thinking about exclusions, inclusions and the role of public space in a democracy—is required.

Conclusions and Implications

Public space is on a trajectory of becoming more and more like the High Line, both in terms of The High Line's explicit popularity with those who are responsible for (new) public spaces, and also in its both reflection and creation of broader cultural-spatial trends visible elsewhere. The concern with spectacle and performance over substance, together with the increasingly disorientating and contradictory role of the government, the spatial manifestations of the financialization of worth under neoliberalism and the enforced social control within these places, are significant spatial hallmarks of contemporary public space, and it is the symbiotic interaction of these factors which serves to work against the potential for political and social change. However, in order to demonstrate and continue to believe in the possibility of change, it is important not to fall into the trap of viewing the current manifestation of public space as somehow inevitable, or as merely the result of structural forces. It is also important to make the argument that public spaces displaying characteristics of the kind outlined above often lead to a lived experience of public space which is unfulfilling—both in terms of a lack of broad appeal across different socio-demographic strata, but also in terms of the lived experiences of those who set foot within them. In short, the experience of The High Line is one which is, in addition to the myriad negative democratic implications of its characteristics, deeply unsatisfying.

The High Line, as a paradigmatic public space under Spectacle Techno-Capitalism poses a set of challenges, particularly in terms of its exclusionary nature and its privileging of a certain set of socio-cultural values to the democratic possibilities of public space. The project for those of us who wish for public spaces to aspire to more than that which the High Line offers us should be to argue and intervene in favor of a set of values about public space (democratic, and open enough to be produced by the creativity of its inhabitants) which stand in opposition to many of the characteristics of public space (and indeed society) at the current conjuncture. How we do that, and discussions over the form which these actions and interventions should take, strikes me as a useful next step in combating the myriad problems inherent within the functioning of public space under Spectacle Techno-Capitalism.

Works Cited

Amoeba Films (2012). NYC Highline Park: Ten Minute Tour. *YouTube:* https://youtu.be/RKLucigE1yI.

Appleton, Josie (2016). *Officious: The Rise of the Busybody State.* London: Zero.

Aspen, Johnny (2013). Oslo – The Triumph of Zombie Urbanism. In Rodolphe El-Khoury and Edward Robbins (eds.), *Shaping the City: Studies in History, Theory and Urban Design.* London: Routledge.

Bliss, Laura (2017). The High Line's Next Balancing Act. *The Atlantic Citylab*: https://www.citylab.com/solutions/2017/02/the-high-lines-next-balancing-act-fair-and-affordable-development/515391/.

Brash, Julian (2011). *Bloomberg's New York: Class and Governance in the Luxury City.* Athens, GA: University of Georgia Press.

Brash, Julian (2017). Park (In)Equity. In Christoph Lindner and Brian Rosa (eds.). *Deconstructing the High Line: Postindustrial Urbanism and the Rise of the Elevated Park.* New Brunswick, NJ: Rutgers University Press.

Cataldi, Michael, David Kelley, Hans Kuzmich, Jens Maier-Rothe and Jeannine Tang (2011). Residues of a Dream World: The High Line, 2011. *Theory, Culture and Society,* 28:7-8, 358–389.

Citadel Security Agency (2018). Park Security: http://www.citadelsecurity-agency.com/new-york-park-security/.

City of New York (2005). West Chelsea Zoning Proposal: http://www1.nyc.gov/assets/planning/download/pdf/plans/west-chelsea/westchelsea.pdf.

City of New York (2009). Mayor Bloomberg, Speaker Quinn And Friends Of The High Line Announce Opening Of First Section Of New York City's Newest Park: http://www1.nyc.gov/office-of-the-mayor/news/257-09/mayor-bloomberg-speaker-quinn-friends-the-high-line-opening-first-section-of.

Dao, Dan Q, Tazzi Phillips, Time Out New York Staff Writers (2017). The Best New York Attractions. *Time Out New York*: https://www.timeout.com/newyork/attractions/new-york-attractions.

David, Joshua and Robert Hammond (2011). *High Line: The Inside Story of New York's Park in the Sky*. New York, NY: Farrar, Straus and Giroux.

Debord, Guy (1970). *Society of the Spectacle*. Detroit, MI: Black & Red.

Du Gay, Paul (1996). Organizing Identity: Entrepreneurial Governance and Public Management. In Du Gay, Paul, and Stuart Hall. *Questions of Public Identity*. London: Sage.

Fisher, Mark (2009). *Capitalist Realism: Is There An Alternative?* London: Zero.

Florida, Richard (2004). *The Rise of the Creative Class*. New York, NY: Basic.

Friends of the High Line. About the High Line. *The High Line*: http://www.thehighline.org/about.

Gibson, Eleanor (2017). 18 Rail to Trail Projects Following in The High Line's Footsteps. *Dezeen*: https://www.dezeen.com/2017/06/27/18-rail-to-trail-projects-high-line-network-north-america/.

Halle, David and Elisabeth Tiso (2014). *New York's New Edge: Contemporary Art, the High Line, and Urban Megaprojects on the Far West Side*. Chicago, IL: University of Chicago Press.

Harvey, David (1989). From Managerialism to Entrepreneurialism: the Transformation of Urban Governance in Late Capitalism. *Geografiska Annaler, Series B, Human Geography*, 71:1.

HR&A (2018). The High Line Transformation. *HR&A*: https://www.hraadvisors.com/portfolio/the-high-line/.

Kayden, Jerold S. (2000). *Privately Owned Public Space: The New York City Experience*. Hoboken, NJ: Wiley.

Loughran, Kevin (2014). Parks for Profit: The High Line, Growth Machines and the Uneven Development of Urban Public Spaces. *City and Community*, 13:1.

Low, Setha, with Dana Taplin and Suzanne Scheld (2005). *Rethinking Public Parks*. Austin, TX: University of Texas Press.

Moss, Jeremiah (2016). Zombie Urbanism (interview with Jonny Aspen). *Jeremiah's Vanishing New York*: http://vanishingnewyork.blogspot.de/2016/08/zombie-urbanism.html.

Moss, Jeremiah (2017). *Vanishing New York: How a Great City Lost its Soul*. New York, NY: Harper Collins.

New York Economic Development Corporation (2011). Economic Snapshot: https://www.nycedc.com/sites/default/files/files/economic-snapshot/EconomicSnapshotAugust2011_0.pdf.

Oursouffof, Nicolai (2009). On High, A Fresh Outlook. *New York Times*, 9 June 2009: https://www.nytimes.com/2009/06/10/arts/design/10high.html.

Reichl, Alexander J. (2016). The High Line and the Ideal of Democratic Public Space. *Urban Geography*, 37:6, 904–925.

Rosa, Brian, and Christoph Lindner (2017). Introduction: From Elevated Railway to Urban Park. In Christoph Lindner and Brian Rosa (eds.). *Deconstructing the High Line: Postindustrial Urbanism and the Rise of the Elevated Park*. New Brunswick, NJ: Rutgers University Press.

Sorkin, Michael (1992). Introduction. In Michael Sorkin, (ed.), *Variations on a Theme Park: The New American City and the End of Public Space.* New York, NY: Hill and Wang.

Symonds, Alexandria (2011). In Which We Mark Graves Like Birthplaces. *This Recording:* http://thisrecording.com/today/2011/10/3/in-which-we-mark-graves-like-birthplaces.html.

Zukin, Sharon (2010). *Naked City: The Death and Life of Authentic Urban Places.* New York, NY: Oxford University Press.

III. Labor, Technological Utopias and Emancipatory Potentials

Infrastructures of Digital Capitalism: On Automation and Labor

Astrid Zimmermann

The hope that technology could evolve into a tool for emancipation is by no means a novel argument. In his essay "*Economic possibilities of our Grandchildren*, published at the onset of the Great Depression, John Maynard Keynes (1931) argued that the technological innovations within industrialization would usher in a society beyond scarcity, in which everybody's basic needs would be catered to, with a fifteen-hour work week and time for leisure, culture and the free development of the individual. As we know today, Keynes's post-scarcity utopia did not come into being.

Neither did others' sanguine visions. In a similar vein, Daniel Bell (1974) anticipated the beginning of a post-industrial society of stability and growth in the early 1970s in his book *The Coming of a Post-Industrial Society*. Bell predicted the advent of an information-based economy and a steady evolution into post-industrialism based on technology and knowledge, opposing the classic Marxist argument that capitalism is bound to violently break under its own contradictions. Shortly after the publishing of Bell's book, the financial crisis of the 1970s dampened the optimistic hopes around technology's impact.

Today, a similar kind of technological optimism is being revitalized around digitization and the utopian promise of labor reduction. When discussing the emancipatory potentials of technology, a recurring argument presents the supposed democratizing affordances that are implied in the innovations of digitization.

In 1995, Jeremy Rifkin argued that capitalism's development of technology and the increases in automation that go along with it would finally initiate *The End of Work*. In his more recent publication, *Zero Marginal Cost Society* (2014), Rifkin posits that the immediacy and virtuality of digitization would drive the marginal costs of commodity production close to zero. As his argument goes, the production of collaborative commons and the model of the sharing economy will eventually overcome capitalism. Similarly, Paul Mason argues in *Post-Capitalism* (2015) that the process of digitization should be understood as conceptually antithetical to the basic tenets of capitalism, since digitization allows for the free circulation of digital commodities. In that sense, the digitization of productive forces is assumed to pave the way to a post-capitalist economy as technology progresses.

Interestingly, both Mason and Rifkin ground their analysis in early writings of Marx. In fact, this somewhat utopian, and arguably selective interpretation of Marx cannot only be found in the works by Rifkin or Mason but has also been articulated by a number of Marxist scholars, especially among Post-Operaists and Autonomous Marxists. The Autonomists too understand capitalism's latest evolvement with technology as qualitatively different from previous modes. The emancipatory role of technology is here not so much seen in its tendency to, as Rifkin and Mason suggest, automate jobs out of existence, but rather believed to lie in technology's ability to bring about a new kind of worker subjectivity whose labor can no longer be contained by capital. New levels of global connectivity are believed to foster a more networked, collaborative form of production and technology is hoped to have the ability to turn the globe into an even playing field of what has been called "immaterial labor" (Lazzarato 1996, 133-134).

In these Marxist accounts, the consensus is that something changed within the process of the generation of value after the crisis of Fordism in the 1970s, and that this change is comparable in significance to the shift from agrarian production to industrialization. In the current case, this change within capitalism is ascribed to the rise of digital technologies. Where factory-based single-site production stood as the emblem of the Fordist economy of industrial mass production, today's economy is commonly analyzed on the basis of highly-integrated, globally-dispersed digital networks of production, historically unprecedented levels of labor automation and the internet as a kind of meta-structure organizing the economy. Where the hegemonic form of labor during Fordism used to be standardized work in the factory, labor in the digital economy is understood to become increasingly cognitive due the high levels of technicization and computerization involved (see Moulier-Boutang 2011).

The application of technology within production is however still ambiguously debated. On the one hand lies the hope that technology's potential to fully automate production processes could free the worker from the repetitive, standardized, alienated relations of wage labor and that the internet could be deployed as a space to collaboratively produce and share digital commodities with close to zero costs. In reality, however, labor relations have actually become more precarious, the polarization of wages is worsening and an ever-increasing rather than diminishing share of the global population is getting integrated into the labor market.

While there is no doubt that technology has impacted the organization of work and that automated machinery and digital algorithms can now perform tasks previously performed by workers, overly affirmative accounts of digitization obscure the fact that technology is still ultimately bound up and situated within very material social relations. Contrary to the claims about the immaterialization of labor, I will argue that the integration of technology is in fact intensifying labor since the wireless spaces of information-based work have not evenly materialized.

Technological advancement has certainly enabled processes of automation and led to a decrease in industrial labor in the Global North, as clearly demonstrated in regions such as the American Rust Belt, but this deindustrialization has been accompanied by an expansion of the global reach of production chains and newly emerging zones of industrialization elsewhere, and digitization plays a crucial role in pushing and managing the flow of these globally unbundling chains of production. Capitalism's latest technological advancements, argued to enable an immaterial regime of production, are rooted in the physically-grounded production of these technological innovations, which are the product of a complex, globalized division of labor, with highly exploitative, often unregulated forms of manual labor in the marginal zones of capitalist development.

Immaterial Labor: The Problem with the Autonomist Critique

The concept of immaterial labor is based on the idea that technological innovations of capitalism are, in an Althusserian sense, overdetermined and the analytical focus of immaterial labor lies precisely in these aspects of overdetermination and the new political possibilities of the networked, globalized post-Fordist working-class. Within this context, technology is, in its most basic sense, understood as an objectification of scientific knowledge, and so to speak, as an objectification of a collective labor process, which suggests that the potential for the creation of societal commons is structurally implied within these technologies—even though the collective quality of these labor processes remains obscure within the contemporary economic system. The critical point here is that structural aspects of capitalist technologies are understood to transcend the logics of capital.

This line of argumentation can be traced back to Marx's early work and an argument he sketched out in the fragment on machinery in the *Grundrisse*. As Marx anticipates there, the process of production and the generation of profit will depend less on living labor and more on the integration of science, knowledge and technology as capitalism develops. The Autonomists argue that this continuous scientification and technicization of production is exemplified in the current stage of capitalism by its reliance on immaterial labor, just as Marx had anticipated in the *Grundrisse*. The argument goes that capital, as it seeks to increase its productivity by further developing the means of production, must necessarily develop technologies that contradict the capitalist logic of value. This reasoning follows from Marx's understanding of technology as an objectification of the *general intellect*. In the most basic sense, this refers to an understanding of the production of knowledge as a collaborative, social process. Scientific knowledge should then be understood as nothing other than "the general productive forces of the social brain" (Marx 1973, 622). The production of commons, as opposed to commodity goods for profit, is thus believed to be structurally implied in this process. Autonomists then suggest that through the integration of technology—here, too, understood as an objectification of the *general intellect*—production is bound to become more social, more collective and more collaborative. However, since the knowledge objectified in technological machinery is appropriated by capital, it must keep the emancipatory affordances of technology in check.

The Autonomist reading of the *Grundrisse* then proposes that the further capitalism advances its means of production, the less "capitalist" it becomes since it endeavors to increase productivity and reduce labor time. The emancipatory hope is that this must lead to an overall decrease in work while at the same time increasing productivity, and thus material wealth. In turn, this contradiction is hoped to develop to the point where human labor might be transcended altogether.

From this vantage point, rather than running on raw materials, the current regime of capital accumulation is believed to mainly rest on immaterial resources, such as knowledge, cognition, ideas, creativity and information. As Maurizio Lazzarato for instance argues, the immateriality of the current hegemonic form of labor concerns not only the immaterial, "informational content" of the commodity being produced, but also the nature of the work being performed as it involves "fixing cultural and artistic standards, fashions, tastes, consumer norms and, more strategically, public opinions" (1996, 132).

Another fundamental characteristic of immaterial labor pertains the supposed destabilization of the dichotomy of manual and mental labor, since "manual labor is increasingly coming to involve procedures that could be defined as 'intellectual'" (ibid., 133) because labor in the post-Fordist industry not only involves high technological proficiency but also capitalizes on the entire subjectivity of the worker. As opposed to the Fordist worker, whose responsibilities were narrowly defined and strictly laid out and dictated, the work responsibilities of the post-Fordist worker are supposedly more flexible, relying on active "cooperation and collective coordination" (ibid., 135). Lazzarato, among others, goes on to suggest that immaterial labor "constitutes itself in forms that are immediately collective, and we might say that it exists only in the form of networks and flows" (ibid., 136). Labor in the post-Fordist age is therefore understood to be implicitly collaborative and communicative, incorporating the worker's entire subjectivity, which is believed to be the raw material on which immaterial labor runs. This new hegemonic form of labor is argued to be anything but repetitive, monotonous and strictly defined, instead it is described as "polymorpheus self-employed autonomous work" performed by "a kind of 'intellectual worker' who is him- or herself an entrepreneur" (ibid., 139). Theories of immaterial labor claim that the constant flow of information in the contemporary networked economy have a communicative, somewhat collective dimension with the potential for social transformation. The opportunities for this kind of interaction are believed to lie in the use of digital technology.

In summary, it can therefore be said that the integration of digital technological innovations into production, according to Autonomists, implies that capital is appropriating communication, or, to be more precise, the cooperative, collective intellect of the workforce while simultaneously controlling and containing the potentially subversive capacities of this collective intellect. The potentials of this new global working class, the "multitude," that performs immaterial labor are argued to lie precisely in these capacities as these technologies—while disseminated for commercial interests—unintentionally open up possibilities for intervention and appropriation as they can be used as a tool for labor organizing and worker solidarity.

This argument has been put forth most prominently by Hardt and Negri, who propose that digital technology harbors the potential to generate a system of globally networked, collaborative production out of capitalist relations. As Hardt and Negri suggest, digitization has systemically changed the relation between capital and labor. In *Empire* they argue that "interactive and cybernetic machines become a new prosthesis integrated into our bodies and minds and a lens through which to redefine our bodies and minds themselves. The anthropology of cyberspace is really a recognition of a new human condition" (Hard and Negri 2000, 291).

This argument is essentially anti-thetical to Marx who had proposed that the adaption of technology within the capitalist relations of production would not lead to a kind of symbiotic synergy between human and machine, as Hardt and Negri propose, but rather deteriorate the worker to a mere "appendage of the machine" (Marx 1887, 451). In contrast, theories of immaterial labor argue that all labor performed in contemporary capitalism shares aspects of interactivity and communication and demands an application of cognitive abilities due the integration of technology—in short, the workers whole subjectivity is being appropriated within immaterial labor to extract value as less labor-time is necessary through the application of machinery.

The underlying premise is that knowledge is now more important than it had been in previous stages of capitalist production, which supposedly paves the way to an overall intellectualization and cognitization of labor. This reasoning implies the supposed impossibility of a fully informational, a fully knowledge-based, or a fully digital capitalism and it further presumes that there is something qualitatively different about digital technologies that separate them from previous technological innovations and fundamentally contradict the logic of capitalism—that being their immateriality. In the end, Autonomist Marxism here builds on the assumption that production is becoming ever more intelligent, in the sense that it relies less on work-intensive labor performed by humans and more and more on efficient, automated technology, and that these inherent potentialities within capitalist production must only be liberated to overcome the exploitative relations of wage labor. In that sense, technological development is understood not only as a means to increase labor productivity, but, and this is crucial, as a kind of civilizatory advancement. Capitalism's push towards innovation and the technologies it generates are believed to disrupt and overturn anachronistic relations of production.

The collectivity and connectivity among workers and labor's immaterial output supposedly enabled by digitization are at the center of Autonomist Marxist critique. This, however, is precisely the crux with Autonomist Marxism. As it places its focus on the interaction between technology and the worker, it largely disregards technology's role within the social relations of capitalism. Digital technologies are, however, still grounded in material, concrete social relations of labor, which are not disappearing or becoming immaterial, even if some of the commodities they produce are. This in turn implies that it cannot be sufficient to exclusively look at technology, but that technology needs to be contextualized within the social relations that produce it, because no matter how digital, technology still cannot transcend the materiality of production.

I do not want to discredit the argument that the application of knowledge is playing an increasing role in production, and that through the substitution of human labor through automated machinery and algorithms, science and technology are being elevated into increasingly major forces of production. My point of critique, however, concerns the fact that this transformation does not develop evenly through all sectors and branches of work, but affects different forms of labor in diverse ways. While theories on immaterial labor state that, in general terms, "the organization of labor becomes increasingly autonomous" and that "control over labor no longer takes on the Taylorist role of direct allocation of tasks" (Vercellone 2008, 6), this organization of labor in fact only affects a comparatively small segment of the workforce—that is, knowledge workers in the focal points of Western urbanization. But their conditions cannot be generalized to describe the social reality of the global working class as a whole. Declaring interactivity and autonomy to be the primary characteristics of labor in contemporary capitalism in general, glosses over entire sectors of labor where Taylorist models of management have not only persisted, but rather been intensified through the digitization and computerization of production.

Uneven Spaces of Labor: On the Moving Contradiction of Capital

Merely pointing to the immaterial quality of digital technologies within labor processes says little about their impact on the organization of labor and technology's role in the realization of value. Looking closer at how these technologies are integrated into the production process unveils why their integration has not, as has been argued by the theorists of immateriality, de-materialized labor. The flaw of Autonomist critique and its claim about the immaterialization of production lies thus in its disregard of the material realities of labor in the fringes of capitalist development and its ignorance toward the hierarchical, racialized and gendered fractions among the global working class—my point being that the main contradiction lies not so much in the potentially quasi-communist and collective affordances of capitalist technology, but rather in, what Marx has termed, "the moving contradiction" (1973, 637) of capital:

> "It [capital] presses to reduce labor time to a minimum, while it posits labor time, on the other side as sole measure and source of wealth. [...] On the one side, then, it calls to life all the powers of science and nature, as of social combination and of social intercourse, in order to make the creation of wealth independent of the labor time employed on it. On the other side, it wants to use labor time as the measuring rod for the giant social forces thereby created, and to confine them within the limits required to maintain the already created value as value." (ibid., 637-638)

In other words, capital tries to reduce labor time as much as possible, while at the same time using labor time as the sole measure of value. This "moving contradiction" manifests itself in the context of contemporary capitalism through the development of automated machinery and algorithmic software that renders whole segments of labor redundant and superfluous, while at the same time increasing the territorial reach of agile production chains, opening up a global disposable resource of cheap labor available to capital.

Cheap labor in mining and extraction, industrial assembly and manufacturing, and low-skill services is then necessary for capital to build the technological machinery through which capital increasingly uncouples itself from the worker in the sphere of production as well as circulation. In other words, while capital drives out labor through automation, it simultaneously absorbs a new low-waged workforce as it globally expands its market boundaries and also absorbs more workers in newly developing sectors. In a similar vein, economists such as David Autor and Doug Henwood call attention to the fact that automation has historically not led to the substitution of human labor, but that the employment-to-population-ratio actually rose throughout the 20th century and the global labor force keeps significantly expanding up until today in times of computerization and digitization (Autor 2015; Henwood 2003).

While technology has not replaced human labor, Autor too argues that it rather influences the kinds of jobs that are available. While automation might be able to substitute what Autor calls "routine tasks" (2015, 11)—that is typical middle-skilled administrative, clerical work, which can easily be codified and algorithmized—Autor identifies two categories of work which can, as of now, not be substituted by machinery. On the one hand these are "abstract tasks" which involve high levels of problem-solving, technical and analytical capabilities and on the other hand "manual tasks" that are minimally reliant on digital data processing, such as service jobs and care work. Put differently, while capital drives out labor through automation, it simultaneously expands its market reach and absorbs more workers in newly developing sectors, such as the rapidly growing low-waged, pink-collar service sector, which currently presents the industry with the highest projected growth rate (Bureau of Labor Statistics 2014).

Capitalism's demand for the most lucrative combination of capital and labor has led the organization of labor to become increasingly fragmented, polarized and globally dispersed. Looking at the increasing segmentation and dispersion of the production process then reveals the social relation between multiple forms of labor required by capital on a global scale and demonstrates that digitization is enabled through a "global ecology of exploitation" (Fuchs 2013, 20). Knowledge-producing, immaterial labor is thus organized within a complex, networked global division of labor encompassing multiple stages of production.

The technological affordances that are understood as a locus for worker autonomy in theories of immaterial labor do not evenly penetrate all spheres of work and lead to an overall intellectualization and immaterialization of labor, but are rather afforded through a displacement of highly exploitative labor relations into areas beyond the central zones of technological and economic development—the crucial point here being that there is an unevenness of development and digitization that allows global disparities of labor costs, wage and environmental regulations to be turned into a productive aspect in the realization of value. The concept of the hegemony of immaterial labor assumes that as capitalism progresses, production becomes more intelligent due to the growing incorporation of science through technology. But as Christian Fuchs has argued, there is a dialectical interconnection between stages of capitalism. In this sense, the "informational productive forces do not eliminate, but sublate other productive forces" (ibid., 10) and therefore, the incorporation of digital technologies has not turned production virtual, cognitive or immaterial, even if certain segments of production operate in this way. Neither the labor force nor the spaces of production can simply be reshaped according to the demands of capital.

For example, the extraction of coal and minerals needed to produce the devices and surfaces of digitization are fixed in certain geographical locations (see Kalt in this volume). Similarly, the labor force itself does not follow the demands of capital: worker resistance, strikes and blockades, demands for labor and wage regulations present a risk of delaying and interrupting the smooth flow of capital. This is precisely where technology plays a crucial role, as its integration into the infrastructures of logistics makes both spatial and temporal obstacles productive for capital. The heightened role of infrastructures further highlights the fact that processes of digitization are enabled through a complex global division of labor which incorporates various stages of production in disparate spaces in the global economy. The role of technology lies in facilitating the globalization of production through transnational supply chains, which in turn allowed for the migration of industrial manufacturing jobs from the Global North to the Global South, which in a neo-colonial fashion is being appropriated as a repository of natural resources and cheap, unregulated labor.

The Material Underside of Immaterial Labor

Consider this reflection by Marx on the industrial integration of technology: "As the use of machinery extends in a given industry, the immediate effect is to increase production in the other industries that furnish the first with means of production" (1887, 295). The argument that the expulsion of living labor as an effect of automation leads to new industries that produce the technologies which enable precisely this level of automation points to the complexities of labor needed to facilitate digitization in the first place. Profits in the digital value chain are thus not solely generated through an integration of technology in the work process to increase productivity, but rather through a dislocation and an extension of markets by capitalizing on global disparities in development. Value is thus generated through a displacement of labor-intensive industries into developing countries. The mobility of capital has the effect of further decreasing wage levels and worker's bargaining power in these countries, as this process establishes the conditions for an international competition between workers. There is thus an array of forms of labor involved in the process of digitization, among them the natural extraction of minerals and subsequently industrial manufacturing, which provide the basis of the digital value chain.

Therefore we must first turn to the sites of extraction. Among the largest suppliers of minerals used in the production of the devices of digitization, such as Tantalum, Coltan and Tungsten, are conflict-ridden areas including the Democratic Republic of Congo and Zimbabwe (United States Geological Survey, 2017). The high demand of Western companies for cheap minerals and cheap labor in the mining industry have been a major force driving the super-exploitative conditions in these countries, as the industries around digital technology stoke the largest demand for minerals extracted in these areas. The informational means of production of digital capitalism—meaning the devices that are needed for the digital processing of flows of information—are thus interconnected to a harshly exploitative, labor-intensive, manual mode of production in the extraction and mining of natural resources in developing countries. In the global division of digital labor, these countries figure as an "economic colony" (Fuchs 2013, 11) from which cheap labor and raw materials are sourced and this seemingly anachronistic, neo-colonial type of exploitation of natural resources and human labor is interconnected to the digital productive forces of immaterial labor.

The assembly process follows the extraction of natural resources. Within the digital value chain, manufacturing processes in the electronics industry are mainly located in low-wage countries, primarily China and Taiwan, where the two largest electronics manufacturing service providers, Foxconn and Pegatron, have their production plants. The de-industrialization in the US and Western Europe is matched with the industrialization of formerly undeveloped, newly industrialized regions, where these industries can be rapidly built up or shut down depending on market demands. Most of the workforce here is comprised of young workers from the countryside who move to urban areas as a result of rural poverty, generating a larger pool of cheap workers demanded by electronic manufacturing (ibid.,13). The uneven development between rural and urban China facilitates the conditions that force rural peasants to abandon their established mode of self-sufficiency and migrate to urban China to look for work, strongly resembling Marx's argument of primitive accumulation.

When describing the process of capitalist expansion and the establishment of capitalist relations of production in newly developing markets, Marx argues that through dispossession and privatization of common land, capital produces a larger proletariat by driving the peasantry off their land and forcing them to sell their labor force as a means of subsistence (1887, 510-521). The expansion of markets does not present a naturally evolving development, but has to be instituted with force. In its structure, the labor in the manufacturing sector of electronics reflects early modes of industrial labor on the assembly line as it is standardized and repetitive, requiring little skill while workers' compliance is achieved through strict control and supervision. The conditions of the Taylorist factory have thus not been outmoded within the organization of labor in digital capitalism, but are an integral part in the global digital value chain.

A glimpse at the global division of digital labor shows how the planetary unevenness in development regarding wage levels, degrees of mechanization and automation, labor productivity, and occupational skills is capitalized on, rather than evened out as an effect of digitization. Technological development in the centers of capitalism is afforded through processes of underdevelopment elsewhere. Rather than declining, there has been an increase in manual and industrial labor, albeit not in the urban centers of the United States and Europe.

The overly affirmative fetishization of technology and the argument that capitalism's technological advancement has fostered a generation of value mainly through its incorporation of science and knowledge, that way making it more "intelligent" and progressive, obscures the continuities of archaic and highly exploitative forms of labor exploitation. The basic social relations of capitalist production have remained consistent and unchanged by the technological advancement of digitization. Regimes of production do not outmode each other, but are rather interrelated with each other and digital technologies operate as a kind of meta-technology combining different regimes of production as digitization conflates the standardized, tightly controlled routine labor of Taylorism with the automation of Fordist mass production and the flexibilized employment conditions of post-Fordism. That is not to deny that there lies potential in the technologies of digitization. However, for these potentials to be realized they must be integrated into a systemic restructuring of precisely these social relations of production.

The Need for Circulation and Acceleration

Not only is digitization embedded within a complex, globally-networked division of labor and class relations, but it simultaneously figures as the organizational logic of managing the labor processes involved. The latter point highlights how technology fosters the expansive reach of capital, making labor and resources available to capital on a planetary scale. The current regime of accumulation is thus dependent on the very material infrastructures that enable the acceleration of the circulation of capital. The geographical fixity of resources needed for digitization in the form of cheap labor as well as raw materials presents an obstacle to the circulation of capital that can be circumvented through the integration of time- and space-compressing digital technologies, enabling a globally integrated network of production. In this case, the role of technology lies in bridging the spatial fixity of cheap labor resources and raw materials. The fact that these resources are bound to a specific geographical locality hinders the smooth circulation of capital, which can be overcome and turned productive through the integration of technology. This points to the crucial role of infrastructures of digital technologies in shaping and extending the boundaries of the market, speeding up the turnover time of capital while at the same time breaking the bargaining power of workers, as this process allows capital to fragment production, thereby bypassing points of struggle and resistance and to move and relocate steps of the production process to wherever regulation and labor costs are lowest.

Value in this case is increased through an acceleration of capital's turnover time, exemplified through the integration of digital technologies in the logistical and infrastructural work needed to manage the acceleration of circulation and the realization of value not through an increase in productivity but through capital's exploitation of wage polarities. The fact that the function of digital technologies lies mainly in the storage and communication of information has the effect of "reducing the costs for transportation while also reducing the time necessary for communication", enabling a new level of "command and control operations" (Lavanda and Mahmoudi 2016, 101). The implications of this are twofold: First, digital technologies enhance and extend the control mechanisms of labor, rather than enabling free, creative work that is more autonomous and cognitive. Secondly, they facilitate the global expansion of the market and the acceleration of its circulation.

Through digital communication networks, information can be shared almost instantaneously, allowing for the spatial fragmentation of production processes and the facilitation and management of the global movement and warehousing of raw materials, intermediate products and commodities. Digital technology is in this regard not only used to administer and supervise the smooth flow of circulation, but also plays a crucial role in processing information—for example tracking shipping, orders or sales—which enables not only the acceleration of value chains, but also allows for the perpetual monitoring of the entire process. The tight control over every stage in the process allows for more flexibility and thus production becomes better tailored to the volatility of market demands. This new agility of value chains has enabled the shift from mass production to cost-efficient just-in-time production systems which require less warehousing and inventory (see Güse in this volume). In this regard, circulation can be defined as a process which, in comparison to production, generates value not through extraction but through acceleration.

Recognizing the fact that commodities are no longer produced at one singular site also implies a perspective of circulation that treats it as a component of production, rather than a step following production. The logics of the accumulation of capital that accelerate the speed of circulation will thus re-configure space and time accordingly, pointing to the heightened importance of infrastructures and logistics. The increasing integration of circulation into production in the development of capitalism has been foreshadowed by Marx in his argument on the expansive nature of capital in the *Grundrisse*. As Marx points out here:

> "While capital must on one side strive to tear down every spatial barrier to intercourse […] it strives on the other side to annihilate this space with time, i.e. to reduce to a minimum the time spent in motion from one place to another. The more developed the capital, therefore, the more extensive the market over which it

circulates, [...] the more does it strive simultaneously for an even greater extension of the market and for greater annihilation of space by time. [...] However, in so far as circulation itself creates costs, itself requires surplus labour, it appears as itself included within the production process. In this respect circulation appears as a moment of the direct production process." (1973, 472-473)

Circulation is a part of production because capital loses value once it stops circulating and since the ever-expanding circulation of capital itself involves labor. For one, this implies that the process of circulation adds value through the labor performed in the infrastructures that enable its circulation. So, not only does the labor involved in transport and logistics become part of the production process, but they do so with the specific aim of increasing the speed of circulation. Moreover, as capital globally extends the boundaries of the market, it continually struggles to condense the amount of time that the overcoming of distance takes to accelerate the velocity of circulation, thus reducing the turnover time of capital and realizing profits in less time. The infrastructures of digital technologies then become a means of turning the obstacles and disruptions of circulation—that is, temporal and spatial distance—productive by compressing space through time. The globalization and flexibilization of markets can thus be understood as what David Harvey has termed "time-space compression" (1989, 284). While capital expands markets spatially, it simultaneously accelerates the overcoming of geographical fixity. In that sense, the speed of informational flows enabled through digitization compresses space through time.

As circulation becomes increasingly important within the generation of value, production is no longer at the core of value extraction. Technology's role in this context is crucial to the creation of value as it increases circulation through, as Marx called it, the "annihilation of space" and a depression of wages by restricting the bargaining power of workers precisely through capital's mobility through the compression of space. Technology's function in the social relations of production is thus not limited to automation, a reduction of labor time, and an increase in labor efficiency. As follows, the use-value of infrastructures and logistics for capital lies principally in its reduction of labor costs through an economic utilization of the global unevenness of wages and regulations. As authors like Keller Easterling (2014) or David Harvey (1996) have pointed out, certain spatial arrangements and processes harbor inherent operational logics and hierarchies. Based on this understanding of infrastructure, I suggest looking at the infrastructures of digital capitalism in a similar way: Technologies of digitization mesh with existing geographies of circulation, executing a kind of infrastructural authority and organizational protocol which provides the framework conditions for the operation of digital capitalism.

Digital technology's integration in the process of circulation has enabled increasingly agile value-chains, which allow for the relocation of industrial enterprises into low-wage zones. As the example of Foxconn has demonstrated, the internal migration within China from rural to newly developed zones of industrial production have generated a highly disintegrated, contingent workforce that is especially vulnerable to extremely exploitative labor relations as their work is largely unregulated and the devices produced through their labor stand in a connection with the digitally-enabled, immaterial labor performed by knowledge workers in the Global North. The increased mechanization and automation that can be witnessed in the Global North are thus being compensated for through a fragmentation of labor in international production chains, allowing for an intensification of labor exploitation for maximum profit as the global unbundling of production chains reduces wage costs.

Instead of evening out polarities, the integration of digital technologies has rather interacted with and reinforced the spatial unevenness of economic activity, promoting the fragmentation of production across space while simultaneously leading to a clustering of economic activities in certain zones of the globe, as evidenced by the mineral mining industry in Congo, industrial manufacturing industry in China and Taiwan, or the clustering of microchip, browser and website firms in California. These geographic configurations of the division of labor are both made useful for as well as reinforced by digitization.

Technology is thus changing the geographies of production that shape who performs what kinds of labor in which locality. As Smith has argued, "uneven development is both the product and the premise of capitalist development" (1984, 155). The comparative advantage of uneven economic geographies, of an uneven distribution of technological advancements and the tremendous global wage gaps are thus not a side-effect but an organizing principle of capitalism. Not only are digital technologies the commodity output of the global expansion of capitalism through the migration of labor and capital to previously non-capitalist markets, but the time-space-compressing innovations in digitization in the forms of communication technologies and data processing are at the same time an integral element facilitating the global push towards expansion and the smooth flow of capital. This generates further downward pressures on wages and labor regulations as digitization has facilitated an international competition between workers rather than marking the onset of capitalism's supposed dissolution through the global unfolding of the *general intellect*.

Conclusions on the Future of Work

The employment of digital technologies eventually hinges on a very material production process through which capital circulates and reproduces itself. Digital technologies surely play a crucial role in the management of this increasingly-globalized production process and the global circulation of capital. But rather than being structurally different, digital capitalism simply constitutes a specific way of organizing production rather than dematerializing or intellectualizing production. As I have argued, capitalism spatially defers its internal crisis tendencies in the current regime of value through an internationalization of capital and a migration of labor-intensive industries into low-wage zones, rather than immaterializing production. The fact that goods and information streams can flow faster and with less disruption across global spacesdoes not eradicate the profound economic inequities between these spaces. Polarizations of power and wealth can thus not be flattened out through technologies of digitization since the geographical clustering of entire sectors utilizes and perpetuates the economic unevenness between spaces of labor. This is not a novel development, but a structural element of capitalism as its economic organization seeks out the most lucrative combination of living labor (workers) and capital (raw materials, technology, machinery)—which are both geographically fixed. Digitization, while having the effect of compressing space, can thus ultimately not transcend the materiality of space.

The exploitation of natural resources and cheap labor in the marginal zones of capitalist development lurk beneath the surface of the seemingly immaterial, cognitive, digital economy. The development of productive forces is thus an ambivalent, contradictory process. The antagonistic possibilities that it entails, on one hand emancipatory while oppressive on the other, are implied within. Technology itself is not inherently progressive nor regressive, but its integration in the relations of production can rather be one or the other. For the emancipative potentials to be realized they need to be situated within a larger political project rather than a mere reliance on technology, which bears the danger of equating technological progress to political progress.

I share the Autonomists' insistence on analyzing the novel possibilities of digital technologies for labor resistance as a potentially threatening barrier to the smooth circulation of capital. However, through the incorporation of time- and space-compressing technologies of digitization, capital, not workers, has gained a crucial advantage as these technologies have opened up capital's access to cheap labor on a planetary scale. While it is true that capitalism has a history of exploiting labor globally, as manifested in histories of colonization, digital capitalism presents a continuity of this tendency rather than a step towards a globally networked, horizontally organized economy where the hierarchies of geographic locality dissolve in the supposedly spaceless digitality of the internet.

The discrepancy between Autonomist Marxism's affirmative understanding of technology and technology's *de facto* role in contemporary capitalism uncovers the profound disparity between material potentialities and socio-political realities. My aim is not to discount the observation that critiques of capitalism must look to the potentials that capitalist production generates—regarding technology, automation and political organization, as the capacities of digitization point beyond the logics of value extraction. But the danger of the discourses I presented lie in their latent complicity in looking at the market as a collaborative network where ideas, skills and knowledge freely circulate—essentially presenting the globalized market as an egalitarian space.

In order to localize and identify moments and opportunities for political agency in contemporary capitalism and escape the ideology that there is no alternative, it is important to discuss the restructuring of labor relations not as an inevitable effect of technological progress that naturally unfolds, but to analyze and recognize the interests that drive these developments instead of shifting the responsibility to an unaccountable, impersonal abstraction like "technology". Otherwise, one runs the risk of neutralizing the economic interests that drive these transformations and overlooking the concrete social relations within which the economy is grounded—no matter how digitally, virtually or immaterially parts of this economy operate. The basic social relations of capitalism still present the organizational scheme of value extraction despite the technological advances of digital technologies. The possibilities that are speculatively drawn out can only be realized through a larger systemic restructuring of precisely these social relations of production—a process which eventually cannot be technologically automated.

Works Cited

Althusser, Louis (1969). *For Marx*. Ben Brewster (trans.). Marxist Internet Archive. https://www.marxists.org/reference/archive/althusser/1965/index.htm (accessed: 13 March 2018)

Autor, David (2015). "Why Are There Still So Many Jobs? The History and the Future of Workplace Automation. *Journal of Economic Perspectives* 29.3, 3–30.

Bell, Daniel (1974). *The Coming of Post-Industrial Society: A Venture in Social Forecasting.* London: Heinemann.

Bureau of Labor Statistics (2014). "Employment Projections: Table 1.4 Occupationswith the Most Job Growth, 2014 and Projected 2024." https://www.bls.gov/emp/tables/occupations-most-job-growth.htm (accessed: 19 June 2017).

Dyer-Whiteford, Nick (1994). "Autonomist Marxism and the Information Society." *Capital & Class* 52.1, 5–34.

— (2015),*Cyber-Proletariat: Global Labour in the Digital Vortex*. Chicago, IL: University of Chicago Press.

Easterling, Keller (2014). *Extrastatecraft: The Power of Infrastructure Space.* London andNew York, NY: Verso.

Fuchs, Christian (2013). "Theorising and Analysing Digital Labour: From Global Value Chains to Modes of Production. *The Political Economy of Communication* 1.2, 3–27.

Hardt, Michael, and Antonio Negri (2000). *Empire.* Cambridge, MA: Harvard University Press.

— (2004). *Multitude: War and Democracy in the Age of Empire.* New York, NY: Penguin Books.

Harvey, David (1989). *The Condition of Postmodernity: An Enquiry into the Origins of Cultural Change.* Cambridge, MA: Blackwell.

— (1996). *Justice, Nature and the Geography of Difference.* Cambridge: Blackwell.

— (2003). *The New Imperialism.* Oxford: Oxford University Press.

Henwood, Doug (2003). *After the New Economy.* New York, NY: New Press.

Keynes, Maynard (1931). "Economic Possibilities for Our Grandchildren." In: *Essays in Persuasion.* London: Macmillan and Co., Ltd.

Lazzarato, Maurizio (1996). "Immaterial Labor. " In: Paolo Virno and Michael Hardt (eds.). *Radical Thought in Italy: A Potential Politics.* Minneapolis, MN: University of Minnesota Press.

Mahmoudi, Dillon and Anthony Lavanda (2016). "Beyond the Screen: Uneven Geographies, Digital Labor and the City of Cognitive-Cultural Capitalism." *tripleC* 14.1, 99–120.

Marx, Karl (1887). *Capital, Vol. I.* Samuel Moore and Edward Aveling (trans.). Friedrich Engels (ed.). Moscow: Progress Publishers. Marxist Internet Archive. https://www.marxists.org/archive/marx/works/download/pdf/Capital-Volume-I.pdf (accessed: January 03: 2017).

— (1973). *Grundrisse: Outlines of the Critique of Political Economy.* Martin Nicolaus (trans.). London: Penguin.

Mason, Paul (2015). *PostCapitalism. A Guide to Our Future.* London: Allen Lane.

Moulier-Boutang, Yann (2011). *Cognitive Capitalism.* Cambridge, MA: Polity Press.

Rikfin, Jeremy (1995). *The End of Work: The Decline of the Global Labor Force and the Dawn of the Post-Market Era.* New York, NY: Putnam.

— (2014). *Zero Marginal Cost Society: The Internet of Things, the Collaborative Commons, and the Eclipse of Capitalism.* Basingstoke: Palgrave Macmillan.

Smith, Neil (1984). *Uneven Development: Nature, Capital and the Production of Space.* Cambridge, MA: Basil Blackwell Publisher Ltd.

United States Geological Survey (2017). "Mineral Commodity Summaries 2017." https://minerals.usgs.gov/minerals/pubs/mcs/2017/mcs2017.pdf (accessed: January 19, 2017.

Vercellone, Carlo (2008). "The New Articulation of Wages, Rent and Profit in Cognitive Capitalism." Paper presented at the conference "The Art of Rent", Queen Mary University School of Business and Management, London.

A Second Gilded Age? Organized Labor in Changing Geographies of Work

Dave Braneck

American labor organizing appears inadequately equipped to face the challenges of an increasingly globalized and automated economy, as well as shifting politics and institutional structures that shape the space in which work and workers are organized. Despite a vibrant history of unionism and labor-based resistance to capital, and at times the state in this country, the labor movement is at a historic weak point just as circumstances for many workers are further deteriorating. Recent years may have brought new lows for the country's unions and labor organizations, but a sense of *déjà vu* seems to have overtaken academics and pundits contemplating American economics and politics writ large. For many, the situation in the United States is nothing new. We must simply look back to the turn of the previous century to understand our current one. To argue that the United States has entered a second Gilded Age has become in many ways a trope in contemporary writing, and this trend has only intensified in the wake of the 2008 financial crisis. As I contend, a striking difference between the periods is mostly ignored: the first Gilded Age was marked by vibrant and radical responses to the power of capital by labor, while recent decades have seen a tremendous decline in the size, influence and actions of organized workers. Regardless of how closely some aspects of current economics, politics or society might mirror the twilight of the 19th century, the labor movement of the early 21st century would be wholly unrecognizable to anyone from the Gilded Age.

This chapter will examine the concept of the 'Second Gilded Age', comparing recent decades with the turn of the 19th century from a labor perspective. To what extent are the periods similar, and how have the conditions of each period shaped labor organizing? If the US truly is in a 'Second Gilded Age', how can the vast differences in the size and influence of the labor movement of each period be accounted for? The Gilded Age comparison is a common yet frequently shallow one. Though the 'Two

Gilded Ages' initially appear to have much in common, from the forceful and far-carrying tremors of changes in technology, to organizational shifts in economy, state and society, the details of these shifts and how precisely they were borne out were markedly different. Just because both eras experienced significant income inequality, intense globalization, a powerful capitalist class, and new developments in technology and the organization of labor does not mean that each of these factors looked remotely similar or had parallel repercussions for workers. Although the comparison is useful, the way it is made frequently misses the detailed contextual differences that do much to set both Gilded Ages apart, especially from a perspective of labor. Though superficially similar, the details of the shifts of each period reveal that most contextual changes of the 'First' Gilded Age fostered an environment ripe for a growing labor movement, while the past 30 years have seen a near universally negative set of shifts from labor's perspective, witnessing the development of an "infrastructural regime" (Vormann 2019) that frequently prevents or coopts labor organizing. These details account for the ascendant labor movement of the late 19th century and the degradation of organized labor and working conditions more generally in the modern period.

This chapter employs a 'long Gilded Age' periodization that runs loosely from 1870 to 1920. This intentionally long view is used for two reasons. The first is comparison's sake: in an indication of its superficial, often arbitrary nature, most of those who perpetuate the trope of two Gilded Ages do so with a very wide historical brush, typically doing little to concretely demark the Gilded Age's beginning and end and failing to differentiate it from the Progressive Era that follows it in most history books. Accounts of a Gilded Age which run from the end of the Civil War until the end of World War I are not entirely uncommon. The second reason is to foreground any continuities and long-term trends and evolutions that occurred during the period, providing a more significant comparison to the modern day. The exact dates of the 'Second' Gilded Age are even less clear. They are rarely stated, and typically imply anything from the last ten years to the late 1970s on. To clearly define a time frame, the end of the Cold War will be used to demark the later period of analysis, running from 1990 until today for the purposes of this article. The later period will be referred to as the 'Second' or 'New' Gilded Age, not necessarily as an endorsement of the concept that the periods are identical, but for clarity's sake.

A broad focus on the United States means that the regional and local nuance that is often key to understanding geographic developments will be difficult to provide, and the nation state will generally (though not always) be viewed as a 'black box' to enable a broader analysis of both periods and the organization of labor. Still, it is important to acknowledge that regional differences in the United States are typically vast, and that this composite view of the US is not meant to imply that something generally true for the nation is always true for all regions. This is doubly so for people in the US, as one's racial or ethnic background, immigration status, religion, gender and a slew of other factors often play an even bigger role in shaping opportunities and challenges in the labor market and society than location. This is also taken into account whenever possible, but broad strokes are painted not in ignorance of these key differences, but in order to provide some form of structural comparison.

The Trope of Two Gilded Ages

Among recent considerations of globalization, technological change, expanding inequality and the shifting nature of work is a common assertion that many of these current factors seem eerily reflective of similar indicators at the turn of the 20th century, and that the US is deep in the throes of a Second or New Gilded Age. The rise of Donald Trump, and his obsession with an ostentatious, gold-plated lifestyle, has only made this argument more common. His unobscured nepotism and graft has also added a corruption angle to the comparison which was generally lacking before the 2016 election. Not a very new argument, it has maintained its salience, and many writers feel little need to provide much evidence to support their claim that recent decades constitute another Gilded Age. Political scientist Larry Bartels was an earlier popular advocate to make the case in 2008's *Unequal Democracy: The Political Economy of the New Gilded Age.* The driving force for Bartels' dusting off Twain's famous moniker was a trend in skyrocketing income inequality which he saw as comparable to that of the First Gilded Age (Bartels 2008, 13). Bartels' generally partisan account emphasizes the political end of today's inequality and its bearings on the healthy functioning of a democracy. James Fallows' recent comparison in *the Atlantic* goes past economics towards a general mood of the period.

"The distortions of that first age—the extremes of wealth and welfare, the sudden dislocations due to technology and trade and ethnic change, the dismay about corrupt and plutocratic politics, the shunting of populist concerns toward racist outbursts—all have their clear counterparts now," he argues (Fallows 2016).

Articles using the term and stressing the comparison have appeared in publications as diverse as *Der Spiegel, The New York Times, Salon, International Journal of Historical Archaeology, Vice* and *Millennium: Journal of International Studies.* A recent *Guardian* article has made the case that the Second Gilded Age phenomenon is now a global phenomenon (Neate 2017). Popular liberal economists like Robert Reich and Paul Krugman use the term extensively, employing their celebrity platforms to reflect on the potential causes and implications of income inequality's continued upward trajectory in the US. Historian Steve Fraser's *The Age of Acquiescence: The Life and Death of American Resistance to Organized Wealth and Power,* written in 2015 and one of the most detailed comparisons of the Gilded Ages, takes the concept of the Second Gilded Age past economic inequality, exploring the public response (or lack thereof) to the conditions of each period. The idea of a New Gilded Age has struck a nerve in an apparently populist moment in American history, and left-leaning politicians like Bernie Sanders and Elizabeth Warren are apt to make the comparison. Even the decidedly more centrist Hillary Clinton was unable to resist the allure of the trope, identifying a "throwback to the Gilded Age of the robber barons" when speaking about inequality in 2014 (Parker 2014).

The image of a rotten society obscured by a golden coating conjured by Twain so long ago is quite persistent and is now back *en vogue.* Still, most authors are content to simply reference Thomas Piketty's famous graph on income inequality from *Capital in the 21st Century* (2014a), regurgitate the notion that the current century closely resembles the end of the 19th, and move on. Those who consider the broader implications of this income inequality—whether on politics, the health of democracy, corruption, or other social factors—are typically reluctant to question the initial comparison. Detailed, all-encompassing attempts to discover just what other factors the eras may or may not have in common are rarely made, and this weakens a lot of the arguments that attempt to extrapolate policy recommendations, social commentaries and deeper analysis out of the comparison. It is true that many of the surface level factors of the Gilded Age and post-Cold War are common, but these similarities fail to tell the whole story. The comparison has staying power because it works superficially or in some regards, but the details of each period, how the monumental shifts in technology, the role of the state, and the organization of labor were enacted, are where major differences between the First and Second Gilded Age quickly become apparent. Despite any parallels, the structural conditions of the First Gilded Age proved fertile soil for labor organizing, while today's Gilded Age brutally stunts worker organizing. It is in the oft-ignored specifics of the periods that potential answers for today's labor morass can be found.

The Rich and Everyone Else: American Income Equality in Both Periods

The yawning crevasse separating the rich and poor in the United States has long been a topic of interest to social scientists and academics, and Occupy Wall Street and Bernie Sanders' surprisingly successful 2016 primary campaign have brought income inequality further into the national limelight. Larry Bartels demonstrates income inequality's typically central role in the Second Gilded Age critique, noting his book is inspired by "the substantial escalation of economic inequality that I refer to as the 'New Gilded Age'" (Bartels 2008, ix). Though historical data on income can be somewhat limited, Piketty's recent publication has greatly bolstered existing figures, allowing for long-term comparisons of wealth and income distribution, private and public capital, wages and taxation. His work has served as fuel for those looking to call attention to inequality and to depict the early 21st century as a repeat of the Gilded Age.

The concentration of wealth in both Gilded Ages is incredible. In 1900, the top 10 percent of income-earners controlled 40.5 percent of the income share, a portion that wouldn't hit such heights in the postwar period until 1986. The top decile's highest share of income during the long Gilded Age was 44.1 percent in 1916, with an average of about 41 percent from 1900 to 1920. Although this is rather astounding, income inequality continued upward after the end of the Gilded Age, with the top decile's income share peaking at 49 percent in 1928. In fact, this trajectory of the 1920s is actually closer to that of the post-Cold War era than the late Gilded Age. The top 10 percent of earners control of the income share was a fairly level average of about 33 percent from 1945-1980, when the current streak of inequality began. In 1990 the top decile controlled 40 percent of income, a percentage that climbed to 47.6 percent in 2000, and 47.9 percent in 2010, with a summit of 49.7 percent (just barely eclipsing the pre-Great Depression high) in 2007(*All statistics in this paragraph are from* Piketty, 2014b).

When considering the top decile's share of income, recent decades certainly have a lot in common with the early 20th century, but it is the 1920s that truly reflect today's income distribution. Looking closer at the percentile level shows that of the 15 percent jump in the income share belonging to the top 10 percent from 1980-2010, "the bulk of the growth of inequality came from 'the 1 percent,' whose share of national income rose from 9 percent in the 1970s to about 20 percent in 2000 […] an increase of 11 points" (Piketty 2014a, 296). This is also more in line with the income distribution that preceded the crash of 1929 than the earlier Gilded Age, and the top 1 percent controlled a pre-World War II income share high of 23.9 percent in 1928, nearly matched by the postwar high of 23.5 percent in 2007 (Piketty 2014b). In both cases, the trend of heightening income inequality during the end of the Gilded Age that is so frequently compared to recent decades only intensified during the 1920s. The stretching maw of a gap in income and wealth in the Gilded Age and in the last 50 years (but even more so since the end of the Cold War) are easily apparent and similar, if not mirror reflections of one another. Still, pre-Fordist income inequality actually peaked in the 1920s and outside of the Gilded Age, highlighting that the most frequent grounds for the comparison is a bit inaccurate, rarely in-depth and exemplifying the extreme fuzziness of the periodization within Second Gilded Age discourse.

Work in the First Gilded Age: Industrialization and the Modernizing State

The globalizations of each period displayed more similarities than vast inequalities of wealth. The flow of people and goods, specifically international trade with the US and immigration to it, was historically quite high in both Gilded Ages. Despite any similarities in inequality or world-spanning trade and integration, it is the specifics of each globalized era, especially their effects on technology, the organization of labor and working people, that in many ways set each time apart.

The heart of the second wave of the industrial revolution in the United States occurred in the window of 1870-1920, during which new technologies left nearly no aspect of life unchanged. This burgeoning age of steel set the tone for modern industrialization. Three of the most important industries of the time, in many ways indicative of the broader technological shifts of the period and the snaking tentacles of ramifications they had reaching in nearly all social and economic directions, were transportation, communication and energy. The US in the Gilded Age was a central hub of industrial expansion and production, which made it a magnet for labor-seeking immigrants, whose very arrival was in many ways made possible through these technological developments. Labor was standardized and reorganized. Business owners in rapidly-growing industries developed new methods of organizing and managing their holdings, leading to the development of a new managerial class and the modern corporation.

The technological industrialization of the Gilded Age was intimately linked to the evolution of the state, which in response to new technologies, social shifts, the aftermath of the Civil War, violent expansion westward and burgeoning imperialism developed many of its modern institutional trappings. The changes of the period "raised demands for national governmental capacities that were foreign to the existing state structure and that presupposed a very different mode of governmental operation" (Skowronek 1982, 8-9). While many of the institutional shifts of the Gilded Age had (at least on paper) democratizing effects or sought to limit the concentration of power by capital, the newly centralized and expanded power of the federal state was frequently used to bludgeon organized labor and defend business interests and the flow of capital and goods. Hard fought for, the Gilded Age saw some of the first major moves towards centralized, national regulatory structures aimed at bringing the same modernization and professionalization of government via civil service and armed forces reform. Even if it was rare for these new institutional structures to be used against business, the general trend of the period was the (oft haphazard) expansion of the state.

The specifics of each era's globalization, particularly changes in technology and state institutions, greatly impacted the organization of labor. Industrial transformation, while on one hand rendering some of the predominant forms of employment that predated the Civil War (agrarian, usually self-employed or coerced via slavery in the South) untenable, ensured the widespread availability of wage labor, often at massive levels organized by particular industry, even if this work was frequently unstable and was almost always grueling. The majority of the regulatory structures put in place to protect workers came towards the end of the era, and the lasting image of work in the Gilded Age is typically one of incredibly dangerous, arduous industrial labor. Although not everyone was sucked into the new industrial workforce, the technological innovations of the period led to a new understanding of what work meant. The general context of primitive accumulation and the development of a modern, professionalized corporate structure set the stage for an evolving working environment. This, along with specific new technologies, saw the rise of industrialized wage labor, particularly clustered around new technologies which had huge labor demands and typically dystopian conditions.

Primitive accumulation, like David Harvey's theory of accumulation by dispossession (2007), is a process of commodification of public lands and goods, typically by force, that through enclosure removes access to resources, forcing people into wage labor (usually exploiting these newly-commodified goods) in order to subsist. Primitive accumulation was used to transform the economy, pushing preindustrial workers into capitalist wage labor. The key first step in creating a profitable industrial economy:

> "[…] rested first of all on transforming the resources of preindustrial societies- their lands, minerals, animals, foodstuffs, fisheries, rivers, workshops, stores, tools, muscle, and brainpower- into marketable commodities produced by wage laborers who had lost or were losing their access to alternative means of staying alive." (Fraser 2015, 11)

Huge swathes of land ceded by the state to new railways ribboning across the continent, the advent of industrial means of producing existing goods and the economies of scale of behemoth corporate entities made self-sufficiency, especially in the volatile and rapidly-consolidating agrarian sector, next to impossible, giving people little choice in whether or not they entered the wage-labor workforce (for a detailed account of this process, see DeDauw's chapter in this volume). In 1820, 80 percent of American workers were self-employed, and the pressures of primitive accumulation ensured that by 1930 this number would drop to a mere 20 percent (Klein 2007, 137). In the 50 years following the start of the Civil War, the number of Americans working for a wage exploded from 1.5 to 5.5 million (Brecher 2014, 8).

The mass sale of land by the state to railroad companies and speculators made farming for self-sustenance nearly impossible. Although the heady stream of new technologies largely made the agrarian-based society envisioned by many of the founders a fever dream of the past, primitive accumulation meant that even those who did remain in the farming industry were no longer independent, and "by the turn of the century, two-thirds of all agricultural work, North and South, was performed by tenants, sharecroppers, or wage laborers (Fraser 2015, 53)." By the end of the Gilded Age, working in the agriculture sector became the exception to the newly industrialized rule, with only 11.7 percent of the labor force working on farms by 1920 (Dubofsky 1996, 3). In the same year, 45 percent of all employed men worked in mining, construction, transportation or manufacturing (ibid., 3). Most of these jobs either did not exist or functioned entirely differently at the beginning of the Gilded Age.

Many of the new industrial jobs required a mass base of unskilled labor, much of which was filled by the 11.7 million immigrants arriving to the US in the last three decades of the 19th century, only 12 percent of whom were skilled workers (Eisner 2014, 45). While these throngs of unskilled workers were the backbone of this new economy, skilled labor remained critical and between 1880 and 1920 "the proportion of the labor force which can be defined as skilled, irreplaceable, and autonomous held constant at about 14-18 percent" (Dubofsky 1996, 4-5). Though industries based on new technologies like coal, steel and rail were major employers and drove this new economy, they required a diversified field of laborers.

The factories, mills and mines of the Gilded Age demanded a steady flow of labor to function at full capacity, often with a tremendous toll on the workers. The era preceded the creation of the National Labor Relations Board (which would eventually be largely captured by corporate interests by the Second Gilded Age), and many legal protections for workers didn't yet exist or were earned through struggle either late in the period or only on a local level. It is estimated that an average of 35,000 workers were killed and over 500,000 were injured annually between 1880 and 1900, with new industries being particularly dangerous (2,000 coal miners died in work-related accidents each year from 1905-1920, while over 89,000 workers in the rail industry were killed on the job between 1890 and 1920. Over 2.5 million were injured in the same period; ibid., 140). These grisly statistics become only grimmer when considering that one in five of all children under fifteen worked for wages at the turn of century, without including the millions that worked on farms (Fraser 2015, 58).

Industrial work was not only dangerous, but exhausting. "In 1890 the work week usually consisted of six ten-hour days. Thirty years later, skilled workers still toiled 50.4 hours and unskilled workers 53.7 hours every week" (Klein 2007, 139). Real wages grew significantly throughout the Gilded Age, but the spoils were mixed, with skilled laborers collecting the majority of the 10-20 percent gains in wages occurring each decade (ibid., 139). Burgeoning industries hired masses of employees, but cyclical booms and busts meant recurrent spikes of unemployment and slashed wages. In 1877, the year of the 'Great Upheaval', the first mass strike in US history, the longest ever depression up to that point had dropped industrial wages by more than a quarter, and an estimated one million industrial workers were jobless (Brecher 2014, 10). While general gains for workers were achieved in the Gilded Age, flashpoints of intense misery and unemployment punctuated the already grueling norm of newly industrialized labor.

Outside of the breathtaking new nature of work itself, the organizational requirements of many of these new industries was also of utmost importance. Clustered around natural resources or key infrastructure, most new technologies had high labor demands (at least in boom times), meaning that they required mass numbers of workers, most of whom had to be located near the resources and industries on which they worked. This, combined with the evolving corporate structure of the era, which saw waves of modernization, consolidation, and often, vertical integration, meant that many corporations (or extraordinarily rich individuals and their families) essentially controlled either entire 'company towns' centered around industry, or all stages of resource extraction and production associated with any given commodity. This consolidation, coupled with a pressing need for such large numbers of workers, had a massive impact on the coordination of labor actions, allowing for labor organizers to relatively easily (assuming that they spoke 15 European languages and weren't immediately clubbed by a foreman) communicate and coordinate with mass numbers of employees along a company's entire supply chain.

Work in the Second Gilded Age: Flexibility and Globalized Logistics

The Second Gilded Age likely has even closer associations with technological changes than the first. Innovations in information and communication technologies, as well as the transportation sector, serve as pictures of the era, and have sparked discussions about how these new technologies may have ushered in a newly globalized information age that has left nary a facet of social, economic and even political life around the world unchanged. The logistics revolution, a recent occurrence in which the concept of logistics has been applied to the management of every point of the supply chain from design to sale, has in many ways made today's mode of globalized production and mass consumption possible (Bonacich and Wilson 2008, 3).

Like the First Gilded Age before it, these innovations in technology and their knock-on effects have a vital relationship with the arrangements of the state, enabled in many ways through the shift towards deregulation of the neoliberal era, or in other cases due to direct investment by the American state in research and development (for more on the logistics revolution and its relation to the state, see Güse's chapter in this volume). Their effects on labor have been equally meaningful, although the United States' shift from the industrial to financial seat in the globalized economic order enabled by these new technologies has mainly been to the detriment of its workers.

Institutionally, the Second Gilded Age saw a dissolution of many of the regulatory structures and social programs aimed at aiding workers and the poor in the name of free trade and budget hawkery. Nearly every big institutional development in the period was a loss for labor. That said, many of the gains of the postwar period have proven more stoic than expected, and even after 30 years of neoliberal shifts the state and regulatory institutions of today are still significantly more robust than their Gilded Age counterparts. This has enabled a pivot in capital's approach to dealing with labor, from the unabetted violence of the First Gilded Age to legal and institutional constraints of the Second.

As the First Gilded Age saw the transformation of a predominantly independent and frequently agrarian workforce into masses engaged in wage work, most typically within new industries, the Second Gilded Age has seen a shift in the scale of production from the national to the global, with financialization and increasingly precarious work arrangements becoming ever more standard. Some aspects of the organization of labor between the periods appear similar: precarity and instability, a mass reserve of labor via the unemployed and a stream of immigrants, and severe inequality of income, yet work itself has evolved tremendously in the last century, generally for the benefit of workers in developed nations. But just because thousands of laborers do not die on the job every year (in the Global North, at least) does not mean things are currently ideal, and many of the more recent shifts in the Second Gilded Age have negatively affected workers in the United States and actively made labor organizing much more difficult.

The context of neoliberal globalization has generally been detrimental to the American working class. Although both can be overstated, capital's increased mobility and the comparatively geographically limited profile of labor created by the neoliberal institutional order and the technological developments fueling the logistics revolution have created a global 'race to the bottom', where capital flight (or its constant threat) depresses wages in sectors across the board. Globalized production pits workers in direct competition with each other with little geographic boundary as capital searches far and wide for the best rate of return (Coe et al. 2012, 157). Chances of this occurring would be scant if not for the newfound technologies in transport and communications, and the neoliberal deregulations of the last 30 (or more) years that surrounded them. Flexible production, which has largely replaced the model of Fordist mass production and drives the organization of modern supply chains, is staked on utilizing new information technologies to provide close control of the production process while fostering tailored production of goods with input coming from around the world instead of one physically-anchored center of production (ibid., 281-2).

The logistics revolution has shaken the organization of labor in US supply chains, leading to significant drops in employment in the skilled labor (and frequently unionized) positions of port longshoremen and rail employees, while lower-skilled positions of port truckers, seafarers and warehouse workers have all experienced heightened rates of contingency-based employment, declines in unionization, deterioration of wages and working conditions, and the racialization of their workforces despite relative growth in employment (Bonacich and Wilson 2008, 239). Not only are the challenges facing these employees directly tied to the logistics revolution (to say nothing of the laborers in big-box retail on the receiving end of their shipments), the shifts of the logistics revolution have helped to make some of the broader changes in the American labor landscape possible, particularly the deindustrialization that saw manufacturing's share of 30 percent GDP after WWII drop to 10 percent in 2011 and the loss of 3.5 million manufacturing jobs since 2000 due to the advent of globalized, flexible production (Fraser 2015, 235).

Flexibility is a keyword in describing the organization of labor in the New Gilded Age, not just when weighing new methods of global production, but in labor itself. The erosion of manufacturing jobs is an indicator of a significant shift facing today's workers, but it doesn't tell the whole story. The United States is still the world's second manufacturing center, following only China (ibid., 248-9). Labor saving technologies mean that the number of employees needed in industry has shrunk, and those that remain face deteriorating conditions which apply to most sectors in the US and include reduced health coverage and pensions, job security and frequently, wages (Greenhouse 2009, 4). These trends are also intimately fused to the financialization of the neoliberal period, with capital moving from production to finance predicating the growth of certain sectors wrought out of the decline of industry. The finance, insurance, and real estate (FIRE) sector has been the fastest growing in recent years, with profits in the financial sector alone increasing 800 percent between 1980 and 2005 (Fraser 2015, 236).

The flexibility that corporations demand in their production has been extended to their corporate structures via subcontracting and outsourcing or forced upon the workforce via contingent labor. This typically involves using temporary staffing agencies or hiring 'independent contractors' and freelancers to fulfill roles that had previously been assigned to full employees. The percentage of Americans employed in 'alternative work arrangements', defined as "temporary help agency workers, on-call workers, contract company workers, and independent contractors or freelancers," while remaining largely steady from 1995 to 2005, rose from 10.7 percent of the workforce in 2005 to 15.8 percent in 2015 (Katz and Krueger 2016, 2). In addition to growing generally, alternative work arrangements have accounted for the vast majority of new jobs created in the last decade (ibid., 2). Importantly, though much of the charge towards flexibility has occurred in low and middle wage industries, it is increasingly being demanded of high-skilled sectors of the economy as well (Ross 2009, 4-5). The utilization of alternative work arrangements, often on a long-term basis, is a means of fragmenting the labor force and skirting unionization by supplementing the workforce with non-organized subcontractors or temporary workers that are by their nature more difficult to organize. Though today's major corporations are by no means smaller than those of the Gilded Age, subsidiaries and outsourcing certain duties to third parties means even work for big companies is a much more fragmented prospect than labor was in the Gilded Age, where concentrations around industrial clusters and 'company towns' were quite normal.

Much has been said of technology's relationship with work in today's 'information age'. As early as the mid-1990s, tech-focused economists and authors were declaring an end of work due to automation and the unleashing of new information technologies. 25 years later, and events outlined in books like Jeremy Rifkin's *The End of Work* have not quite come to pass. The elimination of work remains a serious and looming threat, but not yet today's reality. The same could be said for the much-discussed online, app-based gig economy, which currently only employs 0.5 percent of Americans (Katz and Krueger 2016, 3). If they haven't quite eliminated work as we know it, tech innovations have certainly played a role in the massive productivity boost that saw the productivity of the average American worker rise 85 percent between 1979 and 2012. Meanwhile, wages have been stagnant, going up a mere 6 percent in the same period, shocking considering the explosive incomes of the top decile of earners during this time (Fraser 2015, 346). American workers are more frequently engaged in the service sector, with the percentage of those working in services going from nearly 65 percent in 1960 to 73 percent in 1980 and climbing ever higher to 84 percent in 2008 (Eisner 2014, 125). Although many unions have pivoted to address these changes, the service industry was typically considered difficult to organize and was void of a strong union presence until recent years.

The demographic makeup of the labor force itself now looks dramatically different than in the original Gilded Age, with the increasing number of working women growing the labor pool significantly. In 1890, female labor participation was just under 20 percent, while in the early 2000s it was close to 60 percent (Henwood 2003, 40). General labor force participation is currently roughly 15 percent higher than in the First Gilded Age, putting further downward pressure on wages (ibid., 40). It is also hard to imagine that there are no longer any jobs in the US, considering the mass immigration of the last decades, and that 16.7 percent of the work force is foreign born, typically working in the service, construction and transportation sectors at higher rates and earning $150 less a week on average than their American-born counterparts (Bureau of Labor Statistics 2016). Work has not yet been eliminated in the United States, but it is increasingly fragmented, subcontracted, service-oriented and demanding higher productivity while withholding rewards of increased earnings, all of which has dealt massive blows to workers and organized labor alike.

Intimately linked to state and institutional arrangements and broad technological and societal developments, the organization of labor in both Gilded Ages marks one of the most significant areas of divergence in the two periods. The palpable sense of change that colored many aspects of the lives of those in each era was just as important to work as it was in other areas, but the lurching ruptures of change in labor and its systemization was wildly different in 1870-1920 than 1990-today. The staggering evolutions of the Gilded Age, rooted in industrial capitalism and its development, witnessed the establishment of truly national markets through new technologies and the evolution of a centralized, national regulatory structure. These late 19th century processes, largely executed on the national scale, have been continued on a global scale as established supply chains and markets have spread over the globe; industrial capital has in many was become subservient to financial capital, and some of the regulatory authority around them have shifted to the transnational level. Conversely, the rise of the financialized service economy since the 1990s has seen an erosion of the manufacturing base of labor initially founded in the First Gilded Age and solidified in the Fordist era, which along with the rise of contingent work and the subcontracting of labor has greatly hampered organized labor's prospects.

Labor Organizing in the First Gilded Age: Consciousness and Mass Mobilization

Like many aspects of the two Gilded Ages, organized labor in both eras might seem similar from a distance. Union density in the US today is generally quite close to where it was in the Gilded Age (Fischer 2010). A meager 10.7 percent of the working population is unionized (Bureau of Labor Statistics 2018). As key differences between the two epochs tend to appear on close inspection, labor is no different. Although their proportional sizes are similar, the labor movements of the Gilded Age and the neoliberal era have little else in common. Organized labor between 1870 and 1920 was ascendant, though it suffered many early growing pains, internal divisions and deadly hostile foes in capital and the state. Union memberships grew significantly throughout the Gilded Age, and organized labor was an important part of a broader coalition of the left and progressives pushing for the expansion of the early regulatory state. Unions since 1990 generally continued a decades-long trend of retreat and hemorrhaging members. Battles with capital and the state occurred, but blood was not shed in the streets as it had been 100 years prior, as increasingly insular unions fought (and typically lost) class war in the neoliberal courts or in individualized collective bargaining disputes. Although some mainstream and large unions have managed to shift their focus in recent years, most have been slow to adjust to an increasingly-antagonistic neoliberal context and broader questions of globalization and deindustrialization, forcing them to be more reactive than proactive. The labor movement in each period will be considered to highlight the divergences between labor in the Gilded Ages.

Although it predates the lofty heights of the US union movement of the postwar period, the Gilded Age was greatly shaped by its burgeoning workers' movement. Unionization levels were generally fairly low (union density grew significantly throughout the period, rising and falling erratically based on the fortunes of major unions before steadying at around 10 percent or a bit higher after 1905 or so), but new labor organizations played a pivotal role in aiding workers in dealing with the new realities of industrialization and the centralization of capital power via increasingly organized and powerful corporations (Fischer 2010). Unions were also an important component of the social-political fabric of the era, wherein a spectrum ranging from the radical left to do-good progressive reformers reshaped society (or at least struggled to). It is hard to imagine the turn of the 20th century without unions.

Though labor was ascendant in the Gilded Age, it was by no means a unified and homogenous block. A tension ran through the union movement in its early history, typified by proponents of 'pure and simple unionism' which focused exclusively on achieving gains and protection at the workplace for members and were generally confined to skilled crafts and trades, and 'industrial unionism', which generally drew from a wider base of unskilled laborers and tended to have broader, often revolutionary goals. The American Federation of Labor (AFL), a federation consisting then almost entirely of craft unions founded in 1886, typically avoided engaging in partisan politics and sought not to disturb the larger capitalist system but to build an accord with employers that benefited workers as well (Dubofsky 1996, 70).

The AFL was exclusionary based on its recruitment of skilled workers, as well as race, ethnicity and gender (ibid., 100). More radical (and significantly less stable in membership) were first the Knights of Labor, open to all, which exploded in membership around successful strikes in the 1880s but was essentially dead by the 1890s; and later the Industrial Workers of the World (IWW) (Brecher 2014, 36). Founded in 1905, the IWW was an anti-capitalist federation of unions focusing primarily on the unskilled, marginalized and depressed, and fought for worker control and revolutionary overthrow of capitalism without discriminating on race, gender or immigration status (ibid., 102). The IWW was significantly more political than the early AFL, and was a kind of big tent of the labor-left, consisting of a number of anarchists and syndicalists and maintaining a complex and often fraught relationship with the Socialist Party of the United States (which saw its heyday in the early 20th century), in which the IWW and Socialists were "sometimes fighting, sometimes cooperating, but seldom understanding each other" (Dubofsky 1969, 96). Although these are general snapshots of the major labor federations of the period, it is worth noting that even at a high point in American union activity, a significant spectrum within the movement existed. It likely goes without saying that the IWW did not smile on trade unions utilizing their high-skill positions to command higher wages, often at the expense of unskilled workers, while AFL members resented radical industrial unions attempting to destroy a labor system in which their skilled position was highly privileged.

Whether carried out by unions of the craft or unskilled, industrial variety, or independently of union organization, labor disputes of the period demonstrate general trends and reflect on the larger societal and economic changes of the Gilded Age. Regardless of the political ideologies underpinning major labor organizations, worker actions were first and foremost a response to the punishing conditions of the era's industrial capitalism. Much of the effectiveness of the pitched labor battles of the day was due to the organization of the economy, which was dependent on interconnected technological infrastructures in transportation and energy and the top-down ownership of mass holdings by individual families and corporations. The 'Great Upheaval' of 1877, the "first great American mass strike," spread from a walkout at a small rail town in West Virginia to a series of violently suppressed general strikes ranging from New York to Texas because it exploded along Baltimore & Ohio Rail's web of holdings throughout a huge swathe of the country (Brecher 2014, 11).

The Great Upheaval set the tone for the era. There were 9,668 lockouts and strikes in the 1880s, with 143 strikes and 140 lockouts involving over 600,000 workers in 1886 alone (1886 was a year of struggle, as workers around the country struck en-masse for the 8 hour day) (Dubofsky 1996, 39). Critically, more than a third of the strikes in this period were spontaneous wildcat strikes not initiated by unions, demonstrating the militant mindset of workers of the Gilded Age (ibid., 39). Major flashpoints, from the Homestead strike in 1892 (steel industry), the Pullman Strike in 1894 (rail), Coeur d'Alene in 1899 (mining), to the Seattle General Strike of 1919, are too many to list comprehensively or in great detail but reflect the key technologies of the period. Mass strikes continued throughout the era, and although many of them ended in crippling defeats for individual unions, each represented broader steps towards building solidarity among workers and belief in direct action as a tool, even among craft unions.

Labor Organizing in the Second Gilded Age: Beleaguered and Bureaucratic

If it's hard to imagine the First Gilded Age without unions, one would be mistaken for not noticing their existence in the second. Union density, trending downward for nearly 40 years, is currently barely in the double digits and is particularly low in the private sector, where only 6.5 percent of the workforce is unionized (Bureau of Labor Statistics 2018). Over 20 percent of American workers were in unions as recently as the early 1980s (Bureau of Labor Statistics 2017). Capital's neoliberal assault on working people, an ever-more globalized economy and the introduction of labor-saving technologies in a number of sectors has taken its toll on organized labor, but American unions' reaction to their admittedly dire circumstances has done little to aid their position. While labor struggles of the Gilded Age exploded into mass strikes because they were understood through a framework of class consciousness and solidarity, unionism since the 1990s has often been about self-preservation and an emphasis on bargaining for a better contract, not universal gains. For many of the major federations of unions in the United States, survival has been the most important goal of the era, understandable given the circumstances but largely leading to concessions.

The mainstream of today's labor movement consists of two major federations of unions, the AFL-CIO (the AFL eventually merged with the former breakaway industrial unionist Congress of Industrial Organizations), which currently has over 12 million members, and Change to Win (CtW), which is significantly smaller and consists of unions who broke away from the AFL-CIO in 2005. Though both groups consist of an array of different unions with varied makeups and characters, they generally embody changes underwent by large labor organizations in the Second Gilded Age. The framework of legal collective bargaining for improved contracts has long been the norm in labor organizing, to the extent that this generally limits union flexibility in organizing and can prevent acts of solidarity, as unions have generally moved away from rank and file organizing towards individual contract negotiations and mainstream political engagement. This has also led to a staggering increase in the size of American union bureaucracy, and the United States now has a higher ratio of union officials to members than any other capitalist society (Flanders 2014).

Both the AFL-CIO and CtW are essentially labor arms of the Democratic Party, which limits their room for political maneuver and prevents substantial criticism, or organizing, against the prevailing political and economic order (Aronowitz 2014, 24). Contract-based collective bargaining has by now come to serve capital more than labor, as it severely limits the choice of actions a union can take in a labor dispute. Nearly 90 percent of union contracts today contain a no-strike clause, blunting the weapon wielded so fiercely in the First Gilded Age (ibid., 73). There were a mere 20 major strikes (with over 1,000 workers) per year between 2000 and 2009, compared to over 350 annually during the height of the 1950s, while strikes are also currently much shorter than in decades past and are generally no longer aimed at halting production or creating industry-wide standards, two of the most important historical reasons for striking (Burns 2011, 11, 16–17). The largest unions in the country, beleaguered after years of decline and a toxic environment for labor organizing, have generally lost the will or ability to meaningfully challenge the status quo. Meanwhile, their entrenchment in bureaucratic, legalistic organizing puts unions and their workers at greater risk during today's hostile legal environment, with the recent Janus Supreme Court case, a "sweeping ruling that dramatically undermines" public-sector unions, being only one of the biggest examples of the danger in relying on the legal system while the Trump administration is tasked with appointing its judges (Matthews 2018).

Significantly less common than a century ago, when labor disputes have occurred since 1990 the results have been mixed at best. Of major strikes against Bridgestone-Firestone, Caterpillar, Staley, and UPS in the mid-1990s, the New York City transit strike in 2005, and the Chicago Teachers Union strike in 2012, only efforts by UPS workers and Chicago teachers could be considered partial exceptions to defeat (Post 2016). In 2014, illustrating labor's impotence in the South, the United Auto Workers famously lost an employee vote to unionize a Volkswagen plant despite Volkswagen's actively supporting this measure (DePillis 2014). Still, 2018's wave of teacher's strikes, which rippled through Arizona, Kentucky, Oklahoma and North Carolina, is reason for some measured optimism. Major unions have lost traction in industries in which they were traditionally powerful. Aligned with changes in the makeup of the economy, unions have recently sought to move away from manufacturing and towards services (including the public sector), which although practical for protecting workers, does ignore some of the key nodes of production and transportation in the newly globalized economy (Bonacich and Wilson, 2008, 21).

Service Employees International Union (SEIU) has nearly doubled its membership since the mid-1990s, and in an encouraging sign that also illustrates current major-union priorities, spends half of its budget on organizing workers while others spend below 5 percent (Greenhouse, 2009, 258). The SEIU's unfortunately unique emphasis on rank and file organizing has proffered strategies outside of the typical contract-bargaining dynamic, and they (along with other more progressive organizations) have been involved with movements like 'Justice for Janitors' and 'The Fight for 15', which seek to organize on a broader level and extend benefits outside of union membership. In addition to the existence of a small minority of labor organizations outside the mainstream that have either more radical demands and tactics or work within social movements to address gaps left by major unions, it does appear that even some larger unions are focusing on shifting gears. This includes "efforts to organize immigrants and contingent service workers, the push to internationalize campaigns against multinational employers, and the flourishing of alternatives to work-site bound unions for highly mobile workers whose needs are not met by traditional locals" (Ross, 2009, 9). Even with some glints of potential in today's union movement, it is hard to be ecstatic about labor's recent legacy or future prospects.

Conclusion

Have the last 30 years been a second coming of the 1890s? Are we living in a Second Gilded Age? The key to the trope of the Second Gilded Age rests in its shallow constitution. From a superficial, big-picture perspective, many aspects of the Gilded Age and the Post-Cold War era are similar. Both periods had heightened levels of inequality, quickening and expanding global interconnections, massive changes in the structure of the state, dynamic new technologies as a driving force, and an organization of labor and working conditions predicated on these changes. It is the details of these shifts that tend to set the periods apart, especially from labor's view. Many of these structural evolutions in each period were going in opposite directions: a growing state and increased regulations in the Gilded Age, 30 years of neoliberal deregulation and attacks on the welfare state in the Second Gilded Age; new technologies that brought industrial mass employment to the fore at the turn of the 20th century, labor saving technologies and a globalized system of production capable of bypassing the US at the turn of the 21st; corporate consolidation, gains for workers, and a rising labor movement in the First Gilded Age, stagnant wages, subcontracting, and subdued unions in the Second. Seeking out the details in the construction of the American labor landscape in both eras highlights critical divergences in both periods, particularly how these grander contexts dictate the room organized labor has had to maneuver at each time, which contributed to the biggest difference within the Two Gilded Ages: the state of organized labor.

Much of what makes the periods similar are broad, frequently cyclical factors that are always occurring to some degree. If having new technologies or a pro-business government in the United States makes these eras the same, then yes, the analogy works, but it then also applies to most of the country's history. It is also possible that the postwar era of the Fordist compromise is frequently overstated in its break with some of the tendencies illustrated in the Gilded Age. It was certainly a shift away from what preceded and followed it, but it is not as though everyone in the period was a unionized worker in a factory, or that income inequality, so high in both Gilded Ages, was fully eradicated in the 1950s (especially when inspected along racial or gendered lines). And if we understand neoliberalism as a political project, its ideological underpinnings had been simmering far earlier than the 1970s. Which is to say that these periodizations, though useful, often overblow similarities and divergences for argumentation and simplicity's sake. Even if some things are generally relatively similar in the periods, labor is a massive exception. On close inspection, the detailed differences between the Two Gilded Ages help explain the gap in each period's labor movement, so if it misses these details, the analogy of Two Gilded Ages is not necessarily wrong, it just is not particularly helpful.

Many of the changes specific to the Second Gilded Age, in addition to contributing generally to mountainous income inequality and the deteriorating conditions in the workplace facing most workers in the US, have specifically hampered the labor movement. An institutional framework stressing deregulation and low transportation costs has shaped global trade in the 'smart economy'. Due to the logistics revolution, a national system of industrial production, which along with providing high levels of employment presented key battlegrounds for struggle and solidarity at sites of resource extraction, production and transportation, has grown to a global scale, extending supply lines outside of the United States, moving away jobs and opportunities to challenge capital with it. New technologies have made workers more productive, and therefore, increasingly expendable. Changes in corporate structures and the favored technique of subcontracting work, even when permanent, fractures the workforce and makes unionization more difficult. Neoliberal institutional shifts made these changes possible, while regulatory 'reform' and the capture of the legal structure of collective bargaining have dramatically limited the scope of organized labor's strategies.

Conversely, and somewhat horrifyingly, these shifts cannot be countered without a strong labor movement. One of the historically strongest outlets for resistance to capital has been decimated, which does not bode well for stopping these trends in the future. Many of the underlying processes that led to these shifts, like globalization and technological innovation, are inherently neutral developments that can either benefit or harm groups depending on how they're executed. Unfortunately, at least to date, they seem to generally be used by capital to suffocate labor and the working class, instead of unleashing potential for positive change. A revitalized workers movement would aid greatly in countering or reversing some of these trends, though that is difficult to imagine at the moment. But if we can take lessons from the decline of labor in the Second Gilded Age, maybe the First can be instructive on how to more effectively challenge capital, even if we cannot replicate any of the contextual factors of the period.

Works Cited

Aronowitz, Stanley (2014). The Death and Life of American Labor: Toward a New Workers' Movement. London: Verso.

Bartels, Larry (2008). Unequal Democracy: The Political Economy of the New Gilded Age. Princeton, NJ: Princeton University Press.

Bonacich, Edna and Wilson, Jake (2008). Getting the Goods: Ports, Labor, and the Logistics Revolution. Ithaca, NY: Cornell University Press.

Bureau of Labor Statistics (2016). "Foreign Born Workers: Labor Force Characteristics- 2015." https://www.bls.gov/news.release/pdf/forbrn.pdf (accessed 23 March 2017).

— (2018). "Union Members 2017." https://www.bls.gov/news.release/pdf/union2.pdf (accessed 20 June 2018).

— (2017). "Union Membership Rate 10.7 percent in 2016." https://www.bls.gov/opub/ted/2017/union-membership-rate-10-point-7-percent-in-2016.htm (accessed 26 March 2018).

Burns, Joe (2011). Reviving the Strike: How Working People Can Regain Power and Transform America. New York, NY: Ig Publishing.

Brecher, Jeremy (2014). Strike! Revised, Expanded and Updated Edition. Oakland: PM Press.

Coe, Neil M., Kelly, Philip F. and Yeung, Henry (2012). Economic Geography: A Contemporary Introduction. Hoboken, NJ: Wiley.

DePillis, Lydia (2014). "Auto Union Loses Historic Election at Volkswagen Plant in Tennessee." Washington Post. https://www.washingtonpost.com/news/-wonk/wp/2014/02/14/united-auto-workers-lose-historic-election-at-chattanooga-volkswagen-plant/ (accessed 17 April 2018).

Dubofsky, Melvyn (1996). Industrialism and the American Worker: 1865–1920. Wheeling: Harlan Davidson.

— (1969) We Shall Be All: A History of the Industrial Workers of the World. Chicago: Quadrangle Books.

Eisner, Marc Allen (2014). The American Political Economy: Institutional Evolution of Market and State. New York, NY: Routledge.

Fallows, James (2016). "How America is Putting Itself Back Together." The Atlantic. https://www.theatlantic.com/magazine/archive/2016/03/how-america-is-putting-itself-back-together/426882/ (accessed 12 March 2018).

Fischer, Claude (2010). "Labor's Laboring Effort." UC Berkley Culture and Humanities Blog. http://blogs.berkeley.edu/2010/09/09/labor%e2%80%99s-laboring-effort/ (accessed 4 April 2017).

Flanders, Jon (2014). "Saving Labor from Itself." Jacobin. https://www.jacobinmag.com/2014/03/saving-labor-from-itself/ (accessed 3 March 2018).

Fraser, Steve (2015). The Age of Acquiescence: The Life and Death of American Resistance to Organized Wealth and Power. New York: Little, Brown and Co..

Greenhouse, Steven (2009). The Big Squeeze: Tough Times for the American Worker. New York, NY: Anchor Books.

Henwood, Doug (2003). After the New Economy. New York: New Press.

Katz, Lawrence and Krueger, Alan (2016). "The Rise and Nature of Alternative Work Arrangements in the United States, 1995-2015." Princeton University and NBER.

http://dataspace.princeton.edu/jspui/bitstream/88435/dsp01zs25xb933/3/603.pdf (accessed 14 March 2017).

Klein, Maury (2007). The Genesis of Industrial America, 1870-1920. Cambridge, MA: Cambridge University Press.

Neate, Rupert (2017). "World's witnessing a New Gilded Age as billionaire's wealth swells to $6tn." The Guardian. https://www.theguardian.com/business/2017/oct/26/worlds-witnessing-a-new-gilded-age-as-billionaires-wealth-swells-to-6tn (accessed 16 April 2018).

Dylan Matthews (2018). "The Supreme Court decision gutting public sector unions, explained." Vox. https://www.vox.com/2018/6/14/17437832/janus-afscme-supreme-court-union-teacher-police-public-sector (accessed 20 June 2018).

Parker, Ashley (2014). "Clinton Calls for Expanding Economic Opportunities." The New York Times. https://www.nytimes.com/2014/05/17/us/politics/clinton-calls-for-expanding-economic-opportunities.html (Accessed May 14 2017).

Piketty, Thomas (2014a). Capital in the 21st Century. Cambridge, MA: Harvard University Press, 2014.

— (2014b). "Technical appendix of the book Capital in the 21st Century: Supplementary Tables and Figures." March 2014. http://piketty.pse.ens.fr/files/capital21c/en/Piketty2014FiguresTablesSuppLinks.pdf.

Post, Charlie (2016). "The Forgotten Militants." Jacobin. https://www.jacobinmag.com/2016/08/the-forgotten-militants/ (accessed 26 March 2017).

Ross, Andrew (2009). Nice Work if You Can Get it: Life and Labor in Precarious Times. New York, NY: New York University Press.

Skowronek, Stephen (1982). Building a New American State: The Expansion of National Administrative Capacities 1877–1920. Cambridge, MA: Cambridge University Press.

Vormann, Boris (2019). City Limits: Sustainable Urban Governance in Planetary Infrastructural Regimes. In Helmut Aust and Anél Du Plessis (eds.). *The Globalization of Urban Governance*, 79–84. New York: Routledge.

Ceteris Paribus Ideology: The Green Economy, Technology and the Future of Work

Lasse Thiele

Following the 2007-9 global economic crisis, international institutions converged on fairly similar strategies of "green growth" to overcome both the recession and mounting ecological problems. The reports presented by the OECD (2011), UNEP (2011) and the World Bank (2012) each frame ecological crises as questions of market failure, seeking to address these with market-based solutions such as carbon pricing coupled with offsetting schemes which allow for economically efficient emissions reductions. These are complemented by further regulatory and fiscal measures to foster "green" markets, including targeted subsidies, public procurement policies and the protection of intellectual property rights to safeguard "green" innovation: The multiple crises are essentially to be solved through a wave of eco-efficient technological development. The overall promise is to internalize the previously externalized social and environmental costs of capitalist development and, through a green-tech miracle, create a win-win-win scenario in which the "triple bottom line" of "people, planet, profit" (UNEP 2011, 363, fn. 28) is wholly positive.

The consistency *across* these studies, together forming an almost standardized conception of a *Green Economy* (GE), is arguably not matched by *internal* consistency. Even the most optimistic scenarios presented in these studies fall short of adequate climate change mitigation as calculated by the Intergovernmental Panel on Climate Change (IPCC), despite being based on these same calculations. The "smooth" transition suggested in these studies appears unlikely to achieve the promised dramatic transformation of the global economy—particularly given that no transformation of underlying social relations is envisioned. Consequently, critical discussion of the *Green Economy* has recently intensified (Dale, Mathai, and Puppim de Oliveira 2016; Kenis and Lievens 2015; R. Smith 2016; Tanuro 2013). Even as the political climate has recently shifted away from the implementation of GE policies under the anti-environmental backlash of right-wing populism, the GE remains the liberal mainstream's most comprehensive response to ecological crises that will persist despite resurgent denialism, and arguably be reinforced by it. This chapter thus seeks to contribute to the critical countercurrent by connecting the critique of the *Green Economy* to parallel current debates about future economic developments, and by probing into its generally underexamined labor market agenda.

The hope for technological fixes to complex crises may be punctured by invoking a parallel debate. Heated discussions are currently taking place again over the prospect of intensified technological unemployment, perhaps even the "end of work," in the context of increasing automation and digital production, sometimes taking ecological matters into consideration. Although *Green Economy* models are so technology- and innovation-focused, they neglect to take up these concerns with the broader social and economic implications of accelerated technological development. From a regulationist perspective, this is a severe deficit: Regulation theory posits that any functioning capitalist formation requires an appropriate *mode of regulation* that comprises a complex set of institutions and norms to mediate social antagonisms and guarantee a degree of social cohesion. This very centrally involves labor relations as mediations of class conflict. Thus, those advocating a technology-led GE should be expected to consider the uncertain fate of labor in their technological utopia.

To shine a light on this matter, this chapter presents a thought experiment: What can we learn about the future of work in a supposed *Green Economy* when triangulating it with two other bodies of theory that reflect on future paths of social and technological development, thereby opening to our view a field of tensions and contradictions? In order to map out the conflicting requirements of capital, labor and ecology with regard to technology, GE models will be confronted with degrowth and accelerationist theory. Both approaches not only illustrate that indeed *there are alternatives* but that these alternatives may in important senses be more reality-oriented, based as each is on a more candid consideration of socio-technological developments. Assuming increasing labor productivity in a resource-constrained world, will income eventually have to be decoupled from (shrinking) employment? What about the trade-off, from an ecological viewpoint, between labor efficiency and resource efficiency? Beyond capitalist relations, is a "green" high-tech post-work economy realizable?

Will scarcity due to ecological constraints or abundance through increasing technological capacity emerge as the dominant tendency?

Drawing preliminary conclusions from this confrontation, I will argue that questions of employment and technology are particularly illustrative of the shortcomings of hegemonic *Green Economy* models as viable proposals for 21st-century societies. An engagement with current debates on the future of labor serves to make clear how the GE ignores the complexity of actual and potential social-ecological developments. Institutional proposals for *green growth* generally follow a technocratic, sector-by-sector approach to environmental sustainability within the broader tradition of neoliberalism. These proposals, then, are simply tacked on to an idealized version of the current global free-trade regime. They express what I would call a *ceteris paribus ideology*, rooted in a deeply technocratic worldview that posits the economy as a realm separate from politics or society at large. Consequently, and implausibly, they assume that social relations and the lifestyles they spawn will remain constant during the transition to a *Green Economy*, such that deep changes to economic infrastructure will be achieved while leaving other social spheres, and even important structures and sectors of the economy proper, essentially untouched.

In the following, this study will first dissect the perspective on labor provided by GE studies before introducing the current debate on technology and the rivaling perspectives of degrowth and accelerationism. The field of possibilities and tensions opened up by the triangulation of these three perspectives will then be sketched out, followed by an assessment of this conflictual constellation from the perspective of regulation theory and, finally, a summary and outlook.

Labor in the *Green Economy*: Dominant models and empirical evidence

In this section, I will first outline the positions on labor issues presented in the hegemonic *Green Economy* models before problematizing their stance by reference to recent empirical evidence of labor conditions in emergent "green" sectors. The OECD, the World Bank and UNEP all display a fairly placid attitude towards labor market questions. The OECD argues that only small parts of the workforce will have to adjust at all during the transition to "green" growth (2011, 91). This economic restructuring is to happen according to the familiar neoliberal credos of efficiency and flexibility: "Labor market policies need to be flexible enough to facilitate the movement of workers" (ibid., 51), the latter effectively featuring as chess pieces to be moved across the board of the economy. In the same vein, workers' well-being is to result from market dynamics more than protective policies: "[M]oderate employment protection and strong product market competition are important supports for vigorous job creation." (Ibid., 95) "Green" training and education programs are recommended to address skill shortages, and labor market reforms need "flanking measures" to protect workers "and their families" from "excessive insecurity or inequality." (Ibid., 95–96) Beyond some "adjustment difficulties" for workers (ibid., 90), the institution does not foresee significant trouble.

Indeed, if there is a sense of caution in these recommendations, it is mainly concerned with overly *enthusiastic* hopes for green tech as a massive jobs engine: In its 2015 follow-up study to monitor progress, the OECD reaffirms that "[g]reen growth is unlikely to generate a windfall gain in jobs or a sharp increase in labor market churn." (OECD 2015, 24) In other words, from a macroeconomic perspective, nothing much is expected to happen. The challenge is technical: moving a few jobs from "brown" to "green" industries in as efficiently a manner as possible. The World Bank's (2012, Chapter 4) assessment is very similar, arguing that "odds are that the impacts will be quite moderate" (ibid., 92) and admonishing that potential positive labor market effects hinge on the removal of "labor market rigidities" (ibid., 94); i.e., the completion of neoliberal structural adjustment to ensure maximum flexibility for employers, which is framed as the primary means to counter unemployment. Otherwise, the World Bank worries primarily about short-term skill shortages and concludes that "it is vital to invest in human capital to accelerate growth and to green growth." (Ibid., 102)

UNEP is even quite upbeat, displaying the sort of enthusiasm the other institutions attempt to curb by proclaiming in the introduction that "the greening of economies has the potential to be a new engine of growth, a net generator of decent jobs and a vital strategy to eliminate persistent poverty." (2011, 16) Again, the challenge is framed as a technical one, a matter of devising policies to "close the current skills gap and anticipate the future workforce needs." (Ibid., 572-573) The sectoral analysis in the 600+ pages of the report provides a somewhat more nuanced picture, with the skeptical notes, however, often eliminated or downplayed in the chapter summaries. While agricultural jobs in the Global South are projected to grow considerably with the adoption of more labor-intensive and ecologically sensitive technologies, the prospects for many other sectors, such as fisheries and water provision, involve massive job losses. In yet other sectors, labor market implications of greening are either expected to be relatively neutral, as in the energy sector, or remain uncertain, as in the building sector. Bold projections of a 10 percent increase in employment through the greening of both the waste management and the transportation sectors are undermined by admission to incomplete or distorted data sets.[1] A close reading of the report, thus, already severely compromises the introduction's win-win-win enthusiasm. After all, the prevalent position emerging from these pages aligns the report with the OECD's and the World Bank's languid stance, based as it is on the same neoclassical equilibrium economics—which the authors of one chapter employ to justify their judgment that "[o]verall, a green economy cannot be expected to create or destroy net jobs in the long run." (Ibid., 468)

Interestingly, UNEP had previously co-commissioned a report on "green jobs" with several global labor and employers' organizations (Renner et al. 2008). Advocating a *just transition*, this report displays a decidedly less cheerful tone, acknowledging both that "green" jobs, particularly in "developing" countries, are often in informal sectors with extremely hazardous labor conditions (as in scrap recycling) and that there are several structural obstacles to "greening," including intellectual property rights, entrenched business interests and increased pressures through financialization and international competition. A "purely market-driven process" (ibid., 24) is not seen as a sufficient strategy to achieve a transition.

What little of this skepticism and ambivalence made the cut for UNEP's glossy *Green Economy* report was toned down considerably, particularly with regard to the structural obstacles to a "just" transition, which concept is only rarely mentioned at all.[2] A decade later, the UNEP website still contains a "green jobs" portal, but it contains little more than a summary of the report, a link to the full report—and, ironically, given the basic

1 See UNEP (2011, 318/397). The other job estimates are taken from the respective sectoral chapters of the report.

2 References to other passages of the 2008 study (which is also cited in the OECD report) in the UNEP report notwithstanding.

silence of all these reports on the role of organized labor, a broken link to a "further resource" titled "Strengthening trade union participation."[3]

Tax reforms constitute another common theme throughout the three reports. The general thrust of these arguments is towards a shift from taxation of "goods" such as labor to that of "bads" such as pollution, which is supposed to favor job creation by cheapening the cost of labor (OECD 2011, 39, 92, 97; UNEP 2011, 559). While the OECD holds that these are to be implemented in "ways that do not make the distribution of income less equal" (2011, 40) it is difficult to see how the "lowering of social security contributions" that UNEP (2011, 559) explicitly advocates in return for carbon taxation could not have precisely such an inegalitarian impact, given that carbon taxes are generally envisioned as flat taxes on consumption and thus clearly regressive vis-à-vis (employers') social security contributions. Ironically, this strategy would also mean that social security provisions depend on ongoing carbon emissions. Could there be any more effective way of *installing* politically a trade-off between social and environmental objectives—a trade-off which to debunk as a "myth" is the stated objective of UNEP's (2011, 628) *Green Economy* study?

A recent update from the OECD is still on message in terms of the *Green Economy*'s labor market agenda. The challenges of job losses from productivity-increasing "green" technology and the "megatrends" of digitalization and automation are noted in passing (OECD 2017, 13, 16, 18), but with sufficiently "flexible" labor markets, no harm is projected for overall employment (tellingly, the new report still relies on job projections for 2030 from the 2008 ILO/UNEP study).

It should be noted that proposals for a *Green New Deal* issued by several think tanks in response to the 2007-9 crisis, in line with their generally more neo-Keynesian and social-democratic outlook, focused on job creation more strongly (Barbier 2010; Bowen et al. 2009; Green New Deal

---

3 Cf. http://web.unep.org/about/majorgroups/green-jobs (accessed November 30, 2017) Indeed, the project referred to here did exist from 2007-2009 (cf. http://web.unep.org/about/majorgroups/strengthening-trade-union-participation-international-environmental-processes-joint-unep-%E2%80%93, accessed November 30, 2017), but this "participation" was largely limited to union involvement in the drafting of policy recommendations including UNEP's Green Economy study, which, as explained above, has little substantive to say about labor issues. During the former period, UNEP briefly endorsed the Keynesian notion of a Green New Deal before shifting to the more market-oriented Green Economy concept (Tienhaara 2014).

Group 2008; Pollin et al. 2008). But this was mainly a short- to medium-term plan to jump-start the economy and lead it out of the recession. Inspired by 1930s *New Deal* policies, the idea was to create a sizable number of jobs through massive public investment in infrastructure and incentive schemes to enable the greening of industrialized economies. While the overall impacts of this on economic infrastructure and environmental track records were supposed to be long term, the extra jobs weren't necessarily. And even the study that most ardently makes the case for short-term job creation through green stimulus measures (Pollin et al. 2008) admits that full implementation of its recommendations would fall far short of eliminating unemployment; moreover, while it advocates the creation of two million new jobs in the U.S., it does not consider how many jobs in other sectors would be lost as a consequence of these measures, only claiming that investment in green industries would yield higher job gains *relative* to the same amount invested in fossil fuels (similarly: Bowen et al. 2009, 10). Generally, the *Green New Deal* literature is just as fixated on the traditional ideal of income for full-time work as the more neoliberal GE proposals; it simply envisions a greater (temporary) involvement of the state in the labor market.

Finally, the GE reports tend to treat "green jobs" as a black box: They are jobs, and so they must be desirable. The most substantial argument to this effect is that many "green" activities such as building retrofits and installation and maintenance of renewable energy facilities are inherently local and thus less subject to erosion through global competition (Pollin et al. 2008, 11; Renner et al. 2008). Meanwhile, large-scale offshoring of "green" manufacturing jobs to low-wage locations has long been observable (Boewe and Schulten 2013; Mattera 2009) and arguably, the free-trade agenda pushed in *Green Economy* studies is unlikely to halt such trends. Either way, the *quality* of all these jobs in a social democratic sense—decent pay, job security, good working conditions—is hardly subject to systematic attention, except in a few passages of the UNEP study which point to "serious shortfalls in decent work" (UNEP 2011, 355) in the not-yet-green building sector and admonish that "[i]mproving labour conditions in the waste sector is imperative" (ibid., 293), repeatedly emphasizing that formalization of the sector would be an important step. Even these more sober passages, however, are largely restricted to concerns about physically hazardous working conditions in these yet-to-be-greened sectors.

But even in the newly emerging "green" sectors, as Littig (2013) argues, job quality is quite heterogeneous, many jobs are precariously dependent on subsidies whose long-term availability is uncertain—and what "good" jobs are available tend to be captured by men. A study of the emergent "green" economic landscape in the U.S., commissioned by organizations generally sympathetic to the GE idea, found very low levels of unionization, considerable anti-union activity on the part of employers and wages ranging from poverty-level to fairly high, concluding that "the green economy is not always a humane economy." (Mattera 2009, 34) Lately, the picture is still mixed, with organized labor now trying to get a foot in the door of newly emerging renewable energy branches such as offshore wind in the U.S. (Rosen 2016).

On the face of it, the circumstance that "green" sectors have emerged in the anti-union climate of the neoliberal era is taking its toll, which may explain resistance to "greening" policies on the part of labor constituencies in older industries with a more solid tradition of trade unionism. The rapid growth (and subsequent implosion as political support waned and international competition increased) of the German solar energy industry, for example, relied massively on the availability of specifically politically enabled low-wage labor without job security (Boewe and Schulten 2013). Likewise, the country's wind energy industry shows high rates of temporary and subcontracted work, leading analysts to conclude that its overall labor conditions fall short of the standards established in older industrial branches (Lenz et al. 2017; Meisner 2012). The empirical track record, in other words, is sketchy. But there are also deeper structural forces that complicate the prospects for "green" jobs, to which we will now turn.

But Who Needs Labor Anyway?

The general debate around the potential for technological development to obviate the need for labor is old, famously reflected in the acceptance of *Luddism* into dictionaries as a synonym for opposition to technological change following the 19th-century Luddite uprisings ("Luddism," n.d.). These were an early expression of the contradiction, under capitalism, of labor-saving technology to imply, by tendency at least, immiseration of workers. Marx's recently re-excavated *Fragment on Machines*, written in 1858, anticipates a development in which increasingly "general social knowledge has become a direct force of production." (Marx 2014, 64) As science and machinery displace labor in an endless quest for productivity, capitalist competition ultimately renders not only the labor theory of value but indeed capital itself obsolete—"capital thus works towards its own dissolution as the form dominating production." (Ibid., 57)

The debate over automation and the future of labor again raged in the post-war era of Fordist prosperity, when African-American factory worker and revolutionary Marxist James Boggs anticipated the attendant rise of a surplus population, arguing forcefully that in the new "Age of Abundance," a workless society was eminently possible and that, as "productivity can no longer be the measure of an individual's right to life" (Boggs 1963, 46), income needed to be decoupled from work. Eventually, a commission mandated by U.S. President Johnson brooded over the issue and recommended a guaranteed minimum income to cushion the apprehended blow to economic security (cf. Autor 2015, 3–4). While such measures have not been implemented, the growth of surplus populations over the past half-century has induced significant re-orderings in the global political economy (Clover 2016).

The rapid technological progress in closely connected fields such as machine learning/artificial intelligence and robotics over the past decade revitalized this debate once more and led to widespread discussions on whether technological unemployment may drastically increase in the near future (Autor 2015; Brynjolfsson and McAfee 2014; Frase 2016; Frey and Osborne 2013; Kim et al. 2017; Mason 2015; Rifkin 2014). While skeptics rightly emphasize countervailing forces to such an outcome under capitalism, they still acknowledge the polarizing effect of automation on job markets. What jobs are available to everyone outside a narrow spectrum of well-paid professionals are increasingly service jobs providing little economic security: "a world of domestic servants." (J. E. Smith 2017; cf. Rotman 2015; Butollo and Kalff 2017) While not a *law*, technological unemployment certainly is a capitalist *tendency* to be dealt with, whether by socially progressive (decoupling of income from work) or regressive means (extension of low-paid, insecure forms of employment capable of undercutting machines). *Green Economy* models are centrally premised on the possibility and desirability of accelerated technological progress to overcome ecological constraints to material prosperity. The envisioned decoupling of economic growth from environmental impacts requires dramatic and unprecedented rates of technological advances (for a critical statistical illustration, see Jackson 2009, Chapter 5). In their techno-enthusiasm, the green capitalists echo—and are in turn echoed by—the most cheerful of participants in the automation debate. Unlike the literature cited above, however, they have little to say about large-scale impacts of such developments on patterns of employment and social reproduction, always leaning towards *ceteris paribus* (all else being equal) assumptions.[4]

In the following, in order to broaden the *Green Economy* debate and emphasize downplayed tensions and contradictions, the GE position will be confronted with two theoretical and political projects that understand technological development to be a fundamentally political question and articulate different and in some respects diametrically opposed strategies to tackle social and ecological problems in combination. The names established for these projects over the past few years are *degrowth* and *accelerationism.* For clarity of argument and brevity's sake, my accounts of both will necessarily be somewhat simplified and partial.

Degrowth

Degrowth, for sure, denotes a wildly heterogeneous set of ideas and strategies united by their rejection of capitalist growth societies "as we know them." To clarify the understanding of degrowth used in this essay, I will mainly draw on the rather coherent, anti-capitalist exposition provided by the editors of a recent anthology, *Degrowth: A Vocabulary for a New Era* (D'Alisa et al. 2015).[5] They define degrowth as a project to understand

4 The UNEP report makes reference to historical automation-induced job losses in manufacturing (2011, 247) and the potential for these in agriculture (ibid., 54) and even acknowledges that the same may be expected from measures to green the industrial sector through efficiency improvements—but this would likely be more than offset due to the ensuing rebound effect (ibid., 266–267). Of course, this in turn implies higher resource consumption that undoes the aggregate "greening" effect of the technological improvement: the classical ecological catch-22 of efficiency rebounds. This passage hints at the general dilemma of trying to reconcile capital accumulation, ecological sustainability and full employment. The UNEP/ILO/IEO/ITUC study later disregarded by UNEP, meanwhile, at least refers to the "dual challenge of environmental impact and unemployment" (Renner et al. 2008, 6) in an economy with increasing output and labor productivity and even cites "proposals to reduce individuals' work time in order to share available work better." (ibid.) As previously noted, the OECD (2017) also recently acknowledged the issue without giving much weight to its implications.

5 See also Latouche (2009), Schmelzer and Passadakis (2011) and Exner et al. (2008).

human experience as a qualitative matter which cannot be captured by a capitalist imaginary in which gross domestic product (GDP) reigns supreme and technological progress is equated with social. Not placing faith in purely technology-based solutions to environmental crises or the possibility to redeploy capitalist technology for progressive purposes, "[d]egrowth was thrown explicitly as a 'missile word' to *re-politicize* environmentalism." (Ibid., 9, emphasis in original) The authors agree that counter-strategies should be plural, rising from the grassroots and reflecting a number of concerns instead of the singular capitalist matrix of economic growth: An orientation towards democratic management of the (social and "natural") commons, for example, to reflect social and environmental concerns, as well as a recognition of the centrality of care work, so dramatically undervalued by capitalist logic, production oriented towards use values and just distribution of (scarce) material goods through mechanisms that decouple income from work. Against unsustainable overconsumption, a post-capitalist degrowth society should be characterized by *sufficiency*—the notion that "enough is enough"—, prosperity measured through free time rather than material wealth and a general deceleration of life. Against heteronomy and ubiquitous competition, degrowth aims for autonomy and *conviviality*, thus ensuring collective self-limitation. All of these goals imply, in certain cases, a shift to more labor-intensive technologies to replace ecologically unsustainable and/or inherently centralized and therefore heteronomous ones.

To summarize in simplified terms for the graphic representation in Figure 1 below: Degrowth in this understanding takes an anti-capitalist, techno-skeptical position with a particular focus on ecological restraint and decentralization. Its position on labor is somewhat ambivalent: Significant reductions in labor time and a just redistribution of work are envisioned, but, under conditions of general emancipation, self-determined work may be preferred to resource-intensive, labor-saving technology.

Accelerationism

Unsurprisingly, given its candid label, accelerationism takes a very different angle. Broadly speaking, "[a]ccelerationism sees the intensification of certain tendencies in late capitalist society as a way to escape its gravitational orbit, thereby allowing for a 'repurposing' of the very material infrastructure of capitalism itself, to universally emancipatory ends." (Gardiner 2017, 31) Accelerationism thus seeks to recover the Enlightenment understanding of modernization as an emancipatory process and represents an explicitly "Promethean" approach, stressing the potential of high-tech development to fulfill human needs and desires, now held back only by the fetters of capitalist social relations. I will here confine myself to the "neo-rationalist" variant of left accelerationism, as opposed to both the "libidinal" variant indulged by French poststructuralists and the more nihilistic, pro-capitalist strand associated with Nick Land (for these distinctions, see Cunningham 2015; Gardiner 2017; Mackay and Avanessian 2014), and to its most notable proponents, Nick Srnicek and Alex Williams, who outlined their theoretical and political agenda first in the much-discussed *Manifesto for an Accelerationist Politics* (2014) and then fleshed it out in *Inventing the Future* (2016). Srnicek and Williams share the general accelerationist optimism regarding the "repurposing" of capital's technoscape for universal emancipation, arguing that "the contemporary left should reclaim modernity, build a populist and hegemonic force, and mobilize towards a post-work future" (2016, 69) in order to overcome the limitations of its dominant horizontalist, localist "folk politics" practices. Insofar, their strategy has been judged by critics of accelerationism (Cunningham 2015; Turner 2016) as a more grounded, less spectacular and "heretical" Marxist enterprise than the other, more politically affirmative strands.

All of this is based on the assumption that processes of automation—the necessary consequence of labor-saving capitalist competition—are now, *by tendency*, producing an ever-growing surplus population that cannot be profitably employed (at least not under conditions of "decent" work). This accelerationist agenda is therefore grounded in a significant political-economic tendency which elevates the struggle against wage dependency and for the decoupling of income from work to political primacy. It is not a coincidence that Marx's *Fragment on Machines* (2014) with its emphasis on capital's ultimate self-destruction through the expulsion of "living" labor is a key reference point for contemporary accelerationists.

As an explicitly materialist project, accelerationism does recognize the centrality of environmental crisis and of climate change in particular. Both the *Manifesto* and Mackay and Avanessian's (2014) introduction to a much-cited anthology name this as one of the major challenges by way of introduction, but neither cares to return to the issue in their main argumentation. Besides, the accelerationist position is somewhat indebted to the

Autonomist Marxist strand that assumes "immaterial" labor in the increasingly digitized economy to be a dominant tendency, meanwhile underestimating the stubborn materiality of this high-tech infrastructure, which very much includes the "green" cities supposedly positioned at the cutting edge of environmentally focused innovation and consumption (see the contributions by Zimmermann and Kalt to this volume).

Ecological crisis always looms in the background but is never quite confronted analytically in this literature. The Promethean faith in technology to solve such problems resembles that of *Green Economy* enthusiasts, with the crucial difference that the accelerationists glimpse this possibility *beyond*, not within a capitalist framework. Once the Gordian knot of the relations of production is untied, so the argument goes, this liberation of the forces of production (i.e., workers and technology) carries nearly unlimited potential for sustainable development. This corresponds not just to the Marx of the *Fragment on Machines*, but to the more canonical Marx of the preface to *A Contribution to the Critique of Political Economy*.[6] But as if to cast doubt and confusion about their own optimism, Srnicek and Williams (2016, 145–153) chose to cite, as one successful example of repurposing, the German *Energiewende* (energy transition), arguably a contradictory implementation of green-*capitalist* logic with very mixed results (Sander 2016). McKenzie Wark's critique of the *Manifesto*, more in the spirit of degrowth, consequently expresses skepticism regarding the repurposing of technologies that are fully based on the increasing substitution of energy and natural resources for labor, noting drily that there is "not enough planet left" for capitalist relations to be simply obviated through a technology-driven complete expulsion of labor (Wark 2013, n.p.). To their credit, in their response to their critics Srnicek and Williams frankly admit their analytical weakness regarding climate change (2016, 190).

6 "At a certain stage of development, the material productive forces of society come into conflict with the existing relations of production ... From forms of development of the productive forces these relations turn into their fetters." (Marx 1977, n.p.)

Mapping the Field of Tensions

Figure 1 maps the triangle of positions created in the encounter between *Green Economy* models, degrowth and accelerationism. Accelerationism and the GE appear united in their technological optimism, with degrowth taking a decidedly more skeptical stance. Degrowth and the GE, then, move ecological constraints to the center of their vision of the future, while accelerationism entertains a vision of general abundance once the fetters of capitalist relations are shaken off. Finally, degrowth and accelerationism are allied in their rejection of capitalism and their desire for a post-work society, while the GE follows a there-is-no-alternative path and aims for a market economy with "conventional" full employment. In other words, the Green Economy wants to make economic development sustainable, accelerationists want to free it from its capitalist context in their impatience for a future characterized by accelerated *human* development, and degrowth advocates tend to be disgusted with the "development" trope altogether (which indicates that this position is furthest removed from any position of hegemony, its lack of political viability and its deliberate positioning *apart from* real economic tendencies probably its greatest weaknesses vis-à-vis the accelerationist project).

A further attempt at schematic contextualization may be helpful in order to highlight the curious positioning of the GE in this field. In his *Four Futures*, Peter Frase (2016), assuming that automation will make capitalism as we know it untenable in the medium run, sketches out idealized potential trajectories of future social development according to a two-dimensional matrix: egalitarian versus inegalitarian/hierarchical social relations, and conditions of scarcity—due mainly to ecological crisis—versus abundance. The pair equality/scarcity is referred to as "socialism," inequality/scarcity as "exterminism," equality/abundance as "communism" and inequality/abundance as "rentism." The accelerationist scenario can clearly be identified with the "communist" scenario. Degrowth could be said to come closest to "socialism" in this matrix, although most degrowthers would disagree with the statist organizational model assumed by Frase.

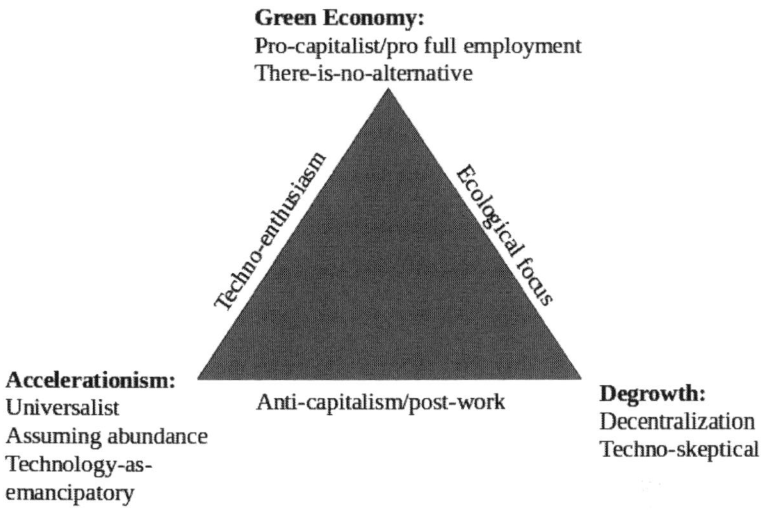

Fig. 1: The Triangle of Possibilities (or, The Field of Tensions)

The *Green Economy*, by contrast, seems to fall outside the matrix altogether. Despite the fact that this approach relies heavily on rapid technological development to overcome ecological constraints, and despite the tendency for technological development under capitalism to raise labor productivity, its proponents mostly refuse to even consider the notion of unemployment-inducing automation that could render capitalist survival problematic. Mirroring capitalist ideology more generally, GE models are based on the general assumption of economic scarcity, here notably including ecological constraints, which is translated into abundance (or "welfare") through rising productivity and output, here complemented by management of natural resources to maximize future yields. The prospect of "rentism" arising from the displacement of labor—i.e., a constellation in which surplus largely arises directly from ownership of means of production rather than exploitation of "living labor," with the attendant problems of securing effective demand and guaranteeing social reproduction—is largely ignored. Such broader considerations appear to fall under the rubric of "indirect" effects on labor markets, which are considered too complex to be included in mathematical models, and therefore effectively disregarded.

The constellation presented here evokes a number of questions—and implies a set of tentative answers. Some are rather speculative at this point, such as the general, and generally unpredictable, question of present and future technological frontiers and their absolute limits. One may also consider the ecological specification of this question: How efficient, how "green," how sustainable can such technology possibly be? Or, mapped onto Frase's matrix: Will the sum total of technological possibilities and ecological constraints ultimately mean abundance or scarcity? And in how far are the results conditioned by social relations? As outlined above, degrowth, accelerationism and the *Green Economy* all provide different assessments on these points.

We also find "objective" goal conflicts, however. One significant choice relates to the issue of automation and the fate of human labor—in other words, the specter of a "green rentism" in which few own the hyper-efficient machines while much of the population is unemployed and without income. Trying to reconcile capital accumulation, full employment *and* ecological sustainability, the old safety valve against technological unemployment—simply ramping up production levels so that total output growth outruns or at least equals productivity growth—is no longer applicable, as it would immediately undermine the ecological imperative. While it is impossible to calibrate the outcome precisely through political measures, a fundamental choice or trade-off, embodied in institutional structures, is involved here. Jason Moore (2016) emphasizes that the rise of capitalism historically entailed a paradigm shift from land (or resource) to labor productivity. The priority was no longer to obtain the maximum utility from a given input of resources (even if it took more work), but to produce a given output with the least possible amount of human labor (even if that required a higher expenditure of energy or material resources). The political question presently would be: Which of the two should be maximized—or how should they be balanced?

Importantly, in a capitalist context, this choice is heavily constrained through the capitalist value form. Resource productivity cannot be directly and systematically maximized as it fundamentally relates to *use* values—whereas labor productivity directly impacts the value, and thus the *exchange* value, of a given commodity. The latter remains the measuring rod of economic activity in a capitalist economy.[7] There is, thus, a general selectivity

7 Of course, measures that increase resource productivity can be profitable under ceteris paribus (all else being equal) conditions. But wherever they negatively impact labor productivity, this profitability is quickly reversed.

to technological development under capitalism, in which the primary criterion is exchange-value maximization; under these conditions, the conceivable frontiers of "green" technological development—the most resource-efficient and non-polluting technical solutions for any particular task—are not immediately accessible. Instead, each technology must proceed through a series of profitability filters, including those at the pre-market stage (where initial investment hinges on expected returns) and, later, on product markets (where competition from cheaper alternatives potentially reduces the market share of the "greenest" option). Of course, each increase in labor productivity implies that additional economic activity—which inevitably entails further resource consumption, directly or indirectly—is required, or else overall employment will decrease. To the degree that resource productivity is to be elevated into a significant criterion, this has to be done through (state) interventions at each stage directed *against* the logic of capital, which under capitalism are ultimately limited by the sine-qua-non condition of general profitability. This explains why a central green-capitalist strategy, the pricing of resource consumption to fully account for the associated negative externalities ("taxing bads not goods"), has so far never been seriously implemented: It would raise (re)production costs to a degree that, while arguably forcing firms into more resource-efficient processes, would undermine profitability, and any move in this direction has been fiercely resisted by capital.

To complicate matters even further at the macroeconomic level, rising labor productivity leads to lower commodity values. Under competitive conditions, this means that less and less surplus value can be realized per unit of output. The result is a dynamic of ever-rising levels of production forced onto capitalist firms just to realize modest rates of accumulation (cf. Clover 2016, Chapter 7). Hence, even when shifting from a labor/employment perspective to the viewpoint of capital, the "crowding out" of labor from production is in itself an ecologically disastrous tendency.[8]

8 Many "immaterial" services—particularly in the financial sector—ultimately still depend for their viability on the "traditional" exploitation of surplus value through very material production in other sectors. In order to outdo the expansionary dynamic outlined above, the speed of effective dematerialization per unit of such production in a capitalist Green Economy—which after all aims to sustain economic growth while reducing overall material throughput—would have to be breathtaking. It would soon require what ecological

These general contradictions are reflected in both degrowth and accelerationist thought, although not always explicitly. The degrowth proposal points towards maximizing resource productivity while counting on overall "socially necessary" labor time to sink in spite of this, since many of the factors shaping social necessity under capitalism would fall away and the world of "professional services" and "domestic servants" would dissolve. Accelerationists are adamant about the "post-work society" while inversely counting on resource productivity to improve as production is reoriented towards use values. Both of these answers may appear conveniently optimistic; while their political priorities diverge, the optimism in each case is grounded in the potential unlocked—and the pressure alleviated—when abolishing the capitalist value form. The leap implied here is primarily *political* rather than technological. Again, the resource-versus-labor-productivity issue cannot be settled in theory, but the problem must be recognized as political, as both approaches do. Whether or not the accelerationist dreams of material abundance despite ecological constraints come to pass, for example, in a post-capitalist accelerationist scenario, this trade-off could in principle be negotiated politically rather than being determined by the sheer systemic necessity of capital accumulation.

The *Green Economy* approach, meanwhile, loath to entertain such heresies, largely skips over this essential political question while selectively addressing the ecological—and putting all faith into solving both through the answer to the technological question, viewed almost in isolation. This applies to the labor dimension of the issue, but is also symptomatic of GE models in general: Within capitalism, the requirements of capital structure the field of political decision-making, with the need to maintain employment as an attendant constraint. The green-capitalist argument consequently hinges on the uncertain possibility of simultaneously increasing labor *and* resource productivity, indefinitely into the future to guarantee capital accumulation under ecological constraints, while *also* providing full employment. As this is unlikely, but resource productivity must still be improved to achieve environmental objectives, sinking labor productivity is only imaginable if surplus value across the economy can be increased otherwise, most likely through harsher wage depression. A "seriously" green

economist Herman Daly (1991, passim) sardonically called an "angelized" economy—an absurd scenario in which the materiality of human existence is somehow suspended through "green" technology.

(i.e., effectively ecologically constrained) capitalist economy therefore seems to imply, by tendency, cut-throat neoliberalism—and chronic instability, as such solutions can only work temporarily. Wages can hardly be pushed permanently below the amount needed for social reproduction and problems of effective demand quickly arise. The way out envisioned by the OECD (2017) is a further shift of employment towards services—under what working conditions, it does not say, but the concurrent demand for "flexible" labor markets and the warning against "wage rigidities" (ibid., 17) suggests that a cut-throat *Green Economy* scenario is not implausible. Indeed, it may be a more realistic variation of the "green rentism" theme, one in which the tendency towards technological unemployment is tempered, once more, by low-paid and insecure forms of employment.

A Green Mode of Regulation?

The prospect of intensified wage depression indicates that just because "we" almost all stand to benefit from limiting climate change and other ecological crises *all else being equal*, this does not mean that there would be no severe social conflicts to be mediated in a hypothetical green-capitalist configuration—particularly since all else never was and is not going to be equal. Some such conflicts and structural contradictions highlighted in the previous section will now be assessed from a regulationist viewpoint.

The necessity of social mediation is central to regulation theory: "A mode of regulation is a set of mediations which ensure that the distortions created by the accumulation of capital are kept within limits which are compatible with social cohesion within each nation." (Aglietta 2015b, 391) This extends far beyond the state and its regulatory function in the narrow sense, but the state is centrally involved, as demonstrated by historical Fordist modes of regulation (see Güse and Braneck in this volume).[9]

In the abstract, the class antagonism between those who own means of production and those who do not certainly persists. Organized interests

9 It should be noted that the regulation approach remains methodologically nationalist and Eurocentric, and the observations in this sector are biased towards a Northern perspective. The implications of the Green Economy agenda for labor in Southern contexts deserve separate attention and probably require different analytical tools.

these days, however, do not neatly represent the capital-labor cleavage; indeed, capital's antagonist can no longer be adequately denoted by "labor" in a historical context in which "traditional" wage labor is subject to multiple corroding and fragmenting factors including (but certainly not limited to) technological unemployment, workers' collective agency has been weakened and "surplus" populations are growing (cf. Clover 2016; Braneck, this volume). In this regard, it is not surprising that the GE reports hardly take notice of labor unions at all. "Green" capitalism's discontents are not as easy to grasp conceptually—let alone to pacify with a coherent set of policies—as those of Fordist times temporarily appeared to be: The interests of middle-class environmentalists, poor communities affected by pollution and a fragmented workforce differently positioned vis-à-vis "greening" efforts all intersect and collide. Of course, their diffuse, conflictual composition is also an obstacle to effective organization and makes them more governable.[10] But asymmetry in class struggle does not make for an economically and socially sustainable accumulation regime.[11]

To relate back to the automation debate, it is unclear how effective demand (and relative social peace) can be sustained if ever larger parts of the population are cut off from substantial sources of income; in Marxist terms, how surplus value can be exploited at the macro-level if "living" labor is increasingly liquidated from the economic process. Reliant as the GE proposal is on a strategy of unleashing high-tech innovation at unprecedented levels—supported by flanking mechanisms, but essentially driven by market competition—, it may be expected to expel significant amounts of labor over time (remember that capital remains structurally compelled to maximize labor productivity, not resource productivity). Ironically, this tendency has been attenuated over the past decades through neoliberal strategies of wage depression and myriad forms of precarious employment, which arguably have not only weakened effective demand but also effec-

10 Obviously, different factions of capital also have antagonistic interests with regard to the Green Economy (Rest 2011; Sander 2016). Nevertheless, when vital general class interests are at stake, they tend to sing in chorus—which may inhibit the implementation of GE policies while defending medium-term class interests.

11 Accumulation regime is another key concept of regulation theory that denotes the more narrowly economic functioning of any capitalist mode of development—basically, the balance between the two departments of production (means of production and means of consumption) and, thus, the realization of effective demand that allows for a smooth accumulation of capital (Aglietta 2015a, Chapter 2; Lipietz 1992, Chapter 1).

tively suppressed (labor-saving) technological innovation by securing cheap labor supplies.[12] The requirement that any green-capitalist solution to this conundrum be respectful of ecological constraints while allowing for ever larger masses of capital to be realized every year further raises the stakes: A functioning "green" accumulation regime faces enormous obstacles.

How, now, to manage these contradictions? In *Green Economy* models, the state is largely restricted to the role of a facilitator, albeit going beyond neoliberal orthodoxy in its ecologically oriented interventions. In order to square the circle and subordinate the forces of capital to ambitious ecological goals, the state would have to be far more active in shaping the economy—and labor relations are no exception to this, particularly given the explosive dynamic indicated in the previous paragraph. Efforts to bend the dynamics of capital in a particular direction—for example, by politically imposing a partial orientation towards the maximization of resource productivity—require extensive, proactive management of contradictions that allows for a stable mode of regulation. Reformist proposals have at least provided some modest hunches in that direction, for example noting the considerable leverage that state agencies on all levels possess to influence labor relations in "green" sectors given the latter's dependence on public subsidies and government contracts (cf. Mattera 2009). This, in turn, may provide organized labor with at least some measure of political leverage.

The model *Green Economy*, however, with its sterilized conceptualization of the relationship between the economy proper, the state and society at large, falls far short of *any* mediation requirements. While my argument here focuses more on functional contradictions than on political conflicts, the outcomes of the former will always be determined on the terrain of the latter. Accordingly, no mode of regulation can simply be devised in theory and implemented from above: It does not only mediate class relations and political conflicts but is also an expression of the latter and thus essentially dynamic. But a model that seeks to formulate a credible political project needs at least a general orientation towards such mediations. The GE implicitly extrapolates the always conflictual and hardly economically sustainable neoliberal mode of regulation into the future, regardless of the emergence of the game-changing factors of ecological constraints and, on a

12 Of course it is by no means certain that the suppressed innovations would have been ecologically beneficial.

high-tech development trajectory, tendentially intensified technological unemployment. In trying to incorporate these and thus credibly connect the GE project with these real or latent social tendencies, a universal basic income is a potential mechanism which would have to be thought through in its articulation with the wider set of GE policies, and in its ecological implications.

But, lest we delude ourselves, it is important to distinguish between the *Green Economy* as an agenda and as a (hypothetical) political reality. In a series of papers, regulationists Ulrich Brand and Markus Wissen outline the contradictory development of "green" capitalism (Brand 2012; Brand and Wissen 2013; 2014). The GE, in their view, assumes an important ideological function as a contemporary strategy for ecological modernization of capitalist economies. At the same time, the implementation of this strategy as a political project is expected to be selective and incoherent at best, taking shape in articulation with ongoing "brown" developments. These green developments would take on highly spatially uneven forms conditioned by successful strategies, on the part of economically powerful actors and regions, of spatio-temporal externalization and problem shifting. The case of labor we are concerned with here illustrates this inherent selectivity and partiality, and the systemic need for new externalizations, rather well.

Thus, even if, against all odds, a "green" mode of regulation were successfully realized, allowing for relatively stable capital accumulation over a few decades with large-scale economic activity in "green" sectors, it is highly unlikely that this would redeem the promise of ecological sustainability. In particular, the ability of such a constellation to keep climate change within "manageable" proportions—which would require immediate radical emissions reductions—appears illusory.

Conclusion and Outlook

The *Green Economy* as conceptualized by major international institutions clearly ignores the complexity of actual and potential social-ecological developments. By simple extrapolation of the last decades' neoliberal reality of financialization, market-oriented regulation and wage depression into the future—albeit in an environmentally enlightened modification—, the GE curiously glosses over the wide-ranging, contradictory implications of any strategy that fundamentally relies on market-driven technological innovation to solve social and ecological crises. Not only does it fail to consider the questions of purpose and *social* worth with regard to work addressed by both degrowthers and accelerationists, it also neglects to grapple with the *functional* contradictions of technological development in a capitalist context, let alone the political conflicts expressed in, and arising from, these.

From a regulationist perspective, it is clear that all else never is equal. Complex social reality will not be controllable through technical engineering. In this view, the GE should be recognized as primarily ideological in function rather than a prefiguration of future social reality: a *ceteris paribus ideology*, since its purpose is precisely to insist on all else to remain equal (or rather unequal). While GE models are short on explicit commentary regarding strategies with which its socially contradictory agenda can be fought through politically, or who will be struggling for it, all cues point towards an intensified, prolonged neoliberal labor regime—whose strategy of cheapening labor has historically stood in the way of innovation. So, even in the capitalist core economies, a meaningfully "green" accumulation regime hardly appears practicable due to the triple specter of effective demand problems, ecological constraints and social unrest. When having to serve capital, labor and ecology at once, it is likely that either of the latter two, or both, will be sacrificed and capital's reproduction costs once again externalized in the *Green Economy*.

So what about the future of labor? Globally speaking, we are arguably far from an "end of work" and shouldn't be misled by isolated impressions from certain economic sectors in the wealthiest regions (see Zimmermann, this volume). Still, there is a solid argument for this general possibility—at least regarding full-time wage labor—, but capitalist class relations are obviously structurally opposed to such an outcome. So far, neoliberalism has found fixes for the *tendency* towards technological unemployment: Most importantly, automation has been circumvented by moving the center of gravity in terms of industrial labor to low-wage regions of the Global South. But in the North, cheap labor strategies abound as well: for example, the proliferation of "bullshit jobs" (Graeber 2013)—many of which, while arguably socially useless in an abstract sense, are indeed necessitated by their concrete capitalist context, such as PR managers or many jobs in finance, accounting and legal services—, of luxury services whose "class content" is even more obvious and of other low-paid, low-productivity (monetarily speaking) service jobs, which have been politically fostered through low-wage policies and in themselves create a disincentive for investments in labor-saving technology.

The much-discussed *sharing* or *gig economy* may be seen as a particularly cannibalistic variant, with the commodification of just about everything and extreme precarization as another socially regressive and temporary fix—if not the last straw—for capitalism's structural contradictions (Booth 2015; see also Pentzien, this volume). There is much to suggest that these tendencies towards insecure employment in services would be intensified in a capitalist *Green Economy*. Contrary to its explicit promise, the latter cannot end the capitalist compulsion to pursue ever new (as well as old) strategies to externalize the costs of accumulation, including to workers and reinforced surplus populations.

While it is unclear if any of these strategies can stem the tide of technological unemployment in the long run, let alone provide a coherent accumulation regime, they certainly have contributed to fending off any systemic challenge to capitalism. Likewise, capitalist ideology—generalized in the unrelenting work ethic—militates against the idea of a post-work society (cf. Frayne 2015). The abolitionist perspective on work is still marginal—but it is precisely for this reason that Srnicek and Williams' political project fills an important gap, as does the "decelerationist" demand for degrowth with its own post-work scenario. For both, un(der)employment, dissociated from its fatal consequences under capitalist circumstances and generalized across societies, becomes a desirable, concrete utopia.

While the paths suggested by both theories are mutually contradictory and certainly require further dialogue, we should register at this point that the *Green Economy*, by marked contrast to both, provides us only with the worst of both present and future: It reaffirms the capitalist work ethic and the material compulsion to work without providing a credible material basis for their future utility and sustainability. The GE, ultimately, does not resolve the—arguably impossible—task of reconciling capital accumulation, full employment *and* ecological sustainability. Among the three, priorities clearly have to be chosen. While the *Green Economy* agenda puts accumulation first and tries to accommodate the others accordingly, the degrowth and accelerationist platforms are more than willing to sacrifice it along with full employment, and thus finally render whatever trade-offs between ecological and social needs persist truly politically negotiable. The degree of material abundance feasible on such trajectories remains to be seen.

Works Cited

Aglietta, Michel (2015a). *A Theory of Capitalist Regulation: The US Experience.* London: Verso.

— (2015b). Capitalism at the Turn of the Century: Regulation Theory and the Challenge of Social Change. In *A Theory of Capitalist Regulation: The US Experience,* 388–445. London: Verso.

Autor, David H. (2015). Why Are There Still So Many Jobs? The History and Future of Workplace Automation. *Journal of Economic Perspectives*, 29.3, 3–30.

Barbier, Edward (2010). Global Governance: The G20 and a Global Green New Deal. *Economics*, 4, 1–35.

Boewe, Jörn, and Johannes Schulten (2013). Das Licht geht aus im "Solar Valley." In *Magazin Mitbestimmung, Hans-Böckler-Stiftung*, 11.

Boggs, James (1963). *The American Revolution. Pages From a Negro Worker's Notebook.* New York, NY: Monthly Review Press.

Booth, Adam (2015, June 10). The Sharing Economy, the Future of Jobs, and "PostCapitalism". *In Defence of Marxism*: http://www.marxist.com/the-sharing-economy-the-future-of-jobs-and-postcapitalism-part-one.htm (accessed November 1, 2017).

Bowen, Alex, Sam Fankhauser, Nicholas Stern, and Dimitri Zenghelis (2009). *An outline of the case for a "green" stimulus.* London/Leeds: Grantham Research Institute on Climate Change and the Environment and Centre for Climate Change Economics and Policy.

Brand, Ulrich (2012). Green Economy and Green Capitalism: Some Theoretical Considerations. In *Journal für Entwicklungspolitik*, 28.3, 118–137.

Brand, Ulrich, and Markus Wissen (2013). Strategien einer Green Economy, Konturen eines grünen Kapitalismus: zeitdiagnostische und forschungsprogrammatische Überlegungen. In Roland Atzmüller et al. (eds.). *Fit für die Krise? Perspektiven der Regulationstheorie,* 132–148. Münster: Westfälisches Dampfboot.

— (2014). Ökologische Modernisierung zu Beginn des 21. Jahrhunderts: Green Economy und Konturen eines grünen Kapitalismus. In Martin Bemmann et al. (eds.), *Ökologische Modernisierung: zur Geschichte und Gegenwart eines Konzepts in Umweltpolitik und Sozialwissenschaften,* 135–159. Frankfurt am Main: Campus.

Brynjolfsson, Erik, and Andrew McAfee (2014). *The Second Machine Age: Work, Progress, and Prosperity in a Time of Brilliant Technologies.* New York, NY: W. W. Norton & Company.

Butollo, Florian, and Yannick Kalff (2017).Entsteht der Postkapitalismus im Kapitalismus? Eine Kritik an Masons Transformationsstrategie. In *PROKLA,* 187, 291–308.

Clover, Joshua (2016). *Riot. Strike. Riot. The New Era of Uprisings.* London/New York, NY: Verso.

Cunningham, David (2015). A Marxist Heresy? Accelerationism and Its Discontents. In *Radical Philosophy,* 191, 29–38.

Dale, Gareth, Manu V. Mathai, and Jose Antonio Puppim de Oliveira (eds.) (2016). *Green Growth: Ideology, Political Economy and the Alternatives*. London: Zed Books.

D'Alisa, Giacomo, Federico Demaria, and Giorgos Kallis (eds.) (2015). *Degrowth: A Vocabulary for a New Era*, New York, NY/London: Routledge.

Daly, Herman E. (1991). *Steady-State Economics*. Washington, D.C.: Island Press.

Exner, Andreas, Christian Lauk, and Konstantin Kulterer (2008). *Die Grenzen des Kapitalismus: wie wir am Wachstum scheitern*. Vienna: Ueberreuter.

Frase, Peter (2016). *Four Futures: Life After Capitalism*. London/New York, NY: Verso.

Frayne, David (2015). *The Refusal of Work: The Theory and Practice of Resistance to Work*. London: Zed Books.

Frey, Carl Benedikt, and Michael A. Osborne (2013). *The Future of Employment: How Susceptible Are Jobs to Automation?* Oxford Martin School: http://www.oxfordmartin.ox.ac.uk/downloads/academic/The_Future_of_Employment.pdf, (accessed November 1, 2017).

Gardiner, Michael E. (2017). Critique of Accelerationism. In *Theory, Culture & Society*, 34.1, 29–52.

Graeber, David (2013). On the Phenomenon of Bullshit Jobs. In *Strike!Mag*, 3: https://strikemag.org/bullshit-jobs (accessed May 15, 2017).

Green New Deal Group (2008). *A Green New Deal*. London: new economics foundation.

Jackson, Tim (2009). *Prosperity Without Growth? The Transition to a Sustainable Economy*. London: Earthscan.

Kenis, Anneleen, and Matthias Lievens (2015). *The Limits of the Green Economy: From Re-inventing Capitalism to Repoliticising the Present*. Abingdon/New York, NY: Routledge.

Kim, Young Joon, Kyungsoo Kim, and SuKyoung Lee (2017). The rise of technological unemployment and its implications on the future macroeconomic landscape. In *Futures*, 87, 1–9.

Latouche, Serge (2009). *Farewell to Growth*, Cambridge/ Malden, MA: Polity Press.

Lenz, Julian, Thorsten Ludwig, and Stefan Timm (2017). *Branchenanalyse Windenergieindustrie. Arbeitsbedingungen und Marktentwicklung aus Sicht von Betriebsräten*. Hans-Böckler-Stiftung: https://www.boeckler.de/pdf/p_fofoe_WP_035_2017.pdf (accessed November 29, 2017).

Lipietz, Alain (1992). *Towards a New Economic Order: Postfordism, Ecology and Democracy*. Cambridge: Polity Press.

Littig, Beate (2013). Green Economy, Green Jobs - und Frauen? Geschlechterpolitische Überlegungen zum aktuellen Nachhaltigkeitsdiskurs. In Erna Appelt et al. (eds.). *Gesellschaft. Feministische Krisendiagnosen*, 60–79. Münster: Westfälisches Dampfboot.

Luddism (n.d.). In *The Free Dictionary* : https://www.thefreedictionary.com/luddism (accessed Nov 16, 2017).

Mackay, Robin and Armen Avanessian (2014). Introduction. In *#ACCELERATE#. The Accelerationist Reader,* 1–46, Falmouth: Urbanomics.

Marx, Karl (1977). Preface. In *A Contribution to the Critique of Political Economy.* Moscow: Progress Publishers: https://www.marxists.org/archive/marx/-works/1859/critique-pol-economy/preface.htm (accessed November 30, 2017).

— (2014). Fragment on Machines. In Robin Mackay and Armen Avanessian (eds.). *#ACCELERATE#. The Accelerationist Reader,* 51–66. Falmouth: Urbanomic.

Mason, Paul (2015). *PostCapitalism: A Guide to Our Future.* London: Allen Lane.

Mattera, Philip (2009). *High Road or Low Road? Job Quality in the New Green Economy.* Good Jobs First: https://www.goodjobsfirst.org/sites/default/files/docs/-pdf/gjfgreenjobsrpt.pdf (accessed Sep 15, 2017).

Meisner, Matthias (2012, August 24). Prekär Beschäftigte in der Windindustrie. *Tagesspiegel:* http://www.tagesspiegel.de/wirtschaft/linke-beklagt-zu-viel-leiharbeit-prekaer-beschaeftigte-in-der-windindustrie/7053210.html (accessed Nov 29, 2017).

Moore, Jason W. (2016). The Rise of Cheap Nature. In *Anthropocene or Capitalocene? Nature, History, and the Crisis of Capitalism,* 78–115. Oakland, CA: PM Press.

OECD (ed.) (2011). *Towards Green Growth.* Paris: Organisation for Economic Co-operation and Development.

— (ed.) (2015). *Towards Green Growth? Tracking Progress.* Organisation for Economic Co-operation and Development: http://www.oecd.org/env/towards-green-growth-9789264234437-en.htm (accessed October 18, 2016).

— (ed.) (2017, June). *Employment Implications of Green Growth: Linking jobs, growth, and green policies. OECD Report for the G7 Environment Ministers.* Organisation for Economic Co-operation and Development: https://www.oecd.org/environment/Employment-Implications-of-Green-Growth-OECD-Report-G7-Environment-Ministers.pdf (accessed June 25, 2018).

Pollin, Robert, Heidi Garrett-Peltier, Heidi, James Heintz, and Helen Scharber (2008). *Green Recovery. A Program to Create Good Jobs and Start Building a Low-Carbon Economy.* Amherst, MA/Washington D.C.: Political Economy Research Institute and Center for American Progress.

Renner, Michael, Sean Sweeney, and Jill Kubit (2008). Executive Summary. In *Green Jobs: Towards Decent Work in a Sustainable, Low-carbon World,* 1–28. Nairobi: UNEP/ILO/IOE/ITUC.

Rest, Jonas (2011). *Grüner Kapitalismus? Klimawandel, globale Staatenkonkurrenz und die Verhinderung der Energiewende.* Wiesbaden: VS-Verlag für Sozialwissenschaften.

Rifkin, Jeremy (2014). *The Zero Marginal Cost Society: The Internet of Things, the Collaborative Commons, and the Eclipse of Capitalism.* Basingstoke: Palgrave Macmillan.

Rosen, Ben (2016, October 15). Unions for green jobs: Why organized labor is getting behind offshore wind. *Christian Science Monitor:* https://www.csmonitor.com/Environment/2016/1015/Unions-for-green-jobs-Why-organized-labor-is-getting-behind-offshore-wind (accessed November 27, 2017).

Rotman, David (2015, June 16). Who Will Own the Robots? *MIT Technology Review*: https://www.technologyreview.com/s/538401/who-will-own-the-robots/ (accessed December 20, 2017).

Sander, Hendrik (2016). *Auf dem Weg zum grünen Kapitalismus? Die Energiewende nach Fukushima.* Berlin: Bertz + Fischer.

Schmelzer, Matthias, and Alexis Passadakis (2011). *Postwachstum: Krise, ökologische Grenzen und soziale Rechte.* Hamburg: VSA-Verlag.

Smith, Jason E. (2017). Nowhere to Go: Automation, Then and Now. *The Brooklyn Rail*: http://brooklynrail.org/2017/03/field-notes/Nowhere-to-Go (accessed December 26, 2017).

Smith, Richard (2016). *Green Capitalism: The God That Failed.* London: College Publications.

Srnicek, Nick, and Alex Williams (2014). #Accelerate: Manifesto for an Accelerationist Politics. In Robin Mackay and Armen Avanessian (eds.). *#ACCELERATE#. The Accelerationist Reader*, 347–362. Falmouth: Urbanomic.

— (2016). *Inventing the Future: Postcapitalism and a World Without Work.* London: Verso.

Tanuro, Daniel (2013). *Green Capitalism: Why It Can't Work.* London: Merlin Press.

Tienhaara, Kyle (2014). Varieties of green capitalism: economy and environment in the wake of the global financial crisis. In *Environmental Politics*, 23.2, 187–204.

Turner, Fred (2016, January 9). On Accelerationism. *Public Books*: http://www.publicbooks.org/on-accelerationism/ (accessed January 6, 2017).

UNEP (ed.) (2011). *Towards a Green Economy: Pathways to Sustainable Development and Poverty Eradication.* Nairobi: United Nations Environment Programme.

Wark, McKenzie (2013, May 14). #Celerity: A Critique of the Manifesto for an Accelerationist Politics. *Speculative Heresy*: https://speculativeheresy.files.wordpress.com/2013/05/wark-mckenzie-celerity.pdf (accessed November 27, 2017).

World Bank (ed.) (2012). *Inclusive Green Growth: The Pathway to Sustainable Development.* Washington, D.C.

Epilogue

Prospects of a Rural Renaissance: Will the Smart Economy Compress Regional Disparities?

Julia Püschel

A central motif in this book has been the role of technology in shaping society. As the essays collected in this volume illustrate in a variety of ways, technology is not an external, exogenous force, but is embedded in power structures and social relationships—shaped in turn by technological innovation. As such, whether a society manages to benefit from a given set of technologies or not crucially depends on active political decision-making, on social norms, and historical context. These decisions also shape our ways of living and our social relations of production. The rise of the smart economy and its focus on software-based solutions for important social challenges, however, often obfuscates our view from the continuing importance of politics. These closing remarks explore the effects of the emergent smart economy on a specific type of social relations—within-country regional disparities—and how they might or might not be changed through the smart economy.

While, since the 1990s, regional inequalities have increased rapidly—with dramatic consequences for economic inclusion, political polarization, social cohesion and even life expectancy—some commentators have noted that recent economic developments might indicate a trend shift, offering new opportunities for economically-disconnected regions. As many argue, peak globalization and the next manufacturing revolution could provide rural provinces with new economic opportunities and even out regional inequalities (Brennan et al. 2015, The White House 2016). But even if we share this optimism, and even if we assume these trends will continue, government has several crucial responsibilities to ensure the materialization of the smart economy's potential.

The renaissance of the rural is not a given. And state intervention is by no means limited to the provision of high-quality, high-speed broadband access. Active government measures will continue to be crucial to reduce regional disparities and the socially polarizing tendencies that come along with them. As such, a reduction of regional divergences will only be possible with active government intervention and will not occur as an automatic result of the smart market economy. As we will see, challenges and opportunities offered to different (rural) regions by the smart economy, highlight the importance of politics along various planes to shape potential futures.

Economic Geographies of Globalization

Technology has always had profound effects on the geographical organization of labor, even if economics as a social science was not always interested in these spatial dimensions of exchange. Until the 1980s, technological development contributed to decreasing inequalities between OECD countries and among regions within these countries.[1] These developments seemed in line with the neoclassical view that there was an automatic and natural tendency for regional inequalities to disappear over time. Divergences in investment opportunities would not stay untapped and technological know-how would diffuse among regions over time (Solow, 1956). Let us ignore for the moment that there have of course been very political reasons for the compression of inequalities during the post-war era—such as cross-regional subsidies, welfare state policies, and regulations—but, be that as it may: economics seemed to provide a powerful, parsimonious explanation for what was happening.

With economic globalization and technological change accelerating during the 1990s and 2000s, however, this pattern changed and regional disparities widened again. Economic globalization led to the relocation of many manufacturing production sites to developing economies with cheaper labor costs and looser health and environmental regulations. For developed economies, the relocations worked in the same direction as structural change: away from manufacturing and towards service jobs. As a result of these long-term developments, whereas employment within manufacturing industries in 2016 made up only 7.9 percent of overall employment in the US, employment in service industries constituted 80.3 percent (U.S. BLS 2017. In 2009, 76.9 percent of all US value added came from

1 The American inter-state income gaps closed at an annual rate of about 1.8 percent (Ganong and Shoag 2017).

services, compared to 21.8 percent from manufacturing (OECD 2010). These changes in economic geography came at a price that was paid for in an uneven manner across societies. According to the Economic Policy Institute, 2.7 million US jobs were lost as a result of increased trade with China, with 2.1 million of these within manufacturing. Low-skilled workers and workers performing relatively routine tasks disproportionately lost their jobs to competitors from lower wage countries.

One crucial feature of the more recent era of globalization, since the 1990s and especially the 2000s, have been the spatial implications of these changes within countries. Employment losses in manufacturing were concentrated in certain regions, often rural, which were seriously affected by relocations and often left in a state of dereliction and unemployment. Manufacturing tended to cluster in rural spaces. The sector had been based on exploiting economies of scale, meaning that production became cheaper with increased volume and when it was agglomerating in proximity to others producing similar goods. The workers who lost their jobs in manufacturing thus had a very hard time finding new work in the service sector. Why? Because these jobs, by contrast, tend to cluster within cities. Those not willing or able to leave their home town, friends and family therefore face a serious problem: unemployment and, given the long-term effects of structural change, little hope in sight.

David Autor and his co-authors (2012) have developed a new methodology to measure the concentrated costs associated with international trade. Their findings suggest that the above-mentioned overall numbers of trade-related employment losses in the US—which seem relatively small—have had far-reaching local consequences in certain areas. The authors analyzed effects within commuting zones and found that not only did unemployment rise and wages decline among manufacturing workers, but the same was true among nonmanufacturing workers in the same communities, implying negative spillover effects of the trade shocks to the local communities which they found to last for about a decade. These findings challenge the widely-held traditional belief in the economics profession that the labor market impacts of international trade are muted by relatively frictionless labor market adjustments. The impacts of international trade, it turned out, do not diffuse over a larger group of workers but rather concentrate among locations.

Regional Disparities and Peak Globalization: Some Optimistic Scenarios

In brief, rural regions in particular can be considered the losers of structural change within countries, whereas most economic growth (including job growth) in recent decades has happened within cities—the engines of economic growth. In 2013, the labor productivity gap between urban areas and other regions was 30 percent for the OECD average, with North America and Europe displaying a higher regional gap than Asia. Regional disparities within countries have started widening again since the 1990s, implying a trend shift from previous decades of reduced regional inequalities. In sum, over the past 20 years, the average productivity gap between the top 10 percent of regions and the lowest 75 percent has grown by almost 60 percent.

These regional gaps have dramatic consequences. In the US, disposable per capita yearly income in 2013 differed by more than 10,000 US dollars between regions (OECD 2016). In 2009, the average hourly wage in Stamford, Connecticut was twice as high as the one in Jacksonville, Florida (Moretti 2011) and the unemployment rate in Iowa City, Iowa was almost six times lower than the one in Flint, Michigan (Kline and Moretti 2013). Even life expectancy differed by almost four years depending on the place of birth within the US (OECD 2016). In addition to these direct effects, these growing geographical disparities have produced further economic, social and political tensions.

Recently, the sense of abandonment and anger in left-behind places was felt in the rise of populism in election outcomes, for instance, in the 2016 Brexit vote in the UK, the election of Donald Trump, or in the 2017 French presidential and German parliamentary elections (Ballas et al., 2017, Jessop, 2017). Autor et al. (2016) have found that Americans in places hit hardest by competition with China voted more extremely than Americans in other regions. And according to Rodriguez-Pose (2018) "the places that don't matter, not the 'people that don't matter', have reacted."

And yet, just as the public discourse begins paying increased attention to the regions left-behind by globalization and technological change, some argue that this period might already be facing its end. As some optimists argue, the latest developments in the smart economy could offer new opportunities for rural areas. For one, they insist, globalization might soon hit its peak, if it hasn't done so already. Indeed, real wages in China have risen considerably since the late 1990s and suggest that we have reached the "end of cheap labor" (Li et al. 2012). Why would one face all the added uncertainties of producing in China as compared to one's home country if labor savings are no longer part of the equation? Right, one would not.

Furthermore, producers of finished goods increasingly prioritize speed-to-market and non-labor costs . The challenges associated with managing complex, international supply chains have become a growing concern for producers of intermediate products. This is why international trade, soaring during the 1990s and 2000s, has been stagnating for over a decade now (Manyika et al. 2016). Anecdotal evidence of firms that are relocating production back to their home countries abounds.

In addition to rising labor costs abroad and the need for production at closer proximity, optimists would point out that we are on the verge of the next manufacturing revolution, enabling production based much less on scale than on customization. Many argue that we might soon see a strong shift towards smaller-scale production, both more local and decentralized than in the previous era. Breakthroughs in machine learning, mobile robotics and new sensor capabilities are currently changing the way we produce (OECD 2017). This might also have major implications for regions currently disconnected from the benefits of globalization.

In the age of traditional economies-of-scale-based production and Fordist mass production, the crucial spatial factor for production was physical infrastructure. Proximity to ports and other major transportation hubs played a significant role. The importance of physical infrastructure also led to regional divergences within low-wage countries like China. Chinese cities in the coastal regions of the East developed as major economic growth nodes with increasing wages and living costs, whereas today mainland (rural) China largely continues to be a relatively poor region where many people struggle to find their basic needs fulfilled (Piketty et al. 2017). In the new, smart economy the importance is shifting towards high-speed access to high-quality broadband connections. As proponents of these technological visions would emphasize, new startups can access software and hardware tools via a huge range of web-based services that had previously only been available to the biggest, most established firms. Particular hopes are placed in 3D printing which enables manufacturing production with significantly lower levels of capital (OECD 2017), at least in theory:

"An AI startup, for example, doesn't need its own server farm to train its software and provide service to customers. The team can rent computing power from Amazon Web Services. [...] Makers can 3D print or mill industrial grade prototypes of physical stuff in a garage or local maker space and send or sell designs to anyone with a laptop and 3D printer via online platforms." (Garrett 2017)

Taken together, these factors seem to indicate that there is new hope for rural areas. In fact, governments do already strive to bridge the digital divide between urban and rural regions to deploy the promised potential of the emergent smart economy. The hope is to attract startups, firms and people who have wanted to escape the city but have been deterred by scant employment opportunities. By enabling home office work and decentralized working arrangements, the attractiveness of rural areas for digital nomads is supposed to be enhanced.

In the US, the federal program BroadbandUSA offers technical and financial help for local regions to get access to affordable broadband (Strickling 2015). In 2012, almost one in four Americans living in rural areas still lacked access to fixed broadband and 14.5 million of the 19 million Americans who did not have access to broadband lived in rural areas (Federal Communications Commission 2012). Audio-visual online meetings and email increasingly enable work from home. In 2009, 25 percent of American workers used telework regularly and the number of people working from home rose to more than 17 million in 2008 (OECD 2011). Donald Trump's effect on these developments remains to be seen.

At the same time that these emancipatory dynamics are in place or at least latent, future studies scholars speak of an increasing desire for the local (Horx 2018). Overall, US labor mobility has reached a historical low. Since the 1980s, the share of Americans who are moving across state lines has fallen by half (Moore 2017). Scholars such as Hall et al. (2009) of the University of Kansas claim that de-urbanization is gaining momentum and that especially young and retired Americans are leaving big cities of more than 4 million people. This does raise a pertinent question: Once everybody in even the most remote villages has high-quality, high-speed broadband access, and even if the division of labor is eventually becoming footloose as a result of the next manufacturing revolution, will we truly see a "renaissance of the rural" (Horx 2018)?

A Rural Renaissance?

People do not just live in cities because of easier access to jobs. An essential problem for many rural areas, driving many into dense urban agglomerations, is a lack of service provision and quality. The availability of such services would be crucial for the inclusion of rural areas within the smart economy. And consciousness about the urban-rural disparity along this dimension is increasing with the stronger connectivity between urban and rural populations. Rural areas are characterized by relatively low population density over large distances, providing weaker incentives for private service providers to deliver services (OECD 2010). Retail is under strong pressure from online possibilities (including shops and banking), and traditionally public services such as postal delivery, proximity to schools and health services are dramatically more difficult to obtain and scarcer in rural than in urban areas. Add to this a tradition of state retrenchment and austerity, and it will be difficult to imagine how disparities would actually be addressed—regardless of the shape and form of smart technologies.

Akin to the rhetoric of the smart city, a utopian idea of smart villages is recently gaining prominence in discourses about economic and social development. This vision claims that smart, software-based technological solutions could offer possibilities to overcome the unique challenges for service provision in rural areas. The solutions relate among others to questions of mobility and healthcare provision. The hope is that mobility could be crucially enhanced by self-driving cars, that the combined transportation of people and packages would create socially beneficial synergies and that new monitoring devices would enable faster responses in case of health emergencies (OECD 2018).

But even if we acknowledge the potential of such new technologies to help improve the provision of some rural services, what is the role of politics in these optimistic scenarios? Hardly surprising, given also the empirical evidence provided in this volume, the government has several crucial roles even if we assume that technology-based services will increasingly be provided by the private sector. Technology cannot substitute for government capabilities, it can only complement them. Importantly, smart villages, and smart cities, for that matter, run on data. Who is going to be able to see and utilize this data? Who will construct the large-scale physical infrastructure and the technical know-how necessary to build smart growth? The public sector has the responsibility of ensuring and preserving privacy.

Most importantly, software is subject to accidents. Driverless cars crash, as does software in general. What happens in such a case if we have decided to provide essential public services like healthcare based on technological improvements alone? The building and maintenance of such infrastructures, questions of risk and liability are public because markets fail to deliver socially optimal results.

From this perspective, the smart city and the smart village appear like extensions of a longer standing tradition of state retrenchment to further shift responsibility for public goods provision towards individuals and private providers. It has become obvious over the last 30 years, that providing essential public goods and services by relying on private providers is problematic. Efficiency of provision does not guarantee social justice and equality (OECD 2010). And neither does efficiency of provision through new technological devices. For these reasons, the sharing economy has been criticized for its implicit exclusivity (Schor et al. 2016). The public sector has a crucial responsibility if it does not want to reinforce within-country inequalities and the broader societal polarizing tendencies that result from such divergences.

This also holds true from another vantage point. In a recent report, the World Bank discusses the preconditions under which software-based technological solutions promise to improve the quality of public service provision. Interestingly, the discussion very much echoes the debates of automation potentials in the labor market. Services that offer most potential to be improved through digital technologies are mainly characterized by routine activities such as cash transfers, licensing and registration services. Political-institutional pre-conditions are more crucial once the activities in question involve judgement discretion and are harder to monitor. Examples of such, often also called complex, tasks include teaching and healthcare. And ensuring social inclusion in public services is a particularly complex and challenging task (World Bank 2016). These are the fields of provision and employment that will continue to rely on human work—and that cannot easily be replaced technologically. It will also remain a political task to make sure that these jobs and services are equally provided across the urban-rural divide.

Moreover, even in the smart economy, scale still matters. Economies of scale may have new sources but they are still crucial. These new dimensions of scale lead to the development of new types of monopolies that foster further regional inequalities as they tend to cluster in space. Machine learning crucially depends on data. The firms with the biggest amount of data available are best at training their machines and the networks and platforms that have most users are more attractive to everyone else. These new returns to scale result in a relatively few superstar firms, which tend to cluster in a relatively few, superstar places. If governments don't ensure redistributive measures, it is hard to imagine a scenario where inequalities and geographical disparities would not persist or even increase.

What can Governments do?

One way in which many local governments have been active is the provision of left-behind places with subsidies to attract key firms and become the place for new industrial clusters. Regions offer tax benefits for relocating companies, subsidies, and sometimes even lower labor standards or reductions in social security payments. Unfortunately, empirical studies suggest that these kinds of incentives are rarely successful in fostering the sustainable, long-term developments of clusters and in raising employment. Such policies are based on views that consider the production set-up as a zero-sum game. Only one region can attract production at the loss of another region. A similar idea has recently gained prominence again with the rise of neo-Mercantilist notions of international trade. In both cases, incentives only work as long as they are actually provided. Once the region (or country) stops offering these benefits, companies often relocate again (Kolko and Neumark 2010). And even the modest employment gains that some studies find come at the cost of neighboring regions, which experience corresponding employment reductions. As a result, it is questionable how big the benefits for the labor force will be in such a case (Kolko and Neumark 2010).

Instead of trying to attract firms from other regions, and thereby merely shifting the pattern of regional disparities by introducing further competition between regions, governments could devote attention to reducing regional disparities. There are ways to actually counter the concentrating tendencies of uneven development in the smart economy. Federal and local governments can intervene by regulating the relevant markets and by providing citizens with capabilities that are required to fully participate in economic life.

The smart economy produces new monopolies that concentrate an immense amount of power. One way to counter these tendencies are better competition laws and stronger enforcement. The rise of digital platform economies, such as Airbnb and Mechanical Turk, in particular, has often led to questions of whether the state can still intervene in these markets via command and control. Jonas Pentzien's chapter in this volume demonstrates that the assumed paradox between more footloose companies and state regulation is an artificial hindrance that blinds us of the possibility of state regulation in these settings. Difficulties in enforcing regulation like competition laws are not the necessary result of the techno-legal structures of platform economies but can rather be traced to competing views with respect to the optimal governance modes among political actors.

Policies need to ensure fair market access and prevent anticompetitive behavior. Network effects and switching costs pose a particular set of challenges in the smart economy. Such market structure features are, however, nothing new and are already regulated in many countries. Just think about telecommunications, railroads and electricity. Challenges are posed, above all, by new interdependencies. Digital platforms, for instance, create new regulating challenges by operating in two-sided markets, charging users and suppliers at the same time (OECD 2017, World Bank 2016). What is necessary is a better understanding of the special market characteristics of the new, smart firms.

Another way to counter the monopolizing tendencies would be to foster the diffusion of non-rival knowledge from the new and relatively few superstar firms. Many new technologies are not being used by a large share of firms within a country. Spreading know-how enables firms and workers to employ new technologies regardless of spatial clusters. The latest technological know-how tends to be employed more frequently in larger, more globally oriented and urban companies. Particularly since 2001, technological know-how within countries has started to disperse less across space. In contrast, the diffusion of knowledge has become quicker and more frictionless from frontier firms in one country to firms with similarly high productivity levels in other countries. One reason for these divergent patterns might be the focus of superstar firms on international rather than local markets (Andrews et al. 2015).

The public sector could play an important role in fostering the distribution of such technological know-how. After all, it has invested significantly in some of the key technologies of the current economy (Mazzucato 2018).

As a response to the structural changes of late 19th century industrialization, the American federal government started to set up land-grant universities. Retrospectively, these significant public investments ensured that the benefits of industrialization were more equally shared among the population (The Economist 2013). Based on the Morrill Acts of 1862 and 1890, the purpose was to provide funds for the creation of higher education institutions to educate the increasingly-demanded farmers and engineers. The federal government offered land to the states, which were supposed to sell it to raise the required funds. The institutions enlarged their missions over time and started to include research and to extend that knowledge to local firms.

In many respects, this historical example sets a precedent for a more even dispersion of knowledge. Research shows that the diffusion of technical know-how from superstar firms to local firms tends to be quicker in countries with high-quality education systems and in countries in which universities and businesses collaborate more intensively (Andrews et al. 2015). In other words, the argument for redistribution as a question of social justice is strong—but even companies would benefit from such burden-sharing in the longer term.

The public sector could invest in adapting the institutions of higher education to the smart economy. This would imply the re-training of the working population and thereby helping local firms to gather the new know-how with respect to machine learning and additive manufacturing. But also providing its citizenry with the basic tools to be competent in ICT, a skill which has by now become a precondition for basic economic inclusion (World Bank 2016). Such digital training should, however, not be the sole focus of adapted education. Due to the unprecedented speed at which technology is developed at the moment, curricula risk being outdated very quickly. And we do not need to refer to the broader societal goals of education to realize that curricula should put more emphasis on generic cognitive and socioemotional skills rather than specialized technical ones. Also, employability and vocational training alone does not an educated citizenry make. If democracy is a social goal that the public can agree on, this dimension of education cannot be thrown under the bus. The technologically most advanced and fair type of service provision cannot replace such a public good.

There might even be an economic argument to bolster this claim. In the smart economy's labor market, socioemotional skills are the skills that are increasingly rewarded. Research already indicates that jobs that are intensive in math skills have contracted, whereas socioemotional abilities are in increasing demand (Heckman and Kautz 2012; Whitmann et al. 2016). Cunnigham and Villasenor (2014) have analyzed 28 studies on the future of work and found that more than half of the skills that employers identified as staying important are likely to fall into the category of socio-emotional skills, 30 percent into higher-order cognitive skills and only 16 percent are related to technical skills. In other words, new economy skills are most importantly emotional intelligence, adaptability and collaboration, followed by critical thinking, creativity and complex problem solving. The third important category includes know-how for ICT specialists as well as basic ICT knowledge of mainstream ICT tools.

Strong generic skills provide the necessary precondition to be able to master the fast-changing technology-specific know-how, regardless of what this know-how might look like in the future (OECD 2017). Furthermore, to ensure that the benefits of the smart economy are widely distributed, societal challenges and social goals should be incorporated into the technical development processes as early on as possible. The OECD stresses the need for a broader, less specialized education by stressing the importance of "funding social science and humanities in integrated co-streams with natural and physical science" to realize this goal (OECD 2017, 279).

Conclusion

It is by no means clear whether globalization will really reverse, come to a halt or just stagnate. The future is open. But in moments of crisis, simple stories, such as that of populists and demagogues seem to gain traction. Will we actually witness a return of manufacturing to the North Atlantic? Will producers just re-locate the factories and the labor embodied within them back from China to the US?

What seems certain is that, even if globalization were to reverse along the lines sketched in these concluding remarks, left-behind regions would not automatically stand to improve from such a change. Although this hope seems to explain a fair share of the more extreme voting behavior in many North Atlantic countries during the last couple of years, several open questions remain: Which types of jobs will be offered in such plants? Which regions attract the re-located manufacturing base? Does re-industrialization imply the re-regulation and redistributive measures of the Fordist past? Closing the regional divide is not simply going to be the natural outcome of technological developments—and regional economic divergence is not only endangering economic inclusion but also social cohesion and political stability.

Future politicians will have to address these questions anew, and not simply revert to another simple answer—that of laissez faire. In such a rethinking and re-inventing of societies, even immense public-sector investments in broadband provision might not be enough to ensure the economic inclusion of "places that do not matter." Public service provision in rural areas remains a vital challenge that has to be addressed by local and federal governments. The public sector should strive to seize the opportunities that smart, technology-based villages offer while critically considering the challenges posed by the objective of social inclusion.

To distribute the gains from new technological developments more evenly—also across space—governments especially need to adapt and strengthen their competition, regulation and education systems. However, all of the above-mentioned policies are unlikely to be a panacea for the development of economically lagging regions. Similar to previous modes of circulation, the smart economy has inherently disruptive characteristics that will continue to lead to uneven developments with concentrated benefits for certain individuals. These developments will recast in new shapes the struggle for social justice and protection that necessitates sound and functioning social and welfare policies to support those that do not benefit from the smart economy.

Works Cited

Autor, David H., David Dorn, and Gordon H. Hanson (2013). The China Syndrome: Local Labor Market Effects of Import Competition in the United States. *American Economic Review*, 103.6, 2121–68.

Autor, David H., David Dorn, Gordon H. Hanson, and Kaveh Majlesi (2016). Importing Political Polarization? The Electoral Consequences of Rising Trade Exposure. *National Bureau of Economic Research Working Paper* No. 22637.

Ballas, Dimitris, Danny Dorling, and Benjamin Hennig (2017). Analysing the Regional Geography of Poverty, Austerity and Inequality in Europe: a Human Cartographic Perspective. *Regional Studies*, 51.1 , 174–185.

Brennan, Louis, Kasra Ferdows, Janet Godsell, and Masrgaret Taylor (2015). Manufacturing in the World: Where next? *International Journal of Operations and Production Management*, 35.9, 1253–1274.

Cunningham, Wendy and Paula Villasenor (2014). Employer Voices, Employer Demands, and Implications for Public Skills Development Policy. *World Bank Policy Research Working Paper* No. 6853, Washington, DC.

Federal Communications Commission (FCC) (2010). Connecting America: The National Broadband Plan: http://www.broadband.gov/plan/8-availability/ [accessed May 15 2018]

Fujita, Masahisa, Paul R. Krugman and Anthony J. Venables (1999). *The Spatial Economy; Cities, Regions, and International Trade*. The MIT Press.

Ganong, Peter and Daniel Shoag (2017). Why has Regional Income Convergence in the US declined? *Journal of Urban Economics*, 102, 76–90.

Garrett, Banning (2017). 'Peak Globalization' and the Future of Democracy: https://www.opendemocracy.net/banning-garrett/peak-globalization-and-future-of-democracy [accessed May 18 2018]

Hall, Arthur P., J. Scott Moody and Wendy P. Warcholik (2009). The County-to-County Migration of Taxpayers and their Incomes, 1995-2006: https://business.ku.edu/sites/business.ku.edu/files/images/general/Research/TR%2009-0306--Taxpayer%20Migration.pdf [accessed May 5 2018]

Heckman, James and Tim Kautz (2012). Hard Evidence on Soft Skills. *National Bureau of Economic Research Working Paper* No. 18121.

Horx, Matthias (2018). Progressive Provinz. In: *Zukunftsreport 2018*. Matthias Horx (ed.), Frankfurt am Main: Zukunftsinstitut, 101–114.

Jessop, Bob (2017). The Organic Crisis of the British State: Putting Brexit in its Place. *Globalizations*, 14.1, 133–141.

Kline Patrick and Enrico Moretti (2013). Place based Policies with Unemployment. *American Economic Review*, 103, 238–243.

Kolko, Jed and David Neumark (2010). Do Some Enterprise Zones create Jobs? *Journal of Policy Analysis and Management*, 29.1, 5–38.

Li, Hongbin, Lei Li, Binzhen Wu, and Yanyan Xiong (2012). The End of Cheap Chinese Labor. *The Journal of Economic Perspectives*, 26.4, 57–74.

Manyika, James, Susan Lund, Jacques Bughin, Jonathan Woetzel, Kalin Stamenov, and Dhruv Dhingra (2016). *Digital Globalization: The New Era of Global Flows*. McKinsey Institute: https://www.mckinsey.com/~/media/McKinsey/Business%20Functions/McKinsey%20Digital/Our%20Insights/Digital%20globalization%20The%20new%20era%20of%20global%20flows/MGI-Digital-globalization-Full-report.ashx [accessed May 5 2018]

Mazzucato, Mariana (2018). *The Value of Everything. Making and Taking in the Global Economy*. Penguin.

Moore, Derick (2017). Overall Mover Rate Remains at an All-time Low. US Census: www.census.gov/library/stories/2017/12/lower-moving-rate.html [accessed May 5 2018]

Moretti, Enrico (2011). Local Labor Markets. In Ashenfelter, Orley and David Card (eds.). *Handbook of Labor Economics*, Volume 4, 1237–313. Amsterdam: North-Holland.

OECD (2010). *OECD Rural Policy Reviews. Strategies to Improve Rural Service Delivery.* Paris: OECD Publishing.

— (2011). *The Future of Families to 2030.* Paris: OECD Publishing.

— (2016). *OECD Regions at a Glance 2016.* Paris: OECD Publishing.

— (2017). *The Next Production Revolution: Implications for Governments and Business.* Paris: OECD Publishing.

— (2018). Enhancing Rural Innovation. Proceedings of the 11th OECD Rural Development Conference. Paris: OECD Publishing.

Piketty, Thomas, Li Yang and Gabriel Zucman (2017). Capital Accumulation, Private Property and Rising Inequality in China, 1978□2015. *National Bureau of Economic Research Working Paper* No. 23368.

Rodríguez-Pose, A (2018). The revenge of the places that don't matter (and what to do about it). *Cambridge Journal of Regions, Economy and Society*, 11.1: forthcoming.

Romer, Paul M. (1986). Increasing returns and long-run growth. *Journal of Political Economy*, 94, 1002–1037.

Schor, Juliet B., Connor Fitzmaurice, Lindsey B. Carfagna, Will Attwood-Charles, and Emilie Dubois Poteat (2016). Paradoxes of openness and distinction in the sharing economy. *Poetics*, 54, 66–81

Solow, Robert M. (1956). A contribution to the theory of economic growth. *Quarterly Journal of Economics*, 70, 65–94.

Strickling, Lawrence E. (2015). NTIA Announces BroadbandUSA Effort to Assist Communities with Broadband Plans. https://www.commerce.gov/news/-blog/2015/01/ntia-announces-broadbandusa-effort-assist-communities-broadband-plans [5 May 2018]

The Economist (2013). *On the inevitability of justice.* 2nd December 2013.

The White House (2016). "President Obama announces winner of new Smart Manufacturing Innovation Institute and New Manufacturing Hub competitions", *Fact Sheet*, June 20, Executive Office of the President, White House Office, Washington, DC: www.whitehouse.gov/the-press-office/2016/06/20/fact-sheet-president-obama-announces-winner-new-smart-manufacturing. [accessed May 5 2018]

U.S. Bureau of Labor Statistics (BLS) (2017). Employment Projections. https://www.bls.gov/emp/tables/employment-by major-industry-sector.htm [accessed May 18 2018]

Whitmore Schanzanbach, Diane, Ryan Nunn, Lauren Bauer, Megan Mumford, and Audrey Breitwieser (2016). *Seven Facts on Noncognitive Skills From Education to the Labor Market.* Washington, DC: The Hamilton Project.

World Bank (2011). *World Development Report 2012*: Gender Equality and Development. Washington, DC: World Bank.

— (2016). *World Development Report 2016*: Digital dividends, Washington, DC: World Bank.

Notes on Contributors

Dave Braneck is a freelance journalist.

Tommaso Burdet works in media and political consulting and runs an internet radio.

Patrick DeDauw is a doctoral student in Earth and Environmental Sciences at the Graduate Center of the City University of New York.

Christian Güse is a doctoral candidate at the Graduate School of North American Studies at Freie Universität Berlin.

Tobias Kalt is a doctoral student in comparative politics at the University of Kassel.

Christian Lammert is department chair and Professor of North American Politics at the John F. Kennedy Institute for North American Studies.

Jonas Pentzien researches the politics of the platform economy at the Institute for Ecological Economy Research.

Julia Püschel is assistant professor of economics at the John-F.-Kennedy Institute for North American Studies at Freie Universität Berlin.

Lasse Thiele is a doctoral candidate in Political Science at the Graduate School of North American Studies at Freie Universität Berlin.

Boris Vormann is professor of politics and head of the politics concentration at Bard College Berlin.

Jeremy Williams is a doctoral candidate at the Graduate School of North American Studies at Freie Universität Berlin.

Astrid Zimmermann works in cultural production and publishing.